Called to Serve

Called to Serve

The Bush School of Government and Public Service

Charles F. Hermann
Sally Dee Wade

Foreword by Mark A. Welsh III

TEXAS A&M UNIVERSITY PRESS
COLLEGE STATION

Copyright © 2017 by Charles F. Hermann and Sally Dee Wade
All rights reserved
Second printing, 2019

This paper meets the requirements of ANSI/NISO Z39.48–1992
(Permanence of Paper).
Binding materials have been chosen for durability.

Library of Congress Cataloging-in-Publication Data

Names: Hermann, Charles F., 1938- author. | Wade, Sally Dee, author.
Title: Called to serve : the Bush School of Government and Public Service /
   Charles F. Hermann and Sally Dee Wade.
Description: First edition. | College Station : Texas A&M University Press,
   [2017] | Includes bibliographical references and index. | Description
   based on print version record and CIP data provided by publisher; resource
   not viewed.
Identifiers: LCCN 2017005402 (print) | LCCN 2017012084 (ebook) |
   ISBN 9781623495657 (ebook) | ISBN 9781623495640(cloth : alk. paper) |
   ISBN 9781623497910 (paper)
Subjects: LCSH: Bush School of Government & Public Service—History. | Bush
   School of Government & Public Service—Graduate work. | George Bush
   Presidential Library and Museum—History. | Public administration—Study
   and teaching (Higher)—Texas—College Station—History. | Political
   science—Study and teaching (Higher)—Texas—College Station—History. |
   Presidential libraries—Texas—College Station—History.
Classification: LCC JF1338.A3 (ebook) | LCC JF1338.A3 U54 2017 (print) |
   DDC 351.071/1764242—dc23
LC record available at https://lccn.loc.gov/2017005402

Contents

Foreword, by Mark A. Welsh III — vii
Acknowledgments — ix

Chapter 1. The President Needs a Library — 1
Chapter 2. A New School on the Horizon — 17
Chapter 3. Trial and Error — 32
Chapter 4. Begin Again — 52
Chapter 5. A Change of Command — 63
Chapter 6. Gaining Momentum and Recognition — 75
Chapter 7. A Robust School in a New Decade — 90
Chapter 8. Continuing Education — 115
Chapter 9. What Are the Graduates Doing? — 124

Postscript — 171
Notes — 179
Index — 187

Galleries of images follow pages 50 and 114.

Foreword

I first learned of the Bush School of Government and Public Service while watching a televised interview of former president George H. W. Bush in the early 2000s. Two things president Bush said in that interview about the Bush School stuck with me. The first was the phrase "our school," which he used multiple times to refer to the college. The second was his reference to "public service as a noble calling," which he eloquently described as the founding principle of "our school." Roughly fifteen years later I found myself standing in front of the statue of President Bush in the courtyard as the newly appointed dean of the Bush School. I thought about those two phrases and realized how lucky I was to serve as a guardian of those ideas.

Still only twenty years old, our school is already a remarkable success story. This book tells the story of its formative years. It introduces the people and events that shaped its growth from a bold idea into an institution of higher learning that has taken its place among the very best in the world.

Chuck Hermann and Sally Dee Wade give us the insider view of the early discussions on possible locations for President Bush 41's presidential library, including the brilliant idea of sweetening the Texas A&M proposal by adding a namesake college to the deal. They introduce us to the visionaries who crafted that proposal, sold it, and then made it reality.

They also introduce us to the brilliant men and women who shaped the direction of the college—politicians, community leaders, scholars, administrators, and staff—people who shared a dream of what the Bush School could become and were willing to put their own skin in the game to make it happen.

The book highlights the pride everyone connected to the Bush School felt, and continues to feel, in being part of Texas A&M University. As the book makes clear, without the other colleges of this great institution, the Bush School would not have succeeded. Texas A&M is a very special place. All of us are honored to serve here.

In these pages, we also meet the enduring product by which our school will forever be judged—our graduates. While still relatively small in number, they have had an outsized impact since the very first graduate entered public service. As you'll read, they are literally changing our world. They make all of us proud each and every day.

The way this book captures the very proud service of our graduates serves as a reminder to all of us that at the core of the Bush School, always, are the values of our namesake. Courage, competence, respect, humility, and selfless service are all words that have been frequently used to describe both President George H. W. Bush's and his wife Barbara's lifetimes of public service. Those of us who have served in the Bush School universally believe in those values, espouse them daily to our students, and celebrate the example he and Mrs. Bush set. We also celebrate twenty years of the Bush School, its wonderful achievements and success to date, and the greatness that lies ahead.

Mark A. Welsh III
Dean, Bush School of Government and Public Service
General, US Air Force (ret.)

Acknowledgments

I (Chuck Hermann) must begin by recognizing the people who make the Bush School a high-quality place to work. The Bush School has been remarkably fortunate to have obtained the involvement of an exceptional staff during its first two decades. Many have been part of the school for much of its first two decades. They have invested time and effort well beyond what would be expected for strong performance. I personally have had the opportunity to work closely with a number of them. Many have helped with this book. Naming them individually and detailing their contributions to the school would require another chapter. That said, there is one I must explicitly recognize—Janeen Wood.

Janeen came to the Bush School in 2005 as the administrative assistant to the director of the Master's Program in International Affairs (MPIA) and continues in that capacity to the head of the Department of International Affairs. Her arrival at the Bush School corresponded with the rapid expansion of the MPIA—we initiated a major research contract with Lawrence Livermore National Laboratory; we launched new reciprocal study-abroad programs with six universities; we started a new interdisciplinary certificate program in China studies and continuously expanded the student enrollment and faculty in the program. I was very successful in expanding her workload, far less so in increasing her compensation. Nonetheless, she stepped into each of these multiple enterprises with energy, competence, and a generous spirit.

Another woman central to my life is Lorraine Eden Hermann. Authors understandably pay tribute to their spouse. I need to explain the magnitude of my debt to Lorraine in conjunction with the Bush

School. Before we moved to Texas so that I could accept the position to start the Bush School, Lorraine, a PhD in economics, was a full professor in the Paterson School of International Affairs at Carleton University in Ottawa, Canada. When we came to Texas A&M, there was no equivalent place for her. The Management Department of the Mays Business School offered her a tenured home but at a reduced rank since she really had limited prior scholarship pertaining to its discipline. A brave heart, she accepted. Now she is a full professor in that department and president of the Academy of International Business, one of their major professional societies. On the side, she has taught at least one course in the Bush School every year since it opened.

And now thoughts from my wonderful coauthor, Sally Dee Wade.

In 1967, the Beatles produced the hit record "With a Little Help from My Friends." That phrase seems most appropriate: Where would I be without my friends? Definitely, this book would never have been written without my friends and especially the encouragement of one friend—Lorraine Eden. I did not plan to write a book about the Bush School; I did not plan to write a book at all, but Lorraine kept saying to me, "Sally, you need to write a book." After a bit of banter, we dropped the subject, but the idea stayed with me because I know to listen to Lorraine.

When Chuck asked if I would be interested in working on a history of the Bush School with him, I jumped at the opportunity, not only for the challenge but also for the opportunity to work again with the Bush School family. The eight years I spent at the Bush School were the most meaningful in my career. When I contacted faculty, staff, and students about our history project, they enthusiastically responded that they would help in any way possible. With the help of the faculty and staff, I contacted outstanding former students. The students responded positively to my requests for résumés and interviews, and we spent hours learning how our Bush School graduates are dedicating their lives to make the lives of people everywhere better. Our students are amazing.

I am also grateful for my support from home. Herb, my husband of fifty-three years, cheerfully agreed and encouraged me to work on this project. He said that we could easily work our schedule around the book. Neither of us had a clue about the amount of time and travel that would be involved. He never complained when our trips to the lake turned into work weekends for me. He never complained when we had to make spur-of-the-moment trips to interview someone involved in the development of the school. He never complained when dinner was "take out." He is the best.

Beyond these individuals who have sustained us directly, we both obtained the help of a great many individuals. One or both of us interviewed each of the following individuals: Jean Becker, Ray Bowen, Lisa Brown, William A. Brown, Andrew Card, Joe Cerami, James W. Cicconi, Ryan C. Crocker, Danny W. Davis, George C. Edwards III, David G. Eller, Daniel Fallon, Robert M. Gates, Charles A. Johnson, Fredrick (Rick) Johnson, Shirley Joiner, Holly Kasperbauer, Sam A. Kirkpatrick, David McIntyre, William Mobley, Jeryl Mumpower, Louis Newman, Michael O'Quinn, Bookman Peters, Sheran A. Riley, Nancy Small, Lori L. Taylor, Arnold (Arnie) Vedlitz, William F. West, and Don Wilson.

In addition we received significant help from the following people: Don W. Bailey, Domonic Bearfield, Derek Dictson, F. Gregory Gause, Mary Hein, Gabrielle Kelleher, Kathryn Meyer, Larry C. Napper, Andrew Natsios, James Olson, Jim Palincsar, Kimberly Reeves, Marc Tracer, Matt Upton, and Janeen Wood. At the Texas A&M University Press we benefited and enjoyed working with Thom Lemmons and Emily Seyl. Despite all this help, we the authors alone are responsible for the material as presented and any errors it may contain.

Called to Serve

1

The President Needs a Library

A Jump-Start for the Library Quest

George H. W. Bush won the election for president of the United States on November 8, 1988. As occurs for every president-elect his life became dominated by the decisions and challenges of preparing for his new administration. Despite the hectic demands, Bush found special time for his family, campaign leaders, and supporters. On the last day of November, he met in Washington with a major contributor and old friend, Michel T. Halbouty. A legend in the oil business, Halbouty achieved enormous success as a calculating wildcatter who ran his own company and wrote and spoke with zeal about the oil business—and his role in it.[1] Over time in Texas, Bush and Halbouty had developed a strong friendship.

Toward the end of his conversation with Bush, Halbouty abruptly advanced an idea distant from the subjects they had been discussing. As Halbouty subsequently related: "It suddenly occurred to me to discuss his Presidential Library,"[2] mentioning to his friend that after his time in office Bush would need to have one. Halbouty proposed his alma mater, Texas A&M University, as a great location. In what undoubtedly is an understatement, Halbouty noted that the president-elect seemed "surprised at my mentioning the Library which, evidently, was the furthest thing from his mind."[3] Although Bush apparently suggested that the library was a subject for much, much later, he told Halbouty that he would consider Texas A&M a fine location.

Suggesting Texas A&M as the site for the future George Bush Presidential Library may have been a spur-of-the-moment thought for Michel Halbouty. But his follow-up was quick, vigorous, and planned. Upon returning to Texas, he contacted his friend Perry Adkisson, chancellor of the Texas A&M University system. He urged Adkisson to query the university regents quickly and let him know whether they wanted to pursue this idea. Several days later Adkisson relayed his board's enthusiasm. Halbouty called Bush's office. He left a message that the Texas A&M officials wished to propose their university as the site for the future Bush Library. Bush dashed off a reply to Halbouty: "This is very flattering; but, Mike, as I think I mentioned, it is way too early for me to reach a decision on this important subject. . . . I hate to get A&M's hopes up. I love A&M, though I have no personal ties to that great school."[4]

The vision of Texas A&M University as the future site for the Bush Presidential Library struck a group of the university system's regents as an exciting prospect. In early January 1989, William McKenzie, chairman of the Board of Regents, appointed a steering committee to create a library proposal. He made Michel Halbouty the chair and included the university chancellor (Perry Adkisson), the deputy chancellor for external affairs (James Bond), the university president (William Mobley), and himself. Other members included Preston Geren, a prominent architect; John Lindsey, a close Houston friend of Bush; and Edmund Pillsbury, director of the Kimbell Art Museum in Fort Worth. Two others were prominent members of the College Station/Bryan local community, Bookman Peters and Louis Newman. Shirley Jones provided staff support, and Michael O'Quinn served as assistant to the chancellor. It was a cleverly crafted committee, combining the leadership of the university and system with close personal friends of the president, expertise on architecture and design, and individuals able to mobilize local support. All had intense loyalty to Texas A&M and strong admiration of the president-elect.

A Commencement Address

The committee hatched an idea to maintain momentum. As vice president, George Bush previously had given a commencement address at Texas A&M. Why not invite him to do so again as president of the United States? If he accepted, they could advance the library site idea in person and present a proposal. William Mobley invited the forty-first president to be the May 1989 commencement speaker. Awaiting a reply from the White House, the Library Steering Committee began conversations with several deans. On April 13 they met with Dan Fallon, dean of the College of Liberal Arts, to explore possible interest among his faculty.

Fallon surprised the committee with specific proposals. Independently—and unaware of the earlier initiative of Halbouty and the regents—several political science faculty had urged Fallon to get the university to pursue initiatives for the Bush Presidential Library.[5] When the new university term began in mid-January, George Edwards, a professor who is a prominent scholar of the American presidency, put on paper the ideas he had been discussing with Bryan Jones, head of the Political Science Department. On January 19 Jones passed Edward's memo to Dan Fallon. Edwards's memo began: "I propose that Texas A&M make an early and concerted effort to have the George Bush Presidential Library located here. . . . It makes sense to move expeditiously."[6] Thus, Fallon told the committee he already had been discussing the idea with faculty and they had strong interests and some ideas.

In mid-April, the White House responded that President Bush would accept the commencement invitation. Suddenly the committee faced a close deadline for an initial presidential library proposal. They would have the opportunity to present a concept personally to Bush on May 12, 1989.

Preston Geren, the architect serving on the committee, explored a possible site for a library and discussed concepts with faculty in both liberal arts and architecture. Shirley Joiner pulled the various suggested elements into a preliminary draft. Ten days before Bush's scheduled arrival, the entire planning committee assembled to review a draft of their preliminary library proposal.[7]

In its final form, the twenty-four-page plan stressed the fit between the president's interests and career activities and the capabilities of Texas A&M. Under Geren's initiative, it included a proposed site and preliminary architectural concepts. The plan also incorporated input from the liberal arts faculty in a page devoted to academic programs to be affiliated with the library. Specifically, it stated: "Given President Bush's wide ranging career and interests, a George Bush Graduate School of Government and Public Service, with special emphasis on research and training in public service and leadership, will be established."[8] From this initial plan, the concept of the Bush School emerged.

Air Force One touched down May 12 at Easterwood Airport in College Station. Every commencement is exciting for the graduates, their families, and friends; however, having the president of the United States participate escalates and expands the excitement. On that day, few in the audience realized that Bush would unveil a policy signaling conditions for changing the Cold War. It constituted the first of three commencement addresses by Bush in the spring of 1989 revealing his new administration's policy toward the apparent changes in the Soviet Union. In his Texas A&M commencement address, he advanced explicit expectations that Mikhail Gorbachev and the leaders of the USSR would need to fulfill if they wanted to bring the Cold War to an end.[9] That address captured worldwide attention.

The group of Texas A&M regents, however, planned to use the visit for a more local purpose. Following a commencement lunch with the president, they wanted to present their ideas for the Bush Presidential Library at Texas A&M. John Sununu, Bush's chief of staff, objected. He insisted that the president's schedule required an immediate return to Air Force One. The president intervened and agreed to a very brief presentation by Michel Halbouty and Perry Adkisson with other committee members present.[10] As the president's party left, they received multiple copies of the Texas A&M preliminary proposal—enough for every principal to have a copy on the trip back to Washington.

Library Selection Process Established

The persistent efforts of Texas A&M pushed President Bush to task someone to organize the selection process for his library. On the trip back to Washington from the College Station visit, he passed that assignment to James Cicconi, assistant to the chief of staff. The president gave Cicconi some instructions concerning bids for his library, including his wish for "a process that would be fair to all, yet, given his many more important responsibilities, keep the issue off his desk until it was ready for decision."[11]

Other places were preparing bids for the library. Early in October 1989 Kenneth Lay, chief executive officer (CEO) of Enron Corporation and chairman of the Board of Regents at the University of Houston, wrote Bush, describing the plans they had made for proposing that the Bush Library be located at the University of Houston. Lay conveyed a note of alarm:

> We have heard from a number of sources . . . that you are strongly leaning toward placing your library on the Texas A&M campus. I am writing you to strongly request that you not make your final decision until you and your staff have at least had an opportunity to carefully review our proposal. Obviously, I am strongly interested in having you select the University of Houston as the site for your presidential library, but I am even more interested in having you select some site in Houston.[12]

Days later Cicconi received a handwritten note from the president: "Jim—Please provide me with all copies of incoming and outgoing on Library."[13] He added that he did not need anything on Texas A&M. Cicconi supplied the list of other queries about locating the Presidential Library. It included

> The University of Houston
> Rice University
> Texas Tech University
> Yale University
> Citizens in Kennebunkport, Maine
> Citizens proposing a private site in Houston[14]

Jim Cicconi already had put a process in place for reviewing inquiries and proposals regarding the Presidential Library. Shortly after Bush gave him the assignment on the trip back from College Station, Cicconi approached Don Wilson, the archivist of the United States who previously had been director of the Ford Presidential Library. Cicconi asked Wilson to provide guidelines for evaluating proposals —drawing on initial guidance from the president—and assessing each plan thoroughly with recommendations to the president. Bush applauded the idea of Don Wilson as an independent evaluator of various proposals and reassured Ken Lay and others at the University of Houston of the existence of a review process for all proposals. He also announced his intent to locate his library in Texas and his preference for affiliation with a university. That statement closed out the queries from Yale and the private groups in Kennebunkport and Houston.[15] For their own reasons, the Texas Tech leadership elected not to follow their initial inquiry with a proposal. Thus, the quest narrowed to the University of Houston, Rice, and Texas A&M.

Don Wilson got to work. Before he submitted his report to the president, he had twice made multiday visits to each site. He also received visitors from the universities in his Washington office and engaged in substantial correspondence. After his first round of visits, he prepared two questionnaires requesting written responses to all items. In one set he posed sixteen questions to all three universities. Additionally each site received eight or nine questions tailored specifically for that institution.[16]

A Formal Texas A&M Proposal

Wilson, with his executive assistant, Bill Stewart, made his first visit to Texas A&M on October 26–27, 1989. The Texas A&M Library Steering Committee had been refining their proposal since Bush's visit in May. In July 1989 they had established an architectural subcommittee, which, in turn, selected the architectural firm CRS Sirrine to develop concepts and explore the site they had in mind. Thus, when Wilson and Stewart arrived in College Station, they received a visual presentation of the concept—including the integration of academic programs—and visits to the proposed site.

In the weeks just prior to the Wilson visit, the Regents' Library Planning Steering Committee had asked Bill Mobley to create an Academic Planning Committee. Mobley assigned Dan Fallon to chair the committee and appointed representatives from the Schools of Architecture (John Greer, Jon Rodiek), Civil Engineering (Donn Hancher), and Business (Jared Hazelton); the head of the university library (Irene Hoadley); and the university archivist (Charles Schultz), as well as faculty from the Departments of History (Larry Hill), Journalism (Peter Roussel), and Political Science (George Edwards, Bryan Jones, Harvey Tucker). It also included the vice president for finance (Robert Smith), the chancellor's administrative assistant (Shirley Jones), and two students (Tim Doolen and Adriana Menchaca). Bryan Jones and George Edwards—the two professors who had independently proposed bidding for the library—played an active role. Before Don Wilson arrived on the campus, the new academic committee advanced their ideas to the Steering Committee and received a favorable response.

After his visit to Texas A&M and before returning to Texas in November for visits to Rice University and the University of Houston, Wilson wrote a brief note to President Bush in which he observed: "The Bush Library is seen as providing the impetus to create a comprehensive research complex that will share the Library site. As described to me by University officials, the complex will house the George Bush School of Government and Public Service." Thus, the idea of a Bush School, which had appeared in both the preliminary proposal and in the briefing to Wilson, was mentioned in the quick report to the president. Bush dashed off a handwritten response to Wilson: "Thanks for that excellent report on your visit to A&M. I was impressed and pleased."[17]

Following Wilson's initial visit to the Texas A&M campus, the Steering Committee and their new partner, the Academic Planning Committee, worked to revise the preliminary proposal they had presented earlier to Bush at the May commencement. Representatives of both committees visited other presidential libraries (including those of Presidents Ford, Carter, Reagan, and the provisional facility for Nixon). They also pored over their notes from the exchanges during the Wilson visit. On January 18, 1990, they submitted the formal proposal.[18]

That twenty-two-page document referenced the public-service character of Texas A&M. It also, perhaps somewhat defensively, noted that College Station is within two hundred miles of 77 percent of Texas residents. It reminded readers that the existing presidential libraries with the largest number of visitors have not necessarily been in large metropolitan areas. The document highlighted two themes that the committees concluded best represented their competitive advantage over Rice and the University of Houston. One emphasized the "beautiful site" proposed for the library on the edge of the campus consisting of ninety pastoral acres with a grove of trees and a running creek. The second theme underscored the academic programs to be associated with the Bush Library. "A special school is being created now; it is hoped that President Bush will allow it to bear his name in the future. The George Bush School of Government and Public Service will offer a master of public administration (MPA) degree, emphasizing the acquisition of analytical skills, character of leadership and management techniques for public service."[19]

Not only are the proposed site and academic programs featured in the proposal, but each is also highlighted in an extended appendix. The proposed site plans appear in ten pages of schematic drawings. The second appendix, "Proposal to Establish a School of Government and Public Service at Texas A&M University," is nearly as long as the formal proposal. The name to be given the school specifies "public service" and thus differs from the designation of other schools such as "public affairs" or "public policy." The committee chose to incorporate in the name of the school a theme that Bush had repeatedly cited—the importance of attracting able people to careers in public service. To drive the point home, they began that appendix by indicating not only the name but also the mission of the school, which must address a need in professional education. They refer to a national need.

> There exists at present a crisis in the public service. The report of the Volcker Commission (the National Commission on Public Service) has documented such crisis in detail and has called for remedial action to attract qualified individuals into public service. As Astrid Merget, dean of Ohio State's School of Public Policy and Management and former president of the National Association of Schools of Public Affairs, noted recently in *Governing*, part of the problem lies within the educational system.[20]

In effect, the committee sought to convey to the president that they will build a school to address a need that he valued and that others declare to be of major importance. The appendix continued with descriptions of the school's goals and curriculum as well as plans for two academic research centers to be associated with the school. First, the Center for Presidential Studies would be designed to become "the leading center for scholarship on the American presidency." Second, a

Center for Public Leadership Studies would draw on "scholars in the social sciences, management, and the humanities [to] . . . enhance our understanding of leadership and encourage its development in the public sector."[21]

Texas A&M's formal proposal for the Bush Presidential Library reflected the significant engagement of two groups under the oversight of the regents' Steering Committee. The first was the Architectural Subcommittee, led by Preston Geren. It continually worked with the firm of CRS Sirrine to advance the site design. The second group, the Academic Planning Committee, was called by Mobley "Dan Fallon's troops." As they continued to refine the proposal, George Edwards, Bryan Jones, and Harvey Tucker engaged fellow political scientists Kim Hill, Arnold Vedlitz, and Charles A. Johnson, as well as Martin Medhurst, a communications faculty member specializing in presidential rhetoric.

Dueling Bids for the Bush Presidential Library

Rice University and the University of Houston submitted their proposals. They also explored the possibility of joint sponsorship of the Bush Library, perhaps located in a Houston public park. On January 17, 1990, Bush hosted a brief meeting at the White House for representatives of the University of Houston and Rice. The background memo that James Cicconi prepared for the president noted: "Both UH and Rice requested a joint meeting to stress their feeling that your library should be located in Houston."[22] Along with representatives of the two universities, the visitors included Kenneth Lay and Rod Canion, CEO of Compaq Computers. The president was joined by First Lady Barbara Bush, John Sununu, Jim Cicconi, and Don Wilson.

The following day the same group hosted three representatives of Texas A&M: William McKenzie, Michel Halbouty, and Perry Adkisson. Reflecting years later on the White House visits of the delegations from the three contending universities, Cicconi observed: "Both the President and the First Lady asked many questions, especially about the academic aspects of each proposal—aspects which seemed to grow more important to the President each time he considered the issue."[23]

Later in the spring of 1990, the advocates of locating the Bush Library in Houston tried a different ploy. William McKenzie received a discreet inquiry in a letter dated March 2: "We sincerely believe that the Bush Library would be best served by a multi-institutionally sponsored facility located in a major metropolitan area such as Houston. Accordingly, this letter will serve as our formal invitation for Texas A&M University to join the six institutions which we represent in cosponsoring the establishment and operation of the library at a site in the Houston area." The letter bore signatures from the chair of the Board of Regents of the University of Houston, chair of the Board of Governors of Rice University, chair of the Board of Texas Southern University, and presidents of Baylor College of Medicine, University of Texas MD Anderson Cancer Center, University of Texas Health Science Center, and the Greater Houston Partnership.[24] The letter was copied to Bush, Don Wilson, and James Cicconi. In passing the letter on to the president, Cicconi correctly noted: "Needless to say, A&M will probably decline the honor."[25]

After the White House meetings—and recognizing the Houston unity ploy was a nonstarter—Don Wilson circulated his set of sixteen questions to all three universities. The questionnaires solicited more information on their approach to specific library issues. Some of Wilson's questions for Texas A&M concerned how the university would attract staff, media, and tourists to its nonurban setting, how the proposed centers would relate to the Presidential Library, and whether Texas A&M would participate in activities if the library were located elsewhere. He then scheduled another round of visits to the universities.[26]

Wilson returned to Texas A&M March 19–20, 1990. During the second visit, the Library Steering Committee provided verbal responses to the questions that Wilson had submitted in advance as well as nine other questions specifically addressed to the Texas A&M proposal. Although both Dan Fallon and George Edwards joined the sessions, the focus of those meetings did not dwell on the Bush School or the academic centers. Instead, the Library Steering Committee seized the opportunity to convey the broad base of support not only within the university but also in the community. The mayors of both Bryan and College Station joined Bookman Peters and Louis Newman, the two businessmen on the Steering Committee, in expressing their enthusiastic support. The city council of College Station renamed the street leading to the proposed library site George Bush Boulevard. Both the university faculty senate and the student government passed resolutions of support. All the participants realized the importance of broad university and community support. A substantial group of Stanford University faculty had strongly opposed placing the Reagan Presidential Library on that campus. That opposition may have cost Stanford the Reagan Library. Closer to home a community group in Houston had expressed opposition to the idea of proposing Hermann Park in Houston as a site for a combined Rice–University of Houston concept for the Bush Library. The A&M Steering Committee eagerly sought to convey to Wilson wide-based, vigorous support for the Bush Library on the campus in College Station.

After his second visit to the University of Houston and Rice University, Don Wilson returned to Washington and prepared his report for the president. He submitted his assessment in a letter on July 17, 1990. It compared the three alternatives along multiple dimensions but made no recommendation: "It is a pleasure for me to report that all candidates, University of Houston, Rice University, and Texas A&M University, are fully qualified sites to sponsor the George Bush Library."[27]

A few days before Wilson submitted his report, Bush had hosted the leaders of major democratic countries—the G7—in Houston (July 10–11, 1990). The heads of state of Canada, France, West Germany, Italy, Japan, and the United Kingdom and the head of the European Commission joined Bush for two days of meetings. The opening ceremonies and some of the meetings were held on the Rice University campus. Rice appeared to have an advantage for the library bid.

Shortly after that summit, writers for the *Houston Chronicle*, the major metropolitan newspaper, joined the local lobbying campaign for the Bush Library. An opinion piece in the *Chronicle* on Sunday, July 15, 1990, appeared under the banner "Bush Could End Library Debate."

> A lot of Houstonians have spent a lot of time and energy pondering what benefits may come to their community because of its role as the host city to last week's summit. One specific question about one possible benefit has not been asked, however. At least, it's not been asked publicly. . . . One can legitimately wonder: Why is there any debate about where Bush's presidential library ultimately will be built? . . . Why does Houston, the president's hometown which has outstanding universities, feel

it must convince Bush to build his library here? One can only assume it is because of the often overwhelming line of patter spun so convincingly by Texas Aggies.[28]

A day later the *Chronicle* offered a story about the earlier visit to the White House of the Houston delegation advocating one of the local universities as the site for the Bush Library. The group had focused on the computer technology Houston universities could offer in collaboration with local companies. "They brought with them a Compaq computer and software developed by Quantum Access, a Houston company specializing in data management software. . . . Bush was described as captivated by what he saw."[29]

The following week (July 22), the *Houston Chronicle* headlined another story "Bush Library Fight Turns into Subtle Game of Chess." The article quotes the president of the Greater Houston Partnership, Jim Kollaer: "I think there is now a sense that the Houston proposals and summit performance were so strong that the president has been given a lot to think about."[30]

"Library Recommendation on the President's Desk" reported the *Chronicle* on September 22, 1990.[31] It would remain there for some time. The urgent tasks of being president of the United States certainly account for the months that elapsed before the president made a decision about his library. Leaders in Houston, however, may have become worried that the president did not seem to find the choice the easy, obvious decision they thought it should be. An editorial in the *Chronicle* on April 2, 1991, declared: "George Bush's home—and heart—are in Houston. The Bush presidential library belongs here too. . . . The rural charms of the Texas A&M campus in College Station . . . are simply no match for Houston's big-city vitality."[32]

Texas A&M Wins

The waiting ended in early May 1991. Don Wilson and Jim Cicconi—the two key advisers to President Bush on his library selection—flew to College Station to meet with the A&M team on May 2. Cicconi said they wanted to review and gain further clarification on academic programs, funding, and—if selected—A&M's postdecision planning.

Cicconi wanted to know what was happening on the academic front. Dan Fallon replied that the first of the two centers—Center for Presidential Studies—had been established with George Edwards as director.[33] Cicconi and Wilson inquired about funding for the proposed school and the centers. Fallon said funds would come from the state and endowments. Questions on other issues followed.[34] Wilson and Cicconi received the answers they needed and quickly informed the president.

On the afternoon of May 3, 1991, President Bush called Ross Margraves, chairman of the Texas A&M Board of Regents, from Air Force One.[35] The Bush Library would be at Texas A&M. The president's formal acceptance letter, also dated May 3, mentioned three features of the A&M proposal that he found especially attractive. In elaborating on these highly valued elements, he began: "In deciding to accept the Texas A&M proposal, I was particularly pleased to note the University's commitment to integrate the library into the academic activities of the University. The school's planned public service school and Center for Presidential Studies will foster strong links between the library and the University."[36] The president continued by noting the attractive library site and the university pledge to secure all needed funds. Before mentioning anything else that influenced his decision, Bush mentioned the proposed school.

The entire community of Bryan–College Station celebrated. "Meanwhile, officials at the University of Houston and Rice University, who also lobbied hard for the coveted library and museum, expressed disappointment, but spoke flatteringly of their College Station rival. 'I'm disappointed but not surprised,' said Kenneth L. Lay, chairman of the UH board of regents."[37] Many in Houston were gracious in their reaction; however, *Houston Chronicle* columnist Jane Ely wrote a scathing piece, "OK, Aggies, Now You Can Gloat."

> OK, so he never promised Houston a presidential library. But, did he have to make an Aggie joke out of it? Sure, maybe A&M always has welcomed him with hurrahs and drawn swords. Perhaps he likes the corps' boots. Or the fine marching band. Did he have to shaft the home folk and a slew of swell Houston-based colleges and universities to show his appreciation to the Aggies? . . . He went with the school alone in the middle of nowhere. . . . Maybe

he just thought having his library built at A&M would be a public service. After all, if there's a library on the premises, maybe that'll be an incentive for the Aggies to learn to read.[38]

Nothing could diminish the excitement the president's decision triggered at Texas A&M and the communities of Bryan and College Station. Soon their rejoicing shifted into the challenging task of creating and executing a plan approved by Bush for construction of his library. Preston Geren, the Aggie graduate and architect who had been influential in selecting the proposed library site and envisioning its development, agreed to continue the plan conceptualization with the firm CRS Sirrine. Perry Adkisson's assistant, Shirley Joiner, who had been key in converting the various ideas into a coherent and convincing library proposal, accepted the position as assistant executive director of the George Bush Library Foundation.

Planning the Presidential Library Complex

Specific plans called for the library complex to consist of three buildings—the library, a conference center, and an academic building. When briefed on the evolving specific design for his library and museum by Cicconi, the president replied in August 1991 from Kennebunkport with short bullet points:

Nothing too flashy
Something that fits at A&M
Not grand but modern
Not requiring undue maintenance
Comfortable, pleasant for browsing, conducive to study[39]

In July 1992, in a break from campaigning for reelection and the duties of his office, President and Mrs. Bush invited William Mobley, the four senior architects, and Shirley Joiner to provide them with an update on the library plans at the White House. President and Mrs. Bush seemed quite pleased with the presentation. The visitors noted that both of them asked questions.[40]

The Texas A&M planners knew that the November 1992 presidential election could force an acceleration of their work. It might reasonably be conjectured, however, that most of them anticipated a second term for the president, with the implication that his Presidential Library would be needed sometime after 1996. After all, less than a year earlier, following the Gulf War, Bush's approval ratings were higher "than (than those of) any other president in the history of public opinion surveys."[41] It was not to be.

Following the end of the Bush administration, Texas A&M offered Don Wilson, who had been extensively involved with the library selection process and a source of guidance, the position of executive director of the George Bush Library Foundation. He accepted. Design of the library and associated buildings accelerated, as did the campaign to raise the necessary funds. The Houston architectural firm HOK was chosen to implement the plans. The Manhattan Construction Company received the bid to build the complex.

From the outset, the bidders for the Bush Presidential Library knew that their proposals would need to comply with the Presidential Libraries Act of 1986. Congress had been concerned that each new presidential library tended to be larger and more complex than its predecessors. This trend escalated the cost to the public for maintaining these facilities. The 1986 legislation established site criteria, specified building size, and required private endowment funds to offset part of the maintenance costs. The Bush Library would be the first constructed and financed under the new rules.

The Bush Presidential Library would be the centerpiece of the three-building complex. Like other presidential libraries, it would be turned over to the federal government for operation after completion. Two other buildings would be owned and operated by the university but would extend and complement the library. One of these would be a conference center with two auditoria, meeting rooms, and a second-floor apartment for President and Mrs. Bush. The second would be an academic building, the physical facility that embodied the university's commitment to link the library complex to the campus learning mission. That building would be home to several academic departments and the Bush School of Government and Public Service.

As the planning continued, multiple personnel changes occurred on the academic side. Some key players in the initial library proposal accepted posts elsewhere. William Mobley left the university, as did Dan Fallon and Bryan Jones. Jones, together with George Edwards, had crafted the concept of academic centers as part of the library proposal, and Jones had been the candidate to head the new Center for Public Leadership Studies. Nonetheless, the second key center came into existence under the direction of Arnold Vedlitz. Meanwhile, Woodrow Jones assumed deanship of the College of Liberal Arts, and Ben Crouch replaced Charles A. Johnson as his deputy. Johnson, in turn, became head of the Political Science Department. All of these individuals, together with George Edwards, would play major roles in turning the plans for the academic dimensions of the Presidential Library into reality.

The first load of documents and artifacts from the Bush administration arrived in College Station in June 1993. With the existence of the Presidential Library still some years in the future, the archivists began their cataloguing and temporary storage in an abandoned bowling alley.

On November 30, 1994, ground was broken for the Bush Presidential Library. A special train brought President and Mrs. Bush; George W. Bush, governor of Texas; Brian Mulroney, former prime minister of Canada; other members of the Bush family; and many dignitaries and guests from Houston. Their numbers were complemented by an invited crowd from the local communities. The event took place inside an enormous tent, and the crowd overflowed into the bright sunshine. Standing at the back of the tent with Ben Crouch was the person just selected to be the founding director of the new George Bush School of Government and Public Service.

2

A New School on the Horizon

Getting Started

After Hermann accepted the offer from Texas A&M University to serve as the first director of the planned Bush School, he flew to Houston in late 1994. The new dean of the College of Liberal Arts, Woodrow Jones, met him at the airport. Before driving the ninety miles to College Station, they visited Bush in his Houston office for a cordial, get-acquainted session. The president expressed his appreciation for Hermann accepting the director position, they posed for photographs, and the session ended. Hermann reflected on that visit: "Only later did I come to appreciate the remarkable nature of the trip. It marked the beginning of my relationship with Dr. Jones and with President Bush. Both would be key to the task ahead."

Hermann's task at Texas A&M entailed the design and implementation of a new master's degree program. Although called a "school," it was to be embedded in the College of Liberal Arts along with typical academic departments such as English, history, and sociology. Hermann and Jones had an effective working relationship. Jones treated him with enormous respect and provided considerable latitude in the planning and operation of the Bush School; however, the relationship seemed different from the relationship Jones had with the other heads of academic departments in his college. He served as Hermann's academic supervisor, but he had to balance the needs and priorities of a dozen academic departments with the needs of the Bush School. Hermann said, "I suspect it was a difficult balancing act because I kept insisting the school has special needs."

The visit with President Bush also signaled his interest and engagement with the school. Although the school was an academic unit of Texas A&M, it would be unlike any other at the university. Bush selected Texas A&M as the site for his library, in part, because the university proposed to establish a new school of public service located next to his library. With his attention came his vast network of friends' interest as well. Bush always emphasized he would not interfere with the school and university's independent operation; however, he and his circle of friends watched with great interest and indicated their willingness to help if asked.

Construction began on the presidential library complex in August 1995. It would be the fall of 1997 before all three major buildings were completed. In the meantime, the Bush School offices were on the top floor of Harrington Tower, home to the College of Education and Human Development. The Bush School operated from a small corner suite on the eighth floor of that building; the remainder of the floor served as the administrative quarters for the dean of education. Jane Conoley, who became dean soon after Hermann's arrival, and her staff were supportive and interested in the new school planning. In the fall of 1995 and early 1996, Hermann began to assemble the first Bush School staff. Theresa Weir started as administrative assistant, and Fredrick (Rick) Johnson became the fiscal officer. Theresa, and especially Rick, became core participants in the early planning for the school.

The elevators in Harrington Tower usually stopped at multiple floors, making the ride to or from the Bush School offices quite slow. The only other option was the stairs; they were easy to descend, but the trip up was arduous. Hermann recalls: "Shortly after moving into the offices, Rick and I devised a game: We would race each other either to the top or to the bottom. One would take the elevator; the other would take the stairs. Going down, the stairs almost always proved faster; however, it took effort to beat the elevator going up. Nevertheless, sometimes the climber won." Hermann went on to say that the organizing work for the Bush School those next two years shared a property of the elevators—slow going. Occasionally, the team found equivalents to the stairs and the work moved rapidly.

In those preparatory years, key tasks included designing the curriculum, obtaining approval of the degree program, recruiting faculty, establishing bylaws, and seeking the first class of students. In terms of required time, most of those undertakings were equivalent to the slow-moving elevators. Like the elevators, however, they eventually reached the desired destination.

One project that moved rapidly pertained to the logo for the Bush School. In his new capacity as executive director for the Bush Presidential Library Foundation, Don Wilson wanted to create symbols and logos that underscored the commonality of all the entities forming the Bush Presidential Library Center. Early versions of the shared design involved red, white, and blue with stars but made no reference to Texas A&M University. Although the Bush Library building would be federal government property, the Bush School would be part of the university. The school's identity with the university was essential in any logo. Rick Johnson sought to remedy that omission and worked quickly with a designer to offer a variation of the original design. The new proposed logo incorporated much of the original concept but included Texas A&M University (without the university colors or seal). The university acknowledged the need for a Bush School logo to fit with the Bush Library complex, and the Library Foundation permitted the proposed modification. Later, Richard Chilcoat, dean of the Bush School, referred to the logo as worth a million dollars in branding.

The Bush School Centers Begin

Rapid early movement also occurred with the establishment of two new research centers that were to be an integral part of the Bush School—the Center for Presidential Studies and the Center for Public Leadership Studies. After his initial visits to Texas A&M in his capacity of evaluating sites for the Bush Presidential Library, Don Wilson had made a suggestion to the university committee. If Texas A&M had an intrinsic interest in the proposed research centers, then it might consider a rapid start-up as a valuable signal of the university's investment in areas of interest to the president.[1] Their early establishment might enhance the Texas A&M proposal. The university had acted on his suggestion. In 1991 the university regents approved establishment of the Center for Presidential Studies with George Edwards as director.[2] With Bryan Jones's departure from Texas A&M, however, the search for a director of the Center for Public Leadership Studies took longer. Fortunately, Arnold Vedlitz had recently completed an administrative post in the provost's office. He agreed to become the director, and the regents formally approved that center in 1993.[3] With limited space in Harrington Tower, both center directors continued to work from their offices in the Political Science Department located next door. (Thus, they were not regular participants in the elevator-stairway races.)

Edwards and Vedlitz worked hard to initiate their programs in those early years. They faced a common obstacle—limited financial resources. The problem was hardly theirs alone. In their campaign for the Bush Library, the regents' Library Planning Committee boldly declared that Texas A&M alumni would contribute all the necessary funds required for the Presidential Library and the proposed academic components. For example, the minutes of that committee for a meeting on May 2, 1991, record its chair, Michel Halbouty, stating that "he guaranteed that neither President Bush nor members of his family would ever be asked to raise one penny for the library." The Academic Planning Committee also reflected similar financial confidence when, in the same meeting, Dan Fallon assured Don Wilson and Jim Cicconi that adequate funding would be provided for the operation of the two centers.[4] Responding to a reporter after Bush selected Texas A&M, Ross Margraves said, "We're going to raise every nickel of it ourselves. . . . We're not going to have any problem whatsoever in raising the funds for this presidential library."[5] Of course, the university financial commitment needed to cover the other two buildings as well as the new start-up academic programs. The belief that former Texas A&M students would quickly contribute the needed millions of dollars probably was never realistic. Furthermore, the timetable for acquisition of the necessary funds became truncated when President Bush did not win a second term.

Don Wilson discovered that raising the necessary funds for the library became his core responsibility. In the process, he also recognized that he would need to seek support primarily from both Texas A&M graduates and the network of friends of George H. W. Bush.

Wilson succeeded in the financial campaign, but the funding challenge became an area of disappointment for Wilson as well as for James Cicconi, the other key player in the Presidential Library selection process.[6]

The Bush Library Foundation was not the only entity facing financial challenges. The dollar shortage also occurred in the College of Liberal Arts—the home of the newly established two centers and the future Bush School. That college faced a budget deficit. Consequently, the start-up funding from the university for the Center for Presidential Studies and the Center for Public Leadership Studies remained minimal. It came primarily in the form of some reduction in teaching to enable both directors to devote more time to their centers. Vedlitz and Edwards scrabbled for money to operate their centers. Each pursued a different strategy.

Arnold (Arnie) Vedlitz pursued competitive research grants. His early strategy entailed assembling interdisciplinary teams of faculty to compete for contracts in three leadership areas—health policy, intergroup relations, and leadership education. In the first two years of operation, associates of the center submitted ten grant proposals and collaborated with other units as partners on several others. An early success resulted from collaboration with the Colleges of Business and Liberal Arts. They won a US Department of Education competition that established Eisenhower Leadership Programs on college campuses. The Texas A&M team created undergraduate leadership courses linked to student teams working on problems for state and local governments. The federal government renewed the grant, and the Colleges of Engineering and Agriculture joined the program so their students might also participate. After federal funding ended, the involved Texas A&M colleges liked the program so well that they sustained the funding for several additional years. In its first years of operation the center received another award for a project that examined the role of local leaders in the use of telecommunication technology for supporting rural health care. That federal program generated more than a million dollars, but only a portion came directly to the center's personnel. The other cooperating partners in the grant received the balance of the awarded funds.

George Edwards pursued a different funding strategy. Primarily he sought private endowment support. Shortly after the center opened,

Lance Tarrance—who supervised opinion surveys in Houston—gifted the center the acquired records of presidential polling data from the Gallup Organization and CBS/*New York Times*. That marked the center's beginning as a major archive for survey data on the presidency. Another early funding source occurred when the university awarded Edwards a professorship established by George and Julia Jordan. Edwards invited his benefactors to learn about his plans for the Center for Presidential Studies. The Jordans found the plans intriguing and in 1994 increased the funding of the professorship. Edwards used those professorship research funds to accelerate his own studies of the presidency and to support several colleagues studying the presidency.

Planning the Degree Program

From the earliest planning for the Bush School, the concept was to provide excellent graduate preparation for public service at an affordable price. The foundation for the degree program was to build on a concept of a public university that emphasized service as a guiding principle. Even though tuition and fees at a public university like Texas A&M remained significantly lower than at private universities, the Bush School recognized that containing the costs would be critical to successfully recruit strong students attracted to the idea of public-service careers. As the Bush School evolved and the costs of a university education rose, the concept of an excellent professional education for those desiring careers in public service—without requiring those students to incur heavy education loans for their graduate experience—became a core principle of the Bush School. Scholarships continue to constitute a key to achieving that goal; however, in the first years of the Bush School, scholarships were important simply to attract the attention of strong, potential students.

In an early effort to create scholarships, numerous friends of President Bush in the Texas congressional delegation were asked whether they might be interested in creating legislation whereby Congress would appropriate a three-million-dollar Bush School scholarship fund in honor of President George H. W. Bush. Joe Barton, Republican congressman from Texas (6th District), a graduate of Texas A&M, took the leadership in the House of Representatives. He introduced the proposal as an element of a bill in the 104th Congress. Congress approved and President Bill Clinton signed the bill on October 19, 1996, as a tribute to Bush. It established scholarships for students who would enter his new school.[7] Next, the school negotiated with the Department of Education, which had been designated in the legislation to administer the funds, to allow the establishment of a scholarship endowment with the appropriated funds rather than to withdraw the entire principle over time until it was gone. That effort also proved successful. Consequently, from the first class, each year a number of students receive Bush Congressional Scholarships from that endowment fund.

Creating a curriculum and a faculty represented a more daunting challenge than the endowment initiative in the organizing years of the Bush School. With the help of Woodrow Jones, Hermann created and chaired the Bush School Advisory Committee. That committee included faculty representatives from economics (Bill Neilson), history (William Brands), political science (Kim Hill), psychology (Winfred Arthur), sociology (Harland Prechel), communications (Scott Poole), and the dean's office (Steve Rholes). The major task involved designing the curriculum for the new school. Here the process, like the Harrington Tower elevator ride, proved to be slow with intermediate stops but was ultimately successful in reaching its destination.

Previously the Department of Political Science had a master's in public administration degree program that was terminated and would be replaced by the new degree to be offered by the Bush School. The Advisory Committee agreed that the new degree plan should maintain the core concepts of public administration but should also draw broadly on the contributions of multiple academic disciplines. The committee met every other week for over a year. The first order of business was to design a mission statement and declaration of the basic assumptions of the degree program. These would serve as the preamble for the intended school bylaws required by the university. Hermann recalls, "I reached out to Professor Paul Van Riper, former head of the Political Science Department and a distinguished scholar in public administration, to help me prepare a draft mission statement and set of bylaws for consideration by the committee. Van Riper and I passed drafts back and forth multiple times. Van Riper crafted the beginning of the proposed mission statement: 'The George Bush School of Government and Public Service educates principled leaders for public service.' Over the years the school's bylaws have been revised and amended multiple times, but Van Riper's mission declaration remains at the school's core. We educate principled leaders for service."

Most of the committee's work involved the design of the curriculum. Kim Hill, who had directed the political science master's in public administration degree program, contributed substantially to articulation of the basic requirements. The entire committee examined and debated the curricula of other schools. To augment their review of these written materials, Hermann visited with deans and key administrators at four schools similar to the one envisioned at A&M as well as the deans of many colleges at Texas A&M: Colleges of Agriculture, Business, Education, Engineering, and Geosciences and the School of Rural Public Health. Most of the deans seemed intrigued with creation of the Bush School and identified subjects and faculty who were engaged in teaching and research related to the plans of the school.

The responses of deans across the campus reinforced the idea that the Bush School could benefit from a strong multidisciplinary program. Members of the Planning Committee, who represented a variety of academic disciplines, shared the conviction of a broad-based instructional design for the professional master's curriculum.

A two-year degree plan was constructed that consisted of core courses in public administration taken largely in the student's first year. These fundamental courses were combined with a series of "career tracks." Each track consisted of three to five courses. Every student would choose one or two tracks to pursue primarily in his or her second year. The initial five career tracks were

Business and Government
Environment and Natural Resources
Health Policy and Management
International Affairs in the Americas
Advanced Public Management

These elective career tracks enabled the school to engage faculty from an array of academic disciplines. More important, they were designed to prepare students for specific domains of public service, which enhanced their preparation for employment.

The curriculum design included several other major features. Between the first and second year each student would work as an intern for an organization engaged in public administration. In the final semester each student would participate in a group research project that addressed a problem specified by a government agency or nonprofit organization. The committee's curriculum design, together with the mission statement and other materials, successfully gained approval through the university, the system regents, and the Texas Higher Education Coordinating Board. The next step: acquire faculty.

Recruiting a Faculty

In 1996 the Bush School hired Donald Deere, a tenured faculty member in the Department of Economics, to serve as the school's associate director. Like Rick Johnson, Deere became totally committed to the school. He played a significant role in recruiting the faculty and implementing the curriculum. Deere worked with individual faculty as they developed their course plans so that each career track had a set of courses that did not overlap but contributed to a common career theme. He worked with them collectively and individually to define expectations for teaching students in a professional master's degree program. In several cases, he arranged for faculty with different areas of expertise to team-teach a course.

From the initial design of the school in the plan submitted to President Bush as part of the Texas A&M proposal for the library, the university established a core concept for the school faculty that became a critical feature. The school would have no faculty of its own but would contract with faculty and their home academic departments to teach one or two (at the most) courses a year in the Bush School. Deere and Hermann served as the only full-time faculty, but even their long-term tenure positions remained in the Departments of Economics and Political Science, respectively. In the parlance of academia, the Bush School would not be a tenure-granting unit for any faculty.

The arrangement had several advantages. First, with the school's salary budget, it could hire more faculty as instructors—paying only a portion of each person's annual compensation—than would be possible if the school had to underwrite every teacher's full-time salary. Second, the school could engage instructors from a range of different academic disciplines. Third, it expanded the awareness of the Bush School across a broad spectrum of departments and colleges at Texas A&M. The initial faculty came from three colleges—Business, Health Sciences, and Liberal Arts—and from the following departments:

Agricultural Economics (1)
Agricultural Education (1)
Communications (1)
Economics (4)
History (1)
Management (4)
Medicine (1)
Philosophy (1)
Political Science (9)
Sociology (1)

After the curriculum had been established, a number of university faculty expressed an interest in teaching a course in the Bush School. Substantial problems arose, however, in negotiating compensation and scheduling with their home departments. Flexibility was the key; there were no one-size-fits-all arrangements. Each department and college required a distinctive plan. Occasionally, however, an agreement insisted on by one department would require revamping arrangements with previously negotiated departments to assure common treatment.

At times it appeared that it would not be possible to conclude agreements to acquire the needed faculty to cover all courses in the intended curriculum. Hermann said, "In one of my meetings with Don Wilson, the executive director of the Bush Presidential Library Foundation, I shared my concerns about the severe difficulties in securing the instructors needed for key courses. He made what I regarded as a wild proposal. Wilson suggested we cancel the entire arrangement for opening the MPA at the school with 'rented' faculty. Of course, I reminded him I was an academic administrator of Texas A&M, who had been hired specifically to open the school with its faculty. Don said no more. At that time I had no idea that Wilson had previously cautioned both Texas A&M and President Bush that the intended design for the Bush School faculty was flawed."[8] In the end, the Bush School secured arrangements for the needed faculty; however, some of Don Wilson's concerns would resurface after several years of experience.

Establishing Expectations of Prospective Employers

On May 3, 1996, the Bush School invited to Texas A&M individuals from organizations representative of those the school's leadership envisioned should want to hire future Bush School graduates. The participants represented a variety of potential employers and public-service leaders, including a sitting member of Congress, a state legislator, representatives of various federal departments and agencies (Health and Human Services, Commerce, Central Intelligence Agency [CIA], Federal Bureau of Investigation [FBI]) and several state agencies, a city manager, and individuals from multiple nonprofit organizations and several private corporations. The guests discussed the skills and abilities their organizations regarded as highly valuable in potential employees. A former dean of the College of Education at Ohio State University, Lavern Cunningham, served as the facilitator, and the discussions focused on such topics as desired personal attributes, knowledge, and skills.

This seminar with typical prospective employers resulted in significant concepts that became incorporated in the plans for the new school. Some suggestions influenced intended admission criteria. The stronger impact involved their advocacy for development of learnable skills. Collectively, they affirmed that even though most Bush School students would likely be at the beginning of their professional careers, they could benefit from acquisition of a set of learnable skills that would enhance their future potential for leadership: for example, communication, management, negotiation, team building, organizing, and managing an agenda. Competence in such skills would not guarantee students as future leaders in public service but would enhance their ability to be effective and make leadership opportunities more likely and successful.

Those consultants' recommendations echoed the characterization of the school in the Texas A&M proposal for the Bush Presidential Library: a school that would prepare future generations of leaders in public service. The particular framework has varied over time, but the concept has been a Bush School cornerstone. In particular, it led to the school's Leadership Program, a full-time Bush School writing consultant and writing workshops, and the student-run Public Service Organization.

The first iteration of these ideas occurred in the design of a Leadership Skills Assessment Center. Winfred Arthur, the faculty member on the planning committee from the Psychology Department, offered to direct this activity. He and a colleague in the Psychology Department created the initial Bush School leadership operation.

Recruiting Students for the First Class

The Bush School was scheduled to open in the fall semester of 1997. With the curriculum in place and the faculty arrangement making progress, the focus shifted to the recruitment of a first class of students. Over twenty-four hundred posters with reply cards were distributed, and a website was established. Several faculty, primarily Donald Deere, visited many four-year colleges in Texas as well as targeted universities elsewhere. The Bush School produced its first full-size recruitment brochure and application package. The school administration envisioned a first class of between fifteen and twenty students and ultimately had an initial class of eighteen, which included nine women, two Hispanics, one African American, and one international student. Each received a scholarship.

Bush School Completion and Dedication

In the late spring of 1997 the academic building in the Bush Library complex was completed. Cicconi, who had left government service, continued to be a key liaison for President Bush during the Bush Library construction. After visiting the campus in July 1994 and finding the primary road between the library complex and the main campus still under construction, Cicconi worried whether Texas A&M would actually bring academic activities to the library complex located at what was then the far edge of the existing campus.[9] He solicited and received repeated verbal and written assurances from faculty and university officials, including Adkisson. Additionally, Charles Johnson, head of the Political Science Department, which was scheduled to move from the center of campus to the library complex, wrote: "We heartily endorse the idea of keeping the Library Center fully connected to the Texas A&M campus."[10] Cicconi need not have worried. In addition to the new Bush School and its two centers, the new academic building became home to the Departments of Political Science and Economics. Furthermore, a significant part of the first floor served as a branch location of the main university library and also housed a small café.

The Bush School personnel began moving into the academic building in spring of 1997. On March 1, President and Mrs. Bush and the Bush Library Advisory Council had a tour of the building. The tour concluded with a briefing in one of the classrooms. The guests received and reviewed the new glossy booklet that included descriptions of the planned courses. At the conclusion of Hermann's remarks, a member of the council, Admiral David Jeremiah—former vice chairman of the Joint Chiefs of Staff—asked a question. He politely noted that the subjects to be taught looked interesting but did not seem to include much on international affairs. President Bush spoke up: "If you look at Chuck Hermann's background, one could conclude that international affairs would be addressed." Hermann recalls, "After the session ended, I went to Admiral Jeremiah to indicate that the university had already proposed the addition of an international affairs degree once the initial master's program was established. He was standing with Mrs. Bush. The three of us had a brief conversation. Mrs. Bush made very clear that any school with her husband's name on it would teach international affairs."

Bush continued to show great interest in the school. As the Bush Presidential Library moved toward completion, the date for its dedication was set for November 6, 1997. Bush expressed his concern that events associated with the opening of the library would likely overshadow the dedication of the school if they occurred on the same day. The idea of a separate dedication emerged. Soon after, Don Wilson and Jean Becker, the president's chief of staff, confirmed that Bush would participate in a separate event dedicating the Bush School. The Texas A&M leadership readily accepted responsibility for an independent event to dedicate the Bush School. The school opening would provide the first public introduction to the new Bush Library complex; it generated considerable interest and media attention.

The Bush School dedication activities occurred on September 9–10, 1997, at the beginning of the fall semester. The two-day event started with a conference on "The President and the Use of Force after the Cold War." The conference featured panels engaging experts from across the country as well as from Texas A&M. That first evening featured a dialogue between Paul Simon, senator from Illinois, and Dick Cheney. Cheney was president of Halliburton, after having previously served as secretary of defense during the Bush presidency. The panel discussions continued the morning of the second day and concluded with observations by President Bush.

Following a lunch hosted by Ray Bowen, president of Texas A&M, the activities moved to a dedication ceremony outside the new home of the George Bush School of Government and Public Service. The stage party included not only President and Mrs. Bush but also Texas governor George W. Bush. The Texas A&M band played the national anthem followed by the first performance of the "George Bush Presidential March," composed by the band director, Ray Toler. Corby Alexander, a member of the first class of the Bush School, offered a prayer of dedication. Two years later he would offer a prayer at the school's first graduation exercise. Hermann remembers, "At the conclusion of my remarks, I made a comment that caught the attention of the media: 'Mr. President, you have a new title. Welcome to Texas A&M University, Professor Bush.'"

An open house at the school followed. In the central hallway a new bronze bust of President Bush occupied a prominent location. An identical bust is in the entrance to the CIA headquarters in Langley, Virginia, which is named for Bush. With a generous donation from Sara and John Lindsey, the sculptor Marc Mellon produced a second casting of the bust. Both the Lindseys and Mellon joined President and Mrs. Bush for the unveiling.

The eighteen members of the first class of the Bush School missed much of the time allocated for the open house. At that time they had a private seminar with President Bush and Governor Bush. It included an extensive question-and-answer session. One member of that class,

Alexandra Kluge, who was from the former East Germany, told President Bush that his actions as president had made it possible for her to live in a united and free Germany and to attend the Bush School.

The festivities ended with an evening concert in the campus Rudder Auditorium, featuring the Aggie Singing Cadets, the Austin Symphony Pops, and Texas A&M graduate Lyle Lovett. The Bush School of Government and Public Service officially opened for business.

3

Trial and Error

An Experimental Exercise

The first two years of the new Bush School might be viewed as a series of experiments. Of course, none of the activities represented controlled research experiments. More generally in an experiment, something is tried that may or may not produce the desired results. If it appears to work, the initiative is continued. If it does not, the search begins for an alternative. Between fall 1997 and the end of the spring semester 1999, a number of experiment-type initiatives were tried at the Bush School. Faculty, students, administrators, and potential donors all served both as investigators and subjects in these exercises. Some things worked well; others did not.

Consider an experiment that worked. The Board of Regents constitutes the governing body for all the educational and research institutions in the Texas A&M University System. Not surprisingly, they asked for a report on the new Bush School of Government and Public Service after the school had been operating for several months. Accompanied by Ray Bowen, Hermann provided an oral briefing. Fred McClure, a graduate of Texas A&M who had served President Bush on his White House executive staff, had returned to Texas and become a member of the Board of Regents. Of course, he had a particular interest in the Bush School and asked about the process used in the selection of students. Hermann recalls, "I described the application forms and the information we sought. McClure knew we had eighteen students in our first class. He responded that given the limited number of students we were admitting, it should be possible to conduct a personal interview with each candidate to augment the written application. After the meeting, President Bowen advised me that such a remark from a regent was closer to a directive than a suggestion."

In selecting the second class, McClure's proposal was employed. The Admissions Committee examined the written applications. All those considered to be plausibly qualified for a professional master's degree were invited to visit the Bush School for a special interview weekend. Those unable to attend had a telephone interview. Whether in person or by phone, each candidate participated in two interviews with different faculty members. Those who came to the campus also engaged in a writing exercise, heard from panels of both current students and faculty, and, of course, toured the campus. Afterward the Admissions Committee received reports with assessments from the faculty interviews, the writing exercise, and current student observations.

The committee found the results invaluable. Furthermore, the campus weekend turned into a valued recruiting experience. If an applicant came to the weekend and was offered admission, acceptance was more likely. Across the years the annual pool of applications to the school has grown substantially—as has the size of each admitted class. The initial interview weekend experiment produced great results. It continues to work as a vital admissions process to this day. Currently most nonresident interviews link the candidate and the faculty interviewers in visual electronic interaction.

In the second year of operation, starting in the fall of 1998, sixty-eight individuals applied and received interviews. Twenty-two were offered admission; twenty enrolled. One-half of the second entering class attended Texas undergraduate institutions. Eleven were women.

Building a Faculty

The new Bush School's multidisciplinary faculty from an array of academic departments constituted a striking experiment and a marked contrast in instruction from the previous Texas A&M master's in public administration degree. That earlier master's program resided exclusively in the Department of Political Science. Its faculty taught the courses. The new Bush School faculty represented multiple departments and colleges. They had begun in early 1997 working together in a series of faculty meetings. As additional faculty members signed up, they joined the group. Some participated in planning meetings even before a formal agreement with their department was negotiated. In addition to getting acquainted with one another, they faced numerous tasks. Implementing a coherent curriculum became a serious challenge.

The two-year curriculum consisted of a series of core courses in the first year followed by a summer internship. In the second year students took a course in ethics and public policy and a course on the characteristics of American society (e.g., race, ethnicity, gender, and social economic structure) that affected public policy. In the last semester as a policy seminar or capstone, students worked in teams for a client on a public policy issue. In addition, in their second year students selected one of five clusters of elective courses designed to prepare them for specific areas of public service. These concentrations were the ones that the multidisciplinary faculty constructed in their months of working together before the school opened.

Each of the five concentrations included multiple courses taught by faculty from different academic departments and colleges in the university. For example, the Health Policy and Management concentration engaged faculty from the School of Rural Public Health; Business and Government brought together faculty from the Political Science Department and the College of Business. The challenge of nonoverlapping coverage and integration across these core-theme concentrations proved substantial.

Courses taken in residence at the university were not the only source of degree credit hours. Students remained enrolled at Texas A&M while undertaking their required summer internships, and they produced credit hours. As a result, the entire degree involved fifty-four credit hours of study—a number larger than comparable programs entailed.

Although not part of the credit-hour curriculum, the Leadership Skills Assessment Center that grew out of the seminar with potential employers (described in chapter 2) constituted another major experiment in the new Bush School. Two faculty members from the Department of Psychology organized and managed that initiative. All entering students participated in this assessment exercise two days before the beginning of the fall semester. Using a variety of simulations, games, and written exercises, the assessment provided students with a confidential estimate of their current performance on a set of skills. These were skills that the US Office of Personnel Management had identified as important abilities for leadership and management in public service. They included written and oral communication, team building, and negotiation skills. Each student received a confidential feedback report and was to configure a personal plan for selective skill enhancement while enrolled at the Bush School. Voluntary workshops were offered periodically during the academic year on various skill sets.

Considerable debate occurred on the success of this particular experiment. All agreed that some of the outside activities (known as the "ropes course") were fun and a great mixer for the entering class. The psychologists, however, wished to focus on activities for which relative performance could be reliably measured. Those concerned with public policy and administration insisted that what was being assessed had to be clearly identified with a specified skill. Scoring relative writing ability proved to be a relatively easy task; team building, less so.

The existing faculty at Texas A&M who agreed to teach in the new school had been engaged by the beginning of 1997; however, faculty recruitment continued to be a major task in the beginning years of the Bush School. The Political Science Department and the Bush School agreed to a joint hire in public administration and successfully recruited Robert Durant. A year later a joint effort with the Department of Political Science and the Office of the Dean of Liberal Arts succeeded in hiring Mitchell Rice, but other efforts between the Bush School and either the Departments of Political Science or Economics were less successful. When employment entailed tenure, that status had to be granted by another academic department. As noted, the Bush School was not a tenure-granting unit. However, if a faculty member taught and engaged in policy research and service at the Bush School, how would that be evaluated by colleagues in the faculty member's home department? Questions arose about balancing workload, salary raises, and possible promotion. Striking an arrangement that proved acceptable to the academic department, the Bush School, and the prospective faculty member proved challenging. By early in the academic year 1998–1999, the challenge led to a dialogue that included the university provost on the concept of a joint tenure process between two academic units. That turned out to be a potential experiment no one wanted to try.

Fortunately, when tenure was not involved, the Bush School experienced much more success. The first occasion occurred when there was an opportunity to accept a CIA officer, James Olson, in residence. In January 1997, Olson and his wife, Meredith, visited the campus. For him to be assigned as an officer-in-residence, the agency required him to teach a course on the role of intelligence in international affairs each semester. Initially, it appeared to be an undergraduate-level course, but Olson seemed to be a good candidate for a visiting appointment, so a special undergraduate course was created. For the first several semesters, Olson team-taught with Martin Medhurst. The course was a complete success. By the time the officer-in-residence term had expired, Jim Olson was offered an appointment at the Bush School teaching graduate seminars. He retired from the CIA and became a full-time member of the Bush master's program. Moving to a full-time appointment teaching Bush School students required that the school cancel Olson's undergraduate course, which infuriated undergraduates. Hermann says, "I received a wave of angry mail from undergraduates who wanted to take Olson's course."

Another successful hire was Kenneth Ashworth, who had completed years of service in Texas state government, ending as administrator of the Texas Higher Education Coordinating Board. He divided his teaching between the LBJ School at the University of Texas and the Bush School. He introduced a variety of game and simulation exercises in his course that proved both exciting and instructive. The same might be said for one of his authored books on public administration with the catchy title, *Caught between the Dog and the Fire Plug, or How to Survive Public Service*.[1] Deborah Kerr first came to the Bush School as a guest speaker in 1998. Her background experience included management in the Texas state government and leadership in a major nonprofit organization, and she was invited to serve as a part-time instructor. Like the others, Kerr proved excellent in the classroom. For several years, Michele Sabino from the Houston Endowment offered a course on management of nonprofit organizations.

These individuals constituted an important dimension of the Bush School's instructional staff. The school's mission seeks to prepare its students for careers in public administration, the conduct of public policy, and international affairs. Most graduates anticipate going into government service or management of nonprofit organizations. They need to learn from a faculty that, in addition to knowledgeable academic experts, includes individuals who have spent much of their careers operating in the public sector. To be effective, such experienced practitioners must have the ability to move from their own particular experience to more general insights and effectively convey them to others: to teach!

The Bush School faculty in its first years represented a remarkably broad and diverse set of instructors. Table 1 identifies the individuals, their field, and the years they taught in the Bush School. The range of expertise and experience they provided was substantial. The new school achieved the university's aspiration of engaging a broad array of faculty expertise from across the College of Liberal Arts and beyond. The continuing challenge remained to fashion the course offerings into a coherent program presented at the appropriate level for graduate students, who lacked the depth of knowledge in any one academic discipline that faculty might expect in their own department. Whatever else, pulling together such a diverse set of faculty to offer an integrated graduate program qualified as a major experiment.

A Bush School Capital Campaign

A capital campaign might not immediately appear to be an experiment, but there is a parallel. The experiment involves finding a fit between the potential donor's passions and interests and the design and presentation of a project needing support. When compatibility is discovered, the experiment succeeds. Such successful fund-raising experiments are critical. A state-funded university educational venture, such as the Bush School, must be augmented by a substantial

Table 1
Bush School–affiliated faculty, 1997–2001

Faculty member	Program / department	1997–1998	1998–1999	1999–2000	2000–2001
Sara Alpern	History	X	X	X	X
James E. Anderson	Political science	X	X	X	X
Richard Kenneth Anderson	Economics				X
Kenneth Ashworth	Visiting professor	X	X	X	X
Sherry Bame	Community medicine	X	X	X	X
Leonard Bierman	Management	X	X	X	X
Richard L. Cummins	Agricultural education			X	X
Donald R. Deere, associate director*	Economics	X	X	X	X
Robert F. Durant	Political science		X	X	X
Lorraine Eden	Management	X	X	X	X
George C. Edwards, director, Center for Presidential Studies	Political science	X	X	X	X
James Griffin	Economics				X
Timothy J. Gronberg	Economics	X	X	X	X
Charles F. Hermann, director*	Political science	X	X	X	X
Kim Q. Hill	Political science	X	X	X	X
Peter Hugill	Geography			X	X
Deborah Kerr	Visiting professor			X	X

Faculty member	Program / department	1997–1998	1998–1999	1999–2000	2000–2001
Jonathan L. Kvanvig	Philosophy		X	X	X
Jan E. Leighley	Political science	X	X	X	X
James W. Mjelde	Agricultural economics	X	X	X	X
William S. Neilson	Economics	X	X	X	X
James M. Olson	Officer-in-residence	X	X	X	X
Marshall Scott Poole	Communications				X
Harland N. Prechel	Sociology	X	X	X	X
Mitchell F. Rice	Political science			X	X
Michele Sabino	Visiting scholar		X		
Paul Van Riper	Political science	X	X	X	X
Arnold Vedlitz, director, Center for Public Leadership Studies	Political science	X	X	X	X
William F. West	Political science	X	X	X	X
B. Dan Wood	Political science	X	X	X	X
Asghar Zardkoohi	Management	X	X	X	X

* Full-time in the Bush School

private endowment to become truly outstanding. Tuition and state funds provide an essential foundation but alone can never yield sufficient resources for an exceptional, innovative learning enterprise. The Bush School needed donors, so the administration embarked on an experiment designed to create a fit between the needs of the school and the interests of potential donors.

Hermann relates, "Soon after I came to Texas A&M, the dean of Liberal Arts, the Texas A&M Foundation, and I agreed on a Bush School Development Campaign of twenty million dollars. Initially, the Bush School shared the development officer assigned to the College of Liberal Arts. A few months later, the Texas A&M Foundation generously stepped up with the assignment of Ron Streibich exclusively to the Bush School. We faced substantial competition in seeking donors for the school, resulting from the major campaign for the Bush Library along with all the other established colleges at A&M that constantly sought donors and, unlike us, had alumni!"

Ron Streibich's office was in Houston because many prospective donors for Texas A&M lived in the greater Houston area. Although Ron came to College Station regularly, over the three years he and Hermann worked together, they often met for a working lunch in the town of Hempstead—about midway between Houston and College Station—to update strategy and plan contacts with potential donors. Hermann explains, "At these lunch sessions, I designated areas of desired gifts and naming opportunities, and—most critically—Ron identified individuals and organizations who might find the Bush School and its undertakings of interest. The result was the first 'Bush School Campaign Plan,' a document running over seventy pages."

Following the identification of potential donors, they hit the road. Hermann says,

> I spoke to groups, and we visited with prospects. It introduced me to more of Texas—Midland, San Antonio, Fort Worth, Dallas, and many other communities. Usually, Ron and I constituted the team, but we had some major help. University president Ray Bowen joined us several times and steered some prospects in our direction. Two members of the Texas A&M Board of Regents proved particularly helpful. John Lindsey set up multiple lunches in the Houston area. Don Powell made introductions in

Amarillo and suggested other contacts. As the executive director of the Bush Presidential Library Foundation, Don Wilson faced the sizable task of raising money for the library, but he offered help on several occasions. President Bush, very understandably, remained adamant that he would not ask for gifts. He stated that that part of his life was over. Nonetheless, he and Mrs. Bush repeatedly hosted prospective donors, and the president quickly wrote personal thank-you notes to all major contributors to the school's campaign.

The combination of a school named for George Herbert Walker Bush and its incorporation as part of Texas A&M University proved marketable, and the school experienced some real success. Ed and Evelyn Kruse and Howard and Verlin Kruse, founders of Blue Bell Creameries, funded an endowed chair.[2] John and Sara Lindsey did the same.[3] The Abell-Hanger Foundation provided an endowment for a policy maker–in–residence. The Cullen Trust and the King Foundation added to the student fellowship program that the 104st Congress had started in honor of the forty-first president. As noted previously, the Jordans substantially enlarged their initial gift in support of the Center for Presidential Studies and created an endowed chair for George Edwards. Compaq Computer Corporation provided a substantial number of computers to start the school. The Korean Foundation established funds for a speaker series.

General Brent Scowcroft had become another enthusiastic supporter of the Bush School. Among his varied contributions, he endowed a faculty chair.[4] Although the campaign still had a way to go to reach its target, on October 8, 1998, President and Mrs. Bush with Scowcroft hosted a dinner for donors to the Bush School and the Bush Library. The following day Bush and Scowcroft invited the guests to watch a taping of their appearance on the Charlie Rose television program.

To recognize and honor donors, the school created a cherrywood wall in the foyer of the Bush School hallway behind the bust of President Bush. It featured silver stars of varying sizes with the names of contributors. Hermann relates one particular experience:

> On one occasion Mrs. Sara Lindsey cornered me and asked about the location of her star. She and her husband, John, had made

separate large gifts, so they each had their own star. But they were at opposite ends of the wall. She protested, "That makes it appear as if we are divorced." We continued to add donor's stars through the following academic year—and we moved Sara Lindsey's star next to that of her husband. That wall remained unchanged from 2000 until 2015, when the space was modified to acknowledge all subsequent donors to the school. However, several faculty offices, including one named for former university president Frank Vandiver, and one classroom named for the amir of Qatar, continue to bear the plaques of donors who asked for that form of recognition.

Not all efforts were successful. Repeated attempts to promote an endowment for a faculty chair in ethics and public policy failed, and the school never hired anyone with that specific teaching and research focus. George Edwards and John Leggett, a faculty member in computer and information science, developed a major proposal for a presidential digital library and worked over a protracted period of time for its promotion—but with no success. Arnie Vedlitz encountered a German American industrialist who expressed great interest in a German-American exchange program to be directed by the Bush School. Vedlitz worked out a detailed proposal, but the prospective donor died before completing the agreement. Ray Bowen had a conversation with a soon-to-retire army chief of staff. They discussed a possible special relationship between Texas A&M and the US Army for the education of their officers designated for international assignments as foreign area officers (FAO). Bowen charged his vice president for research, Robert Kennedy, and Hermann to lead a team developing a program proposal for an operation that would be carried out in the Bush School. After the general retired, no one else associated with the army FAO program showed much interest in the elaborately developed proposal. A similarly unsuccessful effort was made to identify a major donor for whom the academic building would be named. Over more than two years Hermann and Streibich made repeated visits with prospective donors to name the building but had no luck.

In a sense, however, some of these efforts planted significant seeds. The school continued to work with the US Army by hosting a major symposium in December 1998 attended by General Dennis Reimer, army chief of staff; Louis Caldera, secretary of the army; and President Bush. Eventually, Texas A&M, through the Bush School, became one of the universities annually hosting army fellows-in-residence. One of the people called on for a major contribution was Robert Allen. Later, he and his wife provided the gift that led to the academic building being named for them.

Another remarkable story in the development campaign followed the original Abell-Hanger gift to establish a visiting policy maker–in–residence. Arnie Vedlitz suggested initiating that program with Bob Bullock, who was stepping down as the powerful lieutenant governor of Texas in 1999. During his last years in office, Bullock—a leading Democrat—had worked in an unusual bipartisan fashion with Republican governor George W. Bush on key state matters. The invitation was extended to Bullock. Shortly after he retired, the public learned that he had advanced cancer. Within days of the media attention, Bullock called Hermann at the Bush School. He said that he liked the invitation and wanted the school to know that he was going to "beat this thing" and come to the Bush School the next year. He did not achieve that goal and died later the same year. The following year, however, his wife and family established the Bob Bullock Chair in Government and Public Policy at the Bush School of Government and Public Service. The Texas A&M Foundation matched the Bullock family gift to create two new endowed chairs for the Bush School.

The President and the Bush School

The George Bush Presidential Library opening celebration occurred November 6, 1997. President Bill Clinton joined his immediate predecessor and former presidents Jimmy Carter and Gerald Ford along with their wives and former first ladies Nancy Reagan and Lady Bird Johnson. They led a huge crowd of political figures, including Governor Bush of Texas; the soon-to-be governor of Florida, Jeb Bush; and numerous celebrities and well-wishers. The opening of the Presidential Library and Museum marked the completion of the complex that also included a conference center (now the Annenberg Presidential Conference Center) and the academic building that is home to the Bush School (now the Robert H. and Judy Ley Allen Building). As noted earlier, the conference center includes a second-floor office and apartment for President and Mrs. Bush. Although they continued to leave their Houston home in the summers for Kennebunkport, Maine, while in Texas they began to use the apartment on the Texas A&M campus frequently.

Their recurrent presence and accessible, personal styles had dramatic impact. In the early years when his health was robust, Bush would explore the campus. He would occasionally work out at the student recreation center, visit the Corps of Cadets headquarters, and attend home football games. Ray Bowen recalled a Saturday morning when Bush stopped by unannounced at the university president's home on the campus to introduce a friend.[5] Barbara Bush was less likely to roam the large campus, but she made appearances at events and regularly walked their dogs around the pond behind the Presidential Library. On June 9, 1999, several days before his seventy-fifth birthday, Bush made a parachute jump in front of his library.

That parachute jump resulted in one failed Bush School effort to connect with President Bush. The feature wing of the academic building—on the side closest to the Bush Presidential Library—is a two-story structure with a flat roof and bordered the intended parachute landing zone. On the day of the jump, most students were away from campus for summer internships. The few students who remained developed (with the school director) what seemed like a fun project with potential publicity for the school. The idea was to put a huge sign on the school roof facing skyward: "Great Jump, Mr. President." The huge sign appeared on plastic sheeting that would have been visible from the sky near the landing zone. Strong winds required students to make repeated trips to the roof with rocks necessary to secure the sign. Before the jump, the Secret Service discovered the operation. They were not pleased. Unguarded access to a roof immediately adjacent to the jump landing site struck them as a bad idea. The sign came down, and the stairway to the roof was bolted shut. Virtually all other Bush School student encounters with President Bush, however, succeeded.

The Bush School faculty, students, and staff experienced the effects of the Bush interest and presence dramatically. Some of the interactions were informal and random. Friends of the president arranged for the construction of a horseshoe pit, similar to the one Bush had introduced at the White House. It was less than five yards from the side of the Bush School. Students learned that if they went out and "pitched shoes" when Bush was around, he might join them for a game. When he was fishing in the pond behind the library and the school, he would certainly pose for a photograph and a brief exchange. Fishing in the Presidential Library pond was open to all on a catch-and-release basis. When President and Mrs. Bush entertained in their apartment, one or two Bush School faculty would often be included as guests, and on several occasions in the first several years, they hosted receptions specifically for the Bush School faculty.

Not all encounters were casual and social. Many interactions with President Bush centered on the school's educational mission. He agreed to participate in several classes each semester, insisting that the students and instructors be different each time. He preferred a question-and-answer format on an announced topic. Certainly, some of the most powerful and dramatic interactions occurred with speakers whom he and his staff invited to give formal addresses in one of the auditoriums of the Presidential Conference Center. The array of remarkable guest speakers continues to this day, but in the beginning years of the Bush School, the speaker and the president occasionally visited with students in a classroom. In the first years the guests included former heads of state Valéry Giscard d'Estaing, Brian Mulroney, and Lee Kuan Yew plus members of Bush's own administration (e.g., Robert Gates, Brent Scowcroft) and media leaders (e.g., Robert MacNeil).

In 1998 an outside group of distinguished advisers for the Bush School became the Board of Counselors (later renamed the Bush School Advisory Board). President and Mrs. Bush generously agreed to host the first meeting at Kennebunkport that summer. The committee was chaired by Don Powell (then chair of the Texas A&M Board of Regents), who has played a major role throughout the history of the school.[6] Other members at that time included Neil Bush (Interlink Management Corp.), Lynne Cheney (fellow at American Enterprise Institute), Marc Cisneros (lieutenant general in the US Army; retired president, Texas A&M University–Kingsville), Tony Garcia (Texas Railroad commissioner and later US ambassador to Mexico) , Charles Hines (president, Prairie View A&M University), Roger Porter (director, Center for Business and Government, Kennedy School, Harvard University), Condoleezza Rice (provost, Stanford University), William Roper (dean of the School of Public Health, University of North

Carolina), Lynn Schlemeyer (vice president, Compaq Computer Corporation), and Alan Simpson (retired senator, then at the Kennedy School, Harvard University). Most, but not all, attended the Kennebunkport meeting. Jean Becker participated in most of the sessions and later joined the board. For the first Kennebunkport meeting Ray Bowen also sat in on most sessions. The committee received a report on the school's first year and future strategy. The board was invited to offer their assessment and suggestions. Considerable discussion occurred on the admissions process and the composition of the school's faculty.

Hermann recalls,

> President Bush did not attend the sessions, but he and Mrs. Bush hosted cocktails and meals. He found an opportunity to have an informal conversation with Dr. Bowen and me. On that occasion he underscored his pleasure with the school's beginning and his confidence in us as academic administrators. He expressed his layman's surprise, however, that the Bush School seemed buried inside the College of Liberal Arts and wondered how that would affect its future visibility and effectiveness. Dr. Bowen responded that the primary organizing unit of the university beyond individual academic departments was the college, of which there were nine on the Texas A&M campus—the smallest college was geosciences with over a hundred faculty and thousands of students. By contrast, he noted the Bush School had two full-time faculty (as administrators) and under forty residential students. Essentially, Dr. Bowen's response stressed organizational and cost-management considerations. He suggested that it would be valuable for the Bush School to be in an incubator in its formative years. President Bush acknowledged there certainly might be a cost problem, and with that, the substantive conversation ended.

It would come to resonate in later events.

The School's Second Year, 1998–1999

With both first- and second-year classes in residence for the first time, the Bush School had a total enrollment in the fall of 1998 of thirty-eight students. Although space—particularly classrooms—would later become an issue as the school continued to grow, at that time there was extra office space. Consequently, each student was offered a desk in an office. Some offices had three students; others had two. An interesting phenomenon resulted. Most unmarried students spent much of the day, and a good bit of the night, at the Bush School. A remarkably close student community emerged. They quickly formed a student government as well as a student-run Public Service Organization. As the service organization name implied, the students continually organized and conducted community-service projects. Local community organizations snapped them up for grant writing and surveys, reading to children at an early learning center, and using them as able labor for Habit for Humanity home construction.

The two research centers also advanced their work with the Bush School by contributing more resources as well as space. George Edwards became editor of the *Presidential Studies Quarterly* and, as noted previously, continued to seek funding to create a more elaborate survey data archive on the presidency. He encouraged several colleagues to develop programs on aspects of the presidency. H. W. Brands, a historian, established a program on the presidency and foreign relations. Martin Medhurst, a communications faculty member, organized a program on presidential rhetoric. Both programs sponsored academic conferences in the second year of the Bush School's operation.[7]

In the Center for Public Leadership Studies, Arnie Vedlitz established a wide range of interdisciplinary research partnerships that sought research contracts from a variety of public and private sources. Vedlitz was energetic in engaging researchers from the Texas Engineering Extension Service, Texas Transportation Institute, Texas Agricultural Experimental Station, Institute for Biotechnology, and others. In most cases, Vedlitz and his colleagues added an important public policy dimension to proposals that researchers in other fields were developing. They established a healthy success rate. For example, a group of Texas A&M investigators—including those from Vedlitz's institute—won a National Science Foundation (NSF) grant of $336,819 to examine how knowledge was being used in infrastructure decisions in the city of Houston. In effect, that research discovered ways to enhance the success of major public projects in Houston.[8]

Donald Deere correctly asserted that the school's existing centers failed to make full use of an economic perspective in the examination of public policy problems. He urged that better use might be made of the talents of many faculty in the Economics Department, now existing in the same building as the Bush School. Several initiatives were explored. James Griffin (economics) and Ken Meier (political science) developed the concept of a program on markets and government. The Bush School did work with Griffin and an existing center within the Economics Department, directed by Thomas Savings, to convene an academic conference on Medicare. The school helped support another conference, "Increasing Inequality in America," organized by Finis Welch, economics professor. The elusive task remained finding sustainable funding for another center.

In the fall of 1998, Ron Douglas, university provost, requested the Bush School to prepare a formal proposal for a professional master's degree in international affairs. He asked that the design of the degree program include faculty from across the campus because professors in multiple colleges had expertise and interest in international affairs. (Beyond the evident faculty capabilities in the College of Liberal Arts, he noted faculty in the Geography Department in the College of Geosciences and the national security activities of faculty in the Nuclear Engineering Department as examples.) In effect, he sought an even broader multidisciplinary faculty than already existed for the Master in Public Service and Administration (MPSA). That plan presented a special challenge because the current Bush School students were discontent with their present instructors.

Clearly, some innovative teaching was happening at the Bush School. For example, Lorraine Eden, a resident faculty member in the Mays Business School, offered a course on the North American Free Trade Agreement (NAFTA) via closed-circuit television with a parallel course in Ottawa and Mexico City. The instructors at the three sites had constructed a common syllabus and taught the course together once a week, with the students and professors interacting with one another via the closed-circuit television. President Bush and Robert Mosbacher, his former secretary of commerce who had led the NAFTA negotiations, joined a session. Key Canadian and Mexican negotiators also participated.

Other instructors also offered imaginative seminars. Jim Olson's seminars received enthusiastic student assessments. Overall, however, the Bush School students were not pleased with a number of their courses. They felt too many of their professors came to the Bush

School to teach their course and then left, which offered little opportunity for interaction outside class. The students believed that some faculty offered courses more appropriate for academic PhD candidates than a professional master's degree in public administration. The students described many faculty as "rent-a-profs."

Donald Deere; Bill Brands, committee chairman for design of an international affairs master's degree; and Hermann struggled to devise an arrangement for long-term engagement of faculty with the Bush School rather than the current year-to-year contract. The joint-tenure concept had already been rejected as unworkable. Hermann relates, "We began to conceptualize a multiyear joint appointment arrangement but recognized that it would require a framework needing approval by many departments and colleges as well as the university's central administration. Not a quick fix. Meanwhile, we created a consultative committee consisting of students, faculty, and staff to explore more immediate ways to address shared challenges."

Bush School Transformation

In December 1998 at the end of the fall semester of the Bush School's second year of operation, Don Powell convened a second meeting of the school's Board of Counselors. The students asked for and received a two-hour closed session for three of their representatives. Hermann's participation in the meeting was limited due to a serious, but fortunately curable, health problem.

A month earlier, he had experienced a subarachnoid hemorrhage (a hemorrhage between two membranes in the brain), which caused an unwanted flow of blood around the brain. Fortunately, the blood leak sealed itself, but the condition required hospitalization and an extended home stay.

Hermann remembers, "My health situation put me behind in preparing for the Board of Counselors meeting. I did present a chart sketching critical steps for the evolution of the Bush School over the next three years. Don Powell asked that I develop that three-year plan in consultation with University Provost Douglas and President Bowen. That plan was in place in the spring of 1999."

A development—unanticipated by many in the university—occurred in the Texas state legislature. In the budget the legislature included a line item separate from the main appropriation for Texas A&M University for the Bush School, with an undisclosed specification attached. When that budget language was revealed, it stipulated that the school would be required to become an independent unit within the university with its own dean reporting to the provost and president and its own faculty. That came as quite a surprise. At that point Hermann e-mailed Bowen: "Twenty years from now, I hope that the Bush School is such an overwhelmingly valued asset that everyone will pay tribute to you for the enormous difficulty you have borne in getting it underway in a responsible fashion."[9]

Although the legislative move caught most of Texas A&M by surprise, Bowen supported the reorganization. After the meeting with Bush in Kennebunkport the previous summer, Bowen visited the Kennedy School of Government at Harvard University. He reported that faculty and administrators of that school consistently told him their school began to come together as an effective teaching and research unit only after it became an independent organization within the university.[10]

When the Texas bill became law and the university Board of Regents consented to the terms, Ray Bowen and Ron Douglas asked in late spring for Hermann to chair a committee to convert the strategy document into a plan for transitioning to an independent school. The Bush School committee worked intensely both before and after the school's "celebration of completion" ceremony for its first graduates. Corby Alexander, who had offered a prayer at the ceremony opening the Bush School two years earlier, repeated his role. The graduates started what became a tradition of giving a "Silver Star" award to a special faculty member. President Bush spoke to the graduates. Then he joined families and friends as the graduates went outside and pitched their mortar boards. The school transition committee went back to work. Hermann recalls,

> I met in mid-June with President Bowen and Provost Douglas to present our report. They informed me that a committee cochaired by Dr. Condoleezza Rice of Stanford University and Professor Howard Kaplan, Distinguished Professor in Texas A&M's Sociology Department, would lead a committee to search for a Bush School dean. An interim dean would be designated later in the

President Bush welcomes Texas A&M University dean of the College of Liberal Arts, Woodrow Jones, and newly appointed director of the Bush School of Government and Public Service, Chuck Hermann. Photo used with permission of Alexander Fine Portrait Design.

The feature wing of the Bush School under construction in 1996 behind Maurice East, dean of the Elliot School of International Affairs, George Washington University, and Lorraine Eden. Photo used with permission of Chuck Hermann.

"Welcome to Texas A&M, Professor Bush!" The dedication of the Bush School and the unveiling of the bust of President Bush occurred September 10, 1997. From left to right: Dionel Aviles, university regent; Ray Bowen, Texas A&M president; Woodrow Jones (partially obscured), dean of the College of Liberal Arts; President George H. W. Bush; Barbara Bush; Donald E. Powell, chair of the Board of Regents; Erle Nye, university regent; and Chuck Hermann. Courtesy of Texas A&M University. Photo by Michael Kellett.

President Bush addresses the crowd at the dedication of the Bush School. Fred McClure, Texas A&M University regent, former White House staff member, and graduate of Texas A&M responds enthusiastically. Courtesy of Texas A&M University. Photo by James Lyle.

President Bush, with his likeness and the sculptor, Marc Mellon, are flanked by the donors, John and Sara Lindsey, at the school dedication. Courtesy of Texas A&M University. Photo by James Lyle.

At their apartment atop the Presidential Library Conference Center, President and Mrs. Bush host some of the initial Bush School faculty: Hank Jenkins Smith, Laurence Lynn Jr., Jan Leighley, and Arnie Vedlitz. Photo used with permission of Specialties Photography, James A. Nowak.

George W. Bush, governor of Texas, and President George H. W. Bush engage in a question-and-answer session with the first Bush School class after conclusion of the formal dedication ceremony in September 1997. Courtesy of Texas A&M University. Photo by Michael Kellett.

Initial Bush School administrative team—Theresa Weir, Donald Deere, and Rick Johnson—at work in the new building. Photo used with permission of Chuck Hermann.

Initial Lawrence Livermore National Laboratory participants in the Bush School's National Security Leadership Certificate Program visit President Bush in his Houston office. From left to right: Greg Herweg, Tom Anklam, Brian Cracchiola, President Bush, Kim Budil, John Knezovich, and Steven Bradley. Photo used with permission of Chuck Hermann.

During the second US-China Conference in Beijing, Jisi Wang, dean of the Peking University School of International Affairs, and Richard Chilcoat, dean of the Bush School, sign one of an expanding set of reciprocal exchange agreements. Witnessing the signing are Qingguo Jia and Chuck Hermann. Photo used with permission of Lorraine Eden.

Bush students in a team-building exercise during orientation prior to their first semester of classes. Photo used with permission of Specialties Photography, James A. Nowak.

Elaine Chao, secretary of labor in the administration of George W. Bush (and undersecretary of transportation in the administration of George H. W. Bush), fields questions from Bush School students and faculty. Courtesy of George Bush Presidential Library Foundation. Photo by Chandler Arden.

Robert Mosbacher, former secretary of commerce, and President Bush discuss the North American Free Trade Agreement during a course that linked the Bush School with classes in Ottawa and Mexico City. Courtesy of Texas A&M University. Photo by Jean Wulfson.

Senator Edward Kennedy in conversation with President Bush and Bush School students Kelley Norton, Julie Siddique, and Ken Vincent. Courtesy of Texas A&M University.

Condoleezza Rice, with Bush School moderator Jeff Engel, speaks at a Scowcroft Institute event while serving as chancellor of Stanford University and a member of the Bush School Advisory Board in the interval between her service in the administrations of both George H. W. Bush and George W. Bush. Photo used with permission of Lorraine Eden.

Becky Gates, wife of Texas A&M University president Robert Gates, stands with Richard Chilcoat (far right) and some of the other riders before setting off in the Bush School's annual fall bicycle ride, "Tour de Brazos County," organized by Jim Olson (far left). Photo used with permission of Lorraine Eden.

Juan Alfaro, selected as class speaker by his colleagues, addresses the 2004 Bush School graduation celebration. From left to right: William West, Chuck Hermann, Jim Olson, Alfaro, Dick Chilcoat, and President Bush. Courtesy of Bush School of Government and Public Service. Photo by Chandler Arden.

President Bush watches the Bush School class of 2002 pitch their mortar boards. Courtesy of Bush School of Government and Public Service. Photo by Chandler Arden.

Celebrating the fifth anniversary of the Bush Library and School under a large tent in the Bush Library plaza. Left to right: Chuck Hermann, founding director; Douglas Menarchik, director of Bush Presidential Library; Richard Chilcoat, dean of the Bush School; President and Mrs. Bush; Robert Gates, university president; Perry Adkisson, former university chancellor; Roman Popadiuk, director of the Bush Library Foundation; and Ray Bowen, former university president. Courtesy of George Bush Presidential Library Foundation. Photo by Chandler Arden.

The Bush School's fifth-anniversary celebration. Left to right: Chuck Hermann, Barbara Bush, President Bush, and Richard Chilcoat. Courtesy of Bush School of Government and Public Service. Photo by Chandler Arden.

Bush School students join Richard Chilcoat shortly before his retirement to celebrate the school's tenth anniversary. Sam Kirkpatrick, executive associate dean, at far right. Photo used with permission of Lorraine Eden.

summer to serve until a first dean could be appointed. They advised that I would not be a candidate for either position. They noted I was a tenured professor in political science and they hoped I would consider staying on in the Bush School as an associate dean to prepare the international affairs degree.

The big experiment for the Bush School of Government and Public Service—borrowing its faculty on temporary assignment from across a broad array of departments and colleges in the university and headed by a director reporting to a dean—ended. So also did the plan for a master's degree in international affairs with a similar multidisciplinary faculty having joint appointments for a fixed period of time. Interestingly, Don Wilson had challenged that organizational concept in the Texas A&M proposal when he was archivist of the United States and was evaluating sites for the Bush Library. He urged that the proposed Bush School have its own dean and faculty. When the Texas A&M officials rebutted his suggestion, he wrote a private memo to President Bush with the same concern.[11] Hermann says, "Of course, I did not know that information when Wilson—then in College Station as the executive director of the Bush Presidential Library Foundation—met with me in the spring of 1997 and listened to my frustration in attempting to assemble a faculty from multiple departments. At that meeting he had shared with me his alternative concept of a school with its own faculty and dean. At that moment, with the school scheduled to open in a few months, I thought there were no alternatives to the existing arrangement."

By the summer of 1999 Don Wilson had left his position, and the new director of the Bush Presidential Library Foundation was Roman Popadiuk, former ambassador to Ukraine. Others who were more immediately associated with the Bush School experiment also left. Robert Durant returned to the University of Maryland. Donald Deere returned to the Department of Economics.

Rick Johnson, the second person hired as a Bush School staff member in early 1996, stayed on as the chief fiscal officer of the Bush School. He and Lee Ann Holland, who had become an administrative assistant to the director of the Bush School, would be key in the transition to a new experiment under the leadership of Robert Gates, interim dean.

4

Begin Again

Robert M. Gates as Acting Dean

In the summer of 1999, Texas A&M University moved to change the status of the Bush School as mandated by the terms of the new state budget. The approved line item authorizing $2.5 million for the school stipulated that it must first become an independent unit within the university with its own dean, who reports to the provost/executive vice president. In June the Texas A&M Faculty Senate passed a resolution outlining "the process of hiring a dean and his or her responsibilities of being in charge of a full-time staff, school governance policies, promotion procedures, tenure procedures and allocation of financial resources."[1] On July 23 the Texas A&M University System Board of Regents, chaired by Don Powell, authorized the change. The following week in Austin, the Texas Higher Education commissioner approved the requested reorganization.

Next, the university had to name an interim dean for the school while a search began for the first permanent dean. Friends of the former president suggested that the university might approach Robert M. Gates to serve briefly in the interim post. The university administration liked the idea and approached him with the offer.

After serving in the US Air Force, Robert Gates spent much of his career in the CIA. While there he earned a PhD in Russian and Soviet history from Georgetown University. He joined the National Security Council staff from 1974 to 1979 before returning to the CIA, where he rose to the position of deputy director. After George H. W. Bush became president, Gates returned to the White House to be deputy national security adviser serving with Brent Scowcroft. Bush appointed Gates director of the CIA in 1991, and he continued there until the end of Bush's presidency. Thereafter, he and his wife, Becky, settled near Seattle, Washington. Gates served on several major boards and had an extensive schedule as a popular public speaker.

After the university contacted Gates with the offer, it fell to Brent Scowcroft and Bush to encourage him to accept the appointment. Gates later reflected: "It certainly was never part of my career plan. . . . I never anticipated anything like this."[2] Scowcroft reportedly made the major pitch to Gates to accept the position at Texas A&M. As Gates tells the story, his friend Scowcroft offered great assurances that it would demand very little time—maybe a few days a week for a short while—it would last only a few months. Gates later recalled: "Neither he nor General Scowcroft had any idea of the extremely protracted process of hiring faculty and administrators in higher education."[3] In later years when the occasion arose, Gates has strongly recommended the Bush School to prospective candidates for the position of dean. But reportedly, he has repeatedly warned candidates that if they get a call from Scowcroft, they should categorically reject his observations about how much time the position requires.

Gates accepted the appointment as interim dean at the Bush School. With the belief that the job would be short term, requiring only an intermittent presence, he took a room in the guest quarters of the campus Memorial Student Union. It resembled a motel room. He kept all his speaking engagements, and Becky stayed at their home in the state of Washington. When he left College Station for a few days, he had to clear all of his belongings from the room. For many home football games that first fall, the room and all others in the Memorial Student Union had been previously booked by someone else. Little did Gates know then, but he would be interim dean of the Bush School for two years.

Gates, who arrived in August 1999, recalled that "he didn't have much of an agenda at first," believing he would not be around long.[4] He did form some early impressions beyond "how hot it was in the autumn compared to the Pacific Northwest." One advantage Gates found by living in a room in the center of campus was a rapid immersion into campus life—with the undergraduates as well as the graduate students at the Bush School. He liked their spirit and was attracted to the widely shared sense of service to others. In contrast with that favorable impression, he became distressed with the poor writing skills and resolved that the Bush School should address that issue. Furthermore, he recalls that he quickly became aware of the "tenuous relationship" of the Bush School with some faculty in the Political Science and Economics Departments, all of which occupied the same building. Many of the instructors, not only from those departments but also from elsewhere in the university, did not seem to have much interest in teaching at the Bush School, and some had an open distaste for the new school.

The faculty discontent seems understandable. Inevitably, the separation of the Bush School from the College of Liberal Arts and its cluster of academic departments created some serious disappointments and occasional anger. After all, members of the College of Liberal Arts had initially suggested a school as part of the university's proposal to attract the Bush Presidential Library. From the outset it had become apparent that President Bush was intrigued with the idea of a professional school of government and public service linked to the proposed library site. At that time the Board of Regents and university officials had called on the dean of the College of Liberal Arts and his faculty to expand and push their ideas. In fact, the Center for Presidential Studies and the Center for Public Leadership Studies—constructed as part of the Bush School plan—had been jump-started with faculty from the College of Liberal Arts as key players to demonstrate the university's commitment.

In its design for the Bush School, Texas A&M University planners had adopted what they understood was the model that Princeton University used for its Woodrow Wilson School of Public and International Affairs. At Princeton many of the faculty affiliated with the Woodrow Wilson School had their primary appointment in another academic unit on the campus. In the same manner, the proposal designers at Texas A&M envisioned they would construct a faculty for the Bush School that drew on personnel whose primary appointments were elsewhere.

Thus, the planners for the new Bush School may have conveyed to the College of Liberal Arts faculty that the Bush School would expand their involvement and enhance the reputation of their college. The planners overlooked the deep endowment of the Woodrow Wilson School that allowed it to provide significant incentives for extensive faculty engagement. Princeton University also had an established and accepted detailed system for allocating faculty time between different units of the university. Both features contributed to effective joint faculty appointments. Without these conditions at Texas A&M, many faculty had little incentive to invest time and energy in the Bush School. Initial expectations on both sides—College of Liberal Arts faculty and the Bush School—suffered.

Gates faced the challenge of constructing a stand-alone Bush School administration and attracting a faculty engaged and invested in the school's professional degree program. He approached Arnold Vedlitz, who currently served as director of the Bush School's Center for Public Leadership Studies. Vedlitz was a professor of political science with previous academic administrative experience. At his suggestion, Gates asked Marshall Scott Poole from the Department of Communications to serve as the interim associate dean for student affairs. Charles Hermann was asked to serve as associate dean for international affairs.

Virtually all the instructional faculty had already entered into an agreement to teach a course in the Bush School for the academic year 1999–2000 before Gates came on board. During the spring term 2000 (during Gates's second semester), it became evident that the search for the first full-time dean would not succeed in the next several months. That task would continue for a second academic year.

As it became apparent to Gates that he would be in charge of the Bush School to a greater degree and for much longer than he originally anticipated, he developed an action agenda. During the spring semester of 2000, his top priority became establishing a more permanent Bush School faculty. He also decided to tackle the challenges facing the two Bush School research centers. In addition Gates recognized that student enrollment had to increase for the Bush School to be a credible stand-alone school, and soon he concluded that a second degree—a master's in international affairs—should be pursued.

Bush School Faculty

Gates began the construction of the school faculty by approaching several members of the Texas A&M faculty who had been significantly involved with the establishment of the school. He asked Arnold Vedlitz and Charles Hermann to continue their major administrative assignments and shift their tenure home to the Bush School as full-time faculty. Gates offered each an endowed faculty chair in the Bush School. Hermann received the Scowcroft Chair in International Policy Studies established for the school by Brent Scowcroft. In a moving ceremony in November 2000, Jan Bullock announced the creation of the Bob Bullock Chair in Government and Public Policy. Gates declared that the initial Bullock Chair would be awarded to Vedlitz.[5]

After an initial year serving as interim associate dean for student affairs, Scott Poole concluded that continued administrative duties would be incompatible with his ongoing research program. Gates approached William West to fill Poole's position. West, a graduate of West Point with a PhD from Rice University, had established himself as an emerging scholar in public administration. He had been an effective and well-liked instructor early in the Bush School's master's program. Gates offered him promotion to full professor in the school with responsibility for the Master of Public Service and Administration.

West, Vedlitz, and Hermann transferred their tenure location from the Political Science Department to the Bush School. Now Gates sought a senior economist and launched a national search. In the end, however, he hired James Griffin of the Economics Department at Texas A&M. Griffin had an impressive record in economic research linked to public policy issues, including energy and technology. Furthermore, he had already engaged with the Bush School by directing the Program in the Economics of Public Policy underwritten jointly with the Economics Department. Griffin's program conducted major conferences in 1999 and 2000. Both resulted in book publications. When the Bob Bullock family gave funds to endow a faculty chair, the university matched their gift. Thus, Gates was able to offer Jim Griffin the Bob Bullock Chair in Public Policy and Finance.

James Olson, retired from the CIA, agreed to stay on as a senior lecturer in the independent Bush School. Both Deborah Kerr and Kenneth Ashworth affirmed their participation on a part-time basis.

Those three appointments continued the Bush School's commitment to have instructors with strong policy experience as well as others with more traditional academic records.

Robert Durant, the original joint appointment between the Political Science Department and the Bush School, had elected to leave the university; thus, Gates had the resources for another senior faculty hire. The Bush School conducted a national search and succeeded in attracting a husband-and-wife team. Hank Jenkins-Smith and Carol Silva came from the University of New Mexico. Jenkins-Smith, an expert on public policy risk assessment and survey research, became the Joe R. and Teresa Lozano Long Chair in Business and Government. Silva, at an earlier point in her academic career, had taught at Texas A&M as an assistant professor in political science but later joined the Bush School faculty.

Some faculty from other departments who had been teaching courses in the Bush School when it had been part of the College of Liberal Arts proved to be valuable instructors. Agreements with these professors and their home departments enabled them to continue offering a course at the Bush School. They joined with the others now based in the school to form the new faculty for Gates's second year. A core Bush School faculty had been established.

Bush School Research Centers

Recall that the initial bid to locate the Bush Presidential Library on the Texas A&M campus featured a professional school of public service and included two research centers. As noted earlier, the Center for Presidential Studies and the Center for Public Leadership Studies started operation before the Bush School opened. By the time Robert Gates became interim dean, both centers had evolved.

The Leadership Center under Arnie Vedlitz continued the strategy of multidisciplinary teams seeking external grants and contracts for research. Funded projects during this time included a contract with the Environmental Protection Agency to explore restoration of the San Antonio watershed; another funded by the Texas Natural Resources Conservation Commission investigated the feasibility of effluent trading in Texas; and the Hewlett Foundation contracted for work on reframing intractable environmental disputes. The Leadership Program also continued its successful project for promoting undergraduate leadership through courses and projects working with public policy agencies.[6] What became evident, however, was that the center's funded research projects often entailed collaboration with scientists and engineers. In these collaborative efforts with technical researchers, the contribution from the Bush School's center focused less on leadership and more on the public policy dimensions of the scientific or technical project.

Robert Gates and Arnold Vedlitz shared a conviction that the frequent practice of the Bush School Leadership Center examining the policy implications of various technical projects provided an important—and usually neglected—dimension. Such endeavors, however, stretched the initial vision of directly studying public leadership. Gates and Vedlitz agreed to reconceptualize the school's research endeavor. They sought and received university permission to replace the Center for Public Leadership Studies with the Institute for Science, Technology, and Public Policy (ISTPP). The title captured the primary focus of the research enterprise. In the parlance of Texas A&M University, an "institute" organizes research inquiry across multiple departments and disciplines, whereas a "center" focuses more specifically on research within one specific department or academic discipline. Under the revised mandate, Vedlitz and his associates urged researchers in engineering, agriculture, public health, and the sciences to consider adding a public policy dimension to any research proposal for which they sought funding.

During these same years the Center for Presidential Studies achieved success organizing academic conferences in each of its program areas. In 1999 and 2000 such conferences included gatherings on "Reinventing the Presidency" (sponsored by the center's Program in American Politics), the "Korean War in Perspective" (Program in the Presidency and Foreign Relations), and "Civil Rights" (Program in Presidential Rhetoric). Furthermore, George Edwards had made the center the editorial home of the journal *Presidential Studies Quarterly*, under his effective editorship.[7]

The center, however, continued to struggle for funds. Conferences without outside support proved costly. The Bush School budget and Edwards's own chair endowment underwrote most costs. One major effort to secure funding to expand the presidential data archive had not succeeded. Adding to the challenge, several of the center's key program leaders, H. W. Brands and Martin Medhurst, began to be recruited by other institutions and would eventually leave Texas A&M. Neither the Bush School nor the home departments of these scholars had plans to replace them with experts specifically interested in research on the presidency.

Edwards decided to restructure the operation and move it into the Department of Political Science, which offered support for the operation of *Presidential Studies Quarterly*. Furthermore, the research of selected doctoral students working under his supervision complemented Edwards's own substantial ongoing research on the presidency. Thus, the two original research centers envisioned as part of the Bush School came to a close. At the same time, the first of the school's new research institutes began operation.

A Master's Program in International Affairs

Gates inherited Hermann's original plan for an international affairs degree designed for a Bush School with no substantial faculty of its own. It assumed that the Bush School would remain in the College of Liberal Arts but would draw on faculty from both that college and others. That design no longer seemed applicable. Consistent with his expectation of serving as dean for only a short period, Gates early in the autumn of 1999 urged Hermann to defer any plans for redesigning an international degree until a new Bush School dean had been appointed. That dean could decide whether to proceed with a proposal for a second master's degree and, if so, how it might be organized.

An alternative international initiative received an immediate green light from Gates. The proposal was to create a Certificate in Advanced International Affairs to be offered online and in residence. The certificate would permit admitted students (completion of bachelor's degree required) to undertake twelve credit hours of online courses to receive the certificate. The certificate would appear on a Texas A&M university transcript. This program would enable the Bush School to quickly develop some additional graduate seminars in international affairs and would not require the online instructors to be full-time faculty residing in College Station.[8]

The initiative came at a time when Texas A&M University sought to encourage departments to explore online instruction. Recall that the previous year (spring semester 1998) Lorraine Eden taught an online course for the Bush School on the implications of NAFTA. That course had helped establish the experience and technology at the Bush School for distance education. The Bush School moved ahead with the Certificate in Advanced International Affairs, that would soon include an online option.

Contrary to his initial expectations, Robert Gates found himself continuing as Bush School dean for a second academic year—2000–2001. He revisited with Hermann the creation of a separate Master's Program in International Affairs. Gates announced he now wanted that new degree pursued on his watch. The state of Texas specifies very explicit guidelines for the establishment of any new degree program at a state university. In addition to the proposed detailed curriculum, the requirements included a demonstration of an unmet need in Texas for the degree, sources of funding for the first two years, a complete budget, and the qualifications of all proposed faculty. The Bush School Master of Public Service and Administration had been transferred from the previously existing degree program in political science for which state approval had been acquired much earlier; thus, the requirements for reconceptualizing that existing degree were significantly less demanding. The proposed new degree in international affairs had no such prior state approval. On seeing the finished international affairs degree proposal, Gates referred to it as "Chuck's second doctoral dissertation."

Space Wars

In his second year, Gates recognized another problem. To be a viable professional school financially and to impact public service, the Bush School had to grow. It continued to increase its enrollment each year. If it added a second degree, the enrollments would jump even more dramatically. That meant more classrooms and some larger ones. With its own faculty and staff, the school clearly needed more office space. The new ISTPP also sought more space.

The academic building that is home to the Bush School had been designed, and construction was well under way before anyone directly representing the school was hired. In the absence of any alternative vision, the space needs of the school had been estimated using the requirements of the existing public administration program in the Political Science Department. That program typically enrolled between twelve and fifteen students per year. Recognizing that there would likely be some enrollment expansion in the new school, five seminar classrooms were envisioned along with corresponding faculty offices and room for the two centers. The largest classroom accommodated twenty students comfortably; the others were smaller. The first remodeling during the Gates years entailed removing the wall between two adjoining classrooms to make one larger space that could accommodate sixty people in theater-style sitting. (Presently, it is still the school's largest classroom.) More and larger seminar rooms remained a priority along with additional office space. Gates and his senior administrators and faculty proposed that the branch of the main university library that shared the other half of the first floor with the Bush School move. No one questioned the desirability of having an extension of the library on what was then the edge of campus to serve the Departments of Political Science (on the second floor) and Economics (third floor), as well as the Bush School. The Bush School administrators proposed, however, that the library be relocated next door in the conference center building in space beneath the second-floor apartment and offices for President and Mrs. Bush. In the face of strong resistance, the university rejected the proposal.

One of the changes that Gates and William West, public administration director, initiated did not affect space immediately but saved students money. They changed the number of credit hours required for the master's degree from fifty-four to forty-eight. The difference resulted from dropping the requirement that students be enrolled at the university during the summer while they completed their internship. Although the internships remained a valuable experience, requiring students to be enrolled during that time and submit sufficient material to determine a grade for the experience proved quite difficult. Students still did internships but stopped paying nonresidential university tuition while doing so. It made the cost of the master's degree from the Bush School more competitive with many top programs in the country. Despite somewhat crowded seminar rooms, the quality and costs of the Bush School appealed to increasing numbers of students. As more of them enrolled, the space wars continued. A few years later the Bush School's space reallocation issue would get another hearing.

The growing number of students quickly led to a new tradition—an annual softball game between the Bush School and students at the Lyndon B. Johnson School of Public Affairs, University of Texas at Austin. Gates provided the funds for the winner's trophy. Whether he knew in advance that his money would be used to purchase a prize featuring a stuffed armadillo prepared by a clearly amateur taxidermist remains a mystery.

5

A Change of Command

Dean Chilcoat Begins

Richard A. Chilcoat (retired lieutenant general, US Army), a graduate of the US Military Academy at West Point, became dean of the Bush School in July 2001. Chilcoat held staff and command positions and leadership in military education while in the army, including combat experience (Vietnam). He served as commandant of the US Army War College and subsequently as president of the National Defense University. Between those two assignments, Chilcoat acted as executive assistant to General Colin Powell, chairman of the Joint Chiefs of Staff.

Chilcoat's appointment as dean furthered several existing relationships for the Bush School. He continued the link with the US Army that began in the school's first years when the retiring army chief of staff had raised the possibility of a special connection to the Bush School. Further, Chilcoat became the first Bush School dean to hold the Edward and Howard Kruse Endowed Chair. Creation of that endowed chair extended the significant relationship between the school and the Aggie founders and owners of Blue Bell Creameries. No one need ever doubt the featured dessert at Bush School dinners.[1]

His leadership at the Bush School received a jump-start when, before classes began, Chilcoat traveled to the state capital in Austin to present the school's proposal for a second master's degree to the

Texas Higher Education Coordinating Board. Their approval signaled that Chilcoat would soon be presiding over a school with two professional master's degree programs.

Less than three months after Chilcoat's arrival and days after the new fall semester began, the attacks of 9/11 occurred in New York, Washington, and Pennsylvania. Chilcoat observed, "Our graduates have a graphic example that they have to be prepared to handle these kinds of situations if they are working at any level—federal, state or local."[2] As the dean and the school continued to consider how best to respond, one of their initiatives was the creation of a graduate Certificate in Homeland Security as well as courses on terrorism and counterterrorism.

A Focus on Leadership

From its outset, the Bush School made a commitment to leadership education.[3] It began with the original Texas A&M proposal to President Bush for his library that included creating a Center for Public Leadership Studies. Later, in May 1996 before the school opened, a productive seminar with prospective employers had made a case to include teaching learnable skills contributing to leadership in the curriculum. Once established, the Bush School pursued that focus. It started with the school's proclaimed mission of "educating principled leaders for public service." The faculty committee that designed the original curriculum included a required course on leadership. Each of the early entering classes took the Leadership Skills Assessment Inventory prior to starting their classes. After receiving the results, each student was expected to design a personal plan for further leadership skills development.

These early efforts had lagged by 2001. The skills assessment inventory proved difficult to interpret. The expectation that students would find the time and ways to implement a personal plan for skills enhancement quickly required a revision. The course on leadership continued—taught by a "borrowed" professor from the Department of Agricultural Education. Some students contended the school's hype about a focus on leadership was not reflected in the actual program. Some faculty questioned whether leadership skills development constituted a viable educational subject—particularly in a professional graduate program.

Chilcoat quickly asserted that leadership skills enhancement constituted a vital feature of the Bush School. In the spring of 2002, he decided on a major new initiative, which would become one of the defining initiatives of his deanship. Chilcoat approached Joe Cerami, requesting that he devise a new leadership program for the school. As part of the effort to build the new international affairs faculty, Hermann had recently hired Cerami as a lecturer in international affairs. Cerami had credentials for Chilcoat's assignment. Like the dean, he understood the US Army approach to leadership since he was a graduate of West Point and had a subsequent army career. He also served as head of the National Security Affairs Department at the War College. At the time he joined the Bush School faculty, Cerami was completing his doctoral dissertation in the School of Public Affairs at Pennsylvania State University on "Policy Innovation and Public Leadership."

Initially, Cerami resisted the dean's request to head a leadership program, noting that civilian public-sector leadership was strikingly different from what they both experienced in the military. The dean acknowledged the difference but stressed that Cerami was acquiring exactly those insights in his doctoral research. Further, the dean argued that Cerami understood that some aspects of leadership could be taught. Chilcoat proposed that Cerami gradually create and implement a leadership program over the next several years.[4]

Cerami, with his assistant director (initially Allison Dunn and then Lindsey Pavelka), developed the Public Service Leadership Program (PSLP). He acknowledged that in designing the program he was influenced by Joseph Nye, dean of the Kennedy School (1995–2004) at Harvard University and its Center for Public Leadership. Initially, PSLP consisted of the required Bush School leadership course and some revised assessment tests designed to establish each student's baseline orientation toward the world on various dimensions with presumed implications for leadership style.

As it developed, the PSLP built exercises to support other elements of the Bush School program. These included the internship that students undertake at the end of their first year, their involvement in various student organizations, and their participation in a team-based capstone in their final semesters. Through a variety of exercises, the Leadership Program encouraged students to consider the leadership aspect of their involvement in these elements of the Bush School education. Having gradually experimented with workshops, assessment tests, and individual counseling during the initial years of the Chilcoat mandate, the program took another step. In 2006–2007 Cerami introduced the Dean's Leadership Certificate. To earn the certificate, students voluntarily completed a series of leadership activities across the two years of their Bush School enrollment. The certificate and PSLP have continually evolved as one of the school's distinctive features.

Reorienting the Master of Public Service and Administration

Previously, Robert Gates had appointed William West to serve as director of the public administration degree program. A year later Bill West faced significant transition challenges. The immediate problem resulted from the original creation of the degree program under strikingly different conditions. The initial degree plan was designed for a multidisciplinary faculty drawn from an array of departments in the College of Liberal Arts and beyond. Although the original program was anchored in political science, public administration, and economics, it drew on the talents of faculty elsewhere, such as history, philosophy, sociology, management, and public health. In the two years Gates directed the Bush School, most courses continued to be taught by these borrowed faculty, even as the school began to acquire several of its own faculty.

Richard Chilcoat had been allocated funds for additional faculty lines and was expected to build the school's own faculty. That task fell primarily to Bill West. Chilcoat gave West broad latitude in pursuing a hiring strategy so long as it contributed to the expansion and reputation of the school. As noted earlier, Hank Jenkins-Smith was hired as the first new senior faculty in 2001. That same year Angela Bies, with experience in nonprofit organization, joined as a new assistant professor.

The major surge in faculty building occurred in the following academic year (2002–2003). Laurence Lynn Jr., previously dean of the

School of Social Service at the University of Chicago, became the holder of the endowed George Bush Chair. Like Jenkins-Smith, Lynn had spent part of his career in the federal government. Shortly after arriving, Lynn noted the Bush School had "a distinctive approach, emphasizing leadership and public management."[5]

The addition of a core faculty for the Master of Public Service and Administration (MPSA) also included hiring a talented group of assistant professors in 2002 and 2003, including Anthony Bertelli, Kim Isett, Donald Moynihan, M. Jae Moon, and Lori Taylor. Many of these able young faculty members made important teaching and research contributions and then moved on to distinguished careers elsewhere. Lori Taylor continued at the Bush School and assumed a major role.

As the full-time Bush School faculty ranks grew, the original curriculum for the MPSA required revision.[6] Two core decisions structured the redesign of the existing master's degree program. First, all entering students selected a focus either on public management or public policy. Each field represents a major orientation to public-sector governance. Public management addresses subjects such as organization and bureaucracy, personnel administration, and budgeting. Public policy focuses on the means of analyzing policy and assessing and evaluating policy outcomes and issues in various types of policy (e.g., energy, natural resources, and education). In the new Bush School curriculum both fields had several required courses and an array of electives. Certain other courses remained central to both domains, such as budgeting, research methods, and leadership.

The second decision undertaken by West and his colleagues involved the abolition of the original set of concentrations (i.e., the cluster of courses in different areas such as Health Policy and Management, Environment and Natural Resources, Business and Government). In part this decision was driven by necessity, as many of those courses had been offered by faculty residing elsewhere in the university who were no longer part of the Bush School. The concept of concentrations—or cluster of courses tackling different dimensions of a subject—was not entirely dropped. Initially, students created their own concentrations by selecting a set of courses with an apparent theme or focus from anywhere in the university. As time passed, however, the program reintroduced specific clusters of courses around a theme—for example, State and Local Government, Security Policy, Nonprofit Policy, and Management.

Students had the option of selecting one of these concentrations or designing one of their own.

Starting a Master's Program in International Affairs

After Chilcoat obtained approval in the summer of 2001 for a Master's Program in International Affairs (MPIA), he appointed Chuck Hermann to serve simultaneously as associate dean for academic affairs and director of the MPIA. During the ensuing year, Hermann's effort focused on creating courses, recruiting a faculty, and enrolling a first class of students to start in the fall of 2002. Hermann and the initial international affairs faculty used the certificate program that Gates had approved in his second year as a way to jump-start graduate instruction before the formal degree got under way.

As a first step in developing the degree in international affairs, the school initiated the previously planned Certificate in Advanced International Affairs. Beginning in fall semester 2001—a year before the formal master's degree would be ready—the graduate certificate program introduced some classes and generated possible candidates for the future degree. The certificate involved twelve credit hours of graduate courses drawn from a menu of available seminars. Jim Olson, who became director of the certificate program, and his assistant, Nancy Small, launched what became the first of multiple Bush School certificate programs. Nancy Small had joined the Bush School staff the previous year. She provided technical knowledge and experience in both residential and online certificate instruction and proved effective at promoting the new undertaking. Those who completed the certificate could apply their credit hours toward the soon-to-start international affairs master's degree or transfer them elsewhere.

After an initial year of selected residential courses in the certificate program, Olson and Small extended it to include online instruction. Thus, it became the vanguard of the Bush School's Distance Education Program available to resident and nonresident graduate students.

The online certificate program furthered the school's exploration of the Internet for education as did another closed-circuit television course similar to the earlier NAFTA class that connected a Bush School class with those in Mexico City and Ottawa. In spring semester

2001 the Bush School and the Elliott School of International Affairs in Washington, DC, conducted a joint course. The seminar—through closed-circuit television between the universities—studied US foreign policy using cases from the Bush administration. In addition to conducting the usual readings and class discussions, members of that administration made guest appearances to discuss a particular case. President Bush started the discussions with the Malta Summit with Gorbachev. Brent Scowcroft discussed dealing with China after Tiananmen; Lawrence Eagleburger (deputy secretary of state, who later became secretary of state) analyzed construction of the Gulf War coalition. Twelve key members of that administration's foreign policy leadership participated—about half of them from the College Station campus. The course ran a second time in the spring of 2002. In addition to experimenting with the video technology, the course helped call attention to the new Bush School degree program.[7]

The degree program officially began with an initial class of twenty in the fall of 2002. The degree dodged the difficult "reinvention" challenges that confronted the school's degree in public service and administration. From the start, the revised plan for the degree envisioned an independent program with its own faculty. Nonetheless, that initial degree had some start-up challenges. Most of the new Bush School faculty positions were designated for the existing MPSA, which faced an urgent need to replace the part-time faculty previously borrowed from other parts of the university. Because the administration anticipated fewer faculty and courses, the master's degree in international affairs initially required fewer credit hours—and courses—than the degree in public service and administration. A required thirty-six hours of course work enabled students to earn a master's in international affairs in three semesters (a year and a half of residency). Before graduating, however, they had to demonstrate proficiency in a language different from their native one.

Prior to the first year of offering the master's in international affairs, Kishore Gawande (PhD, international economics, UCLA) joined Cerami, Hermann, and Olson to establish four full-time faculty. The remaining faculty continued the older model of faculty with primary "homes" elsewhere. To overcome potential problems uncovered in the Bush School's earlier experience with borrowed faculty, some changes occurred. The MPIA bylaws introduced the concept of "associated faculty" tenured elsewhere in the university but with both rights and responsibilities in the Bush School. A vigorous effort began to engage these colleagues regularly with the full-time school faculty. They participated in faculty meetings and the life of the program. Some found an attractive, second multidisciplinary home. Consequently, even as the MPIA secured more full-time faculty, it continued to engage affiliated faculty. This feature of voting affiliated faculty continued until the Bush School established its own departments in 2015 and rewrote the bylaws.[8]

Speakers and Conferences

College Station's geographical location arguably approximates the hub of a wheel with spokes to the major population centers of Texas (Houston, Dallas–Fort Worth, Austin, San Antonio). Nonetheless, it is a long way from Washington, DC, and the bicoastal centers of national politics and commerce. Some—including potential students—occasionally worry that the distance might be a liability for a school of public affairs. A few might contend that a bit of distance encourages an environment more conducive to study and research. All concur that a vigorous schedule of conferences and seminars involving participants from throughout the world provides a bridge to expertise everywhere.

Even in its early years, the school enjoyed a rich menu of key speakers on public policy. In April 2001 Mikhail Gorbachev visited the campus. In addition to a public lecture, he and President Bush spent an hour in a classroom with approximately thirty Bush School students. Although remarkable, that occurrence was far from an isolated event. In the same year, students had the opportunity to hear and interact with Sam Donaldson (ABC News), Lech Walesa (first democratically elected president of modern Poland and Nobel Peace Prize winner), Michael Beschloss (historian), James Baker III (former secretary of state), and Robert Kerrey (Democrat senator from Nebraska), among others.

In subsequent years the pace of speakers at the Bush Library and school accelerated. In 2002, speakers included Tony Blair (prime minister of Britain), Condoleezza Rice (at that time provost at Stanford), Laura Bush, Elaine Chao (US secretary of labor), David McCullough (author of books on several presidents), and Jiang Zemin (president of China). Today on her desk in her office in Beijing, Bush School graduate Lisa Liang keeps a photograph of herself with Bush and Jiang Zemin taken in 2002 when the Chinese president visited the school.

During his visit in 2003, Edward Kennedy, Democratic senator from Massachusetts, held an interview with students after having been introduced to the Bush School program. He volunteered the observation: "I think there's nothing more powerful, personally, and I think anyone fortunate enough to be in these programs . . . receive[s] the best in terms of the kinds of skills which are necessary to make an important difference."[9]

As the school's faculty network grew, presentations by public figures were complemented by scholars presenting their current research. Often these occurred as individual presentations, but occasionally they appeared in organized conferences bringing together academic research to bear on policy questions. For example, within a year of the 9/11 terrorist attacks the Bush School, jointly with the American Society for Public Administration, hosted a conference, "Public Service after September 11, 2001: What Comes Next?" The conference papers led to a special issue of *Public Administration Review*. Other conferences during the first years of Chilcoat's deanship of the Bush School included "A Century of Air Power Leadership" (October 29–31, 2003) and "Strategic Issues for Intelligence Practice in the 21st Century" (February 18–19, 2004).

The Bush School joined with Texas A&M University, the Bush Library Foundation, and the Chinese People's Association for Friendship with Foreign Countries to hold a conference in College Station on China-US relations in 2003. It had several parallel components: plenary sessions and panels featuring policy makers of both countries and leaders of firms interested in business exchanges along with academic workshops to explore shared research interests. The academic sessions explored areas of existing or potential collaborative research. At the conclusion of the conference, it became apparent that the policy makers had found value in the informal exchanges around the periphery of the formal events. Thus encouraged, the conference organizers arranged to repeat the conference two years later in Beijing on November 14–18, 2005. That meeting resulted in a third conference, structured in the same manner, that convened in Washington,

DC, in October 2007. Most Bush School conferences did not have such a protracted "half-life" but regularly promoted exploration of research and policy questions.

Student Engagement

Bush School students, particularly in the early years, displayed a strong inclination to network with one another. Multiple factors likely contributed to this pattern. Their numbers were small, and they took most courses together. As mentioned previously, students in the initial years each had their own office space in the Bush School, which promoted studying and "hanging out" in the building. Furthermore, they were physically separated from much of the rest of the campus. Whatever the explanation, students interacted a great deal.

A student government quickly emerged. The Bush School regularly fielded intramural sports teams. Bicyclists under the tutorage of James Olson engaged in a yearly tour. The annual softball rivalry with the LBJ School at the University of Texas was expanded to include a second combined faculty and alumni game, but still competing for the armadillo trophy. One of the deans of the two competing teams quipped that the "losing team should be forced to take the trophy for the subsequent year."

One distinctive Bush School student organization quickly emerged with the straightforward name Public Service Organization (PSO). Entirely student run—with Bill West serving initially as an adviser—the group used a committee structure to engage in a variety of service projects. Some projects were one-day efforts, such as working a day on construction of a Habitat for Humanity house or volunteering to work a fund-raising event for a local charity. Others required semester or year-long commitments. One team engaged in grant-writing proposals for several local organizations. Another undertook a year-long study for a nonprofit working with low-income settlements on the Texas-Mexico border. One group that read and worked with young children in an early-learning center caught the attention of President Bush. One week he and Mrs. Bush joined the reading team. The PSO remains a vital and very active student operation at the Bush School.

Another student activity resulted from the school's administration. In the day-long seminar in May 1996, potential employers stressed the importance of good writing as one of the learnable skills that would give Bush graduates a comparative advantage. Gates had underscored writing as a critical need. Under Chilcoat, the Bush School followed through with a programmatic investment. The school hired as lecturer a writing expert and coach. Thereafter, every student has completed a writing exercise evaluated by the writing lecturer prior to his or her first semester at the Bush School. Those who score below established standards are required to participate in a series of writing workshops. Other students are encouraged to attend. Beyond the workshops and individual guidance, the writing lecturer created a Writing Certificate. On a volunteer basis, students work with the lecturer to create a writing portfolio that includes various reworked and polished class assignments displaying different kinds of writing ability. Students who complete the entire portfolio effort received a Writing Certificate in a special ceremony. The completed electronic portfolio can supplement a student's résumé in seeking employment.[10]

Robert M. Gates
President of Texas A&M University

At the end of the first year of Richard Chilcoat's term as dean of the Bush School, former interim dean, Robert Gates, became the president of Texas A&M University. That evolution from interim dean to university president probably came as a surprise to both sides. The Texas A&M University System Board of Regents struggled with two candidates. Both Robert Gates and Phil Gramm, former US senator and Texas A&M economist, had strong backers for the position. Gates got the job. As dean he had anticipated only a very brief interlude in College Station initially requiring only a temporary room on campus. Expecting to be a short-term outsider sitting on the Council of Deans and other university committees, Gates felt comfortable speaking out, raising questions, and offering suggestions. His queries peaked interest.[11] Gates realized he liked the university and the university liked him. He came to see Texas A&M as "a unique American institution."[12]

After becoming president of Texas A&M, Robert Gates joined with Richard Chilcoat in a 2002 celebration naming the academic building in the Bush Library complex for Judy and Robert Allen. Their major contribution represented an eventual endowment campaign success that had begun in the first years of the Bush School. Henceforth, the academic building adjacent to the Bush Presidential Library became the Allen Building.

In 2003, Gates announced a bold plan to hire 447 additional Texas A&M faculty. During the next twelve months a careful process unfolded to determine how to allocate the new positions throughout the university to create maximum impact. Ultimately, the Bush School received eight new faculty posts. Previously, an initial surge of Bush School faculty hiring occurred between 2001 and 2003, shortly after the school became an independent unit. It would be several years before the resources for the Gates initiative for the new faculty hires became available and searches could begin. When it happened, the Bush School experienced an extraordinary second wave of faculty building.

Another action undertaken by Gates dealt directly with the Bush School. He instructed the branch of the university library that shared the first floor of the Allen Building to relocate to space next door in the conference center. Previously, as interim dean of the Bush School, Gates had recognized that the school would have to grow in enrollment and in faculty. For the professional graduate program to become effective both within the university and among peer institutions, the scale of the operation had to be increased. To do so, it required more classrooms, office space, and support areas. As interim dean, he had not been successful; as university president, he prevailed.

6

Gaining Momentum and Recognition

Administrative Changes

In the fall semester of 2005, Richard Chilcoat began his second four-year term as dean of the Bush School. When Chilcoat arrived in July 2001, the school had 54 students enrolled in one degree program. Four years later, the two master's degree programs had 135 full-time residential students, and the graduate certificate programs had more than 50. The full-time faculty at the Bush School had grown from nine to eighteen, and active searches for additional faculty were under way.

To accommodate the projected growth, the school, with the support of Robert Gates, acquired additional first-floor space in the academic building. The expansion nearly doubled the number of square feet available to the Bush School. Bill West and Chuck Hermann moved from the second-floor dean's suite to new space on the ground floor. Hermann also relinquished his position as associate dean for academic affairs, given that the fully operational MPIA now demanded full-time attention.

At the same time, Chilcoat required a more permanent administrative structure for a rapidly expanding school. He hired Samuel A. Kirkpatrick as executive associate dean. Years earlier Kirkpatrick served as head of the Political Science Department at Texas A&M. He left to become a dean at Arizona State University. Subsequently, Kirkpatrick assumed presidencies at the University of Texas at San Antonio and then Eastern Michigan University. Sam Kirkpatrick welcomed the opportunity to return to Texas A&M, and Chilcoat was eager to engage his university administrative experience. Kirkpatrick recalls that almost immediately after accepting the position, Chilcoat bombarded him with agendas and priority tasks even before he moved back to College Station. Essentially Kirkpatrick's assignments included formalization of procedures within the school as well as fuller integration of the Bush School into the structure of the university.[1]

At the time the Bush School originally opened next to the Bush Library, the complex was situated at the extreme western end of the university with considerable vacant space between it and other campus buildings. University expansion subsequently has filled much of the empty space, but in the beginning the physical separation of the Bush School visually reinforced the perception that this tiny, but privileged, unit operated largely independently of the rest of the university's large and established academic colleges. The biblical story of the young, favored Joseph with his wonderful coat and his older brothers might have seemed apt. Sam Kirkpatrick had to change this image.

Developing the Master's Program in International Affairs

In 2004, the Bush School jumped to make new faculty hires from the anticipated new university-wide positions designated by Gates. In that fall, two new faculty joined the fledgling Master's Program in International Affairs. Michael Desch became the first occupant of the Robert M. Gates Chair in Intelligence and National Security Decision-Making. Jeffrey Engel, with a new PhD in history, arrived as an assistant professor. Each undertook initiatives that made significant contributions to the program.

As a historian Engel took full advantage of the Bush Presidential Library. His work served as an important bridge that signaled the faculty's use of the library as a resource for research and furthered the bond of the forty-first president with the Bush School. With the support of Bush, Engel edited the diaries that Bush kept while serving as America's first liaison officer (de facto ambassador) in China in 1974–1975. Engel added an extended commentary to the volume *The China Diary of George H. W. Bush*.[2] Then Engel began an extended inquiry into the foreign policy of President Bush. In addition to his own work, he used this knowledge to edit and contribute to several volumes that emerged from Bush School conferences on Bush's foreign policy.[3]

Desch immediately became editor of an academic journal, *Security Studies*. Soon after arriving, Desch joined Roman Popadiuk—who succeeded Don Wilson as executive director of the Bush Presidential Library Foundation—on a road trip for a speaking engagement. During their travel the two discussed the idea of an international affairs research institute at the Bush School. They speculated about naming it for Brent Scowcroft, the highly respected national security adviser in the Bush administration. Popadiuk thought the foundation could secure some of the money that such an enterprise would require. Upon returning to College Station, Desch received the enthusiastic support of Chuck Hermann and the concurrence of Chilcoat. Desch and Hermann set to work designing a proposal, acquiring core resources and the approval of Scowcroft. In March 2007 the Texas A&M Board of Regents gave their approval. Desch became the first director of the Scowcroft Institute of International Affairs. Among other activities the Scowcroft Institute subsequently sponsored conferences on Europe after the fall of the Berlin Wall and on the war to liberate Kuwait from Saddam Hussein. Important in their own right, these activities also furthered the links with President Bush and the Bush Presidential Library Foundation. More generally, the creation of the Scowcroft Institute further established the bridge between policy research and interest in contemporary policy issues.

A year after Desch and Engel arrived, the Bush School added two more international affairs faculty who would play major development roles. Upon retirement Larry Napper, an ambassador in the US Foreign Service, came to the Bush School as a senior lecturer. His distinguished career tracked the devolution of the Soviet Union. He served as the political section chief in Moscow in the 1980s. Later he became director of the State Department's Office of Soviet Union Affairs just as the USSR imploded. Napper's final career post was as ambassador to Kazakhstan, one of the new countries emerging from the Soviet Union breakup. To Texas A&M loyalists, Napper held one other significant credential: He was a graduate of the university—an Aggie! Napper quickly demonstrated a knack for teaching as well as policy analysis. A short time after his arrival, when Mike Desch accepted an appointment as a departmental chair at Notre Dame, Napper served as the director of the Scowcroft Institute for five years (2009–2013), which took shape and direction under his leadership.

Another new faculty member in 2005 was Christopher Layne, named an associate professor, who had both a PhD and a JD and had practiced law for almost a decade. Within a year of his arrival he published two books (*The Peace of Illusions* and *American Empire*). Layne demonstrated effectiveness in international affairs theoretical debates in academic meetings and among the pages of major scholarly journals. He established a new course on grand strategy. He soon earned promotion to full professor and on Desch's departure held the Robert Gates Chair. Later, Chris Layne would be the first Bush School faculty member to be selected for the university's elite group of distinguished professors. Layne and Napper represented two different, but necessary, dimensions of the international affairs faculty. Because the Bush School is a professional graduate school in international affairs, the program needs both experienced experts who practiced the conduct of foreign and security policy and creative scholars engaged in cutting-edge, policy-applicable research.

Beyond the classroom, the expanding international affairs faculty sought to provide a richer international foundation for students in the degree program. Typically, one-third to one-half of the entering class has had some type of experience abroad. The number with more than short-term tourist or military experience, however, has always been substantially less. Increasing firsthand international opportunities and understanding constituted an important part of the educational mission. Knowledge of other languages serves as an essential gateway.

As noted previously, all international affairs degree students are required to demonstrate proficiency in at least one language other than their native tongue prior to completion of their degree. The language exam consists of a telephone interview with a trained examiner in the selected language, using a nationally established proficiency rating scale. In addition to an on-site language lab and a cluster of language study groups, students have sought intensive language study abroad—usually in the summer after their initial year. Those students studying a particularly challenging language for native English speakers (e.g., Arabic, Mandarin) may spend a semester abroad in a country where that language is spoken.

The program began to enter reciprocal student exchange agreements with similar schools in China, Korea, Germany, India, and Canada. In reciprocal exchanges registered students at each of the two universities swap places for a semester. The exchange need not be simultaneous but must balance within a contracted time period. Such reciprocal exchanges, although demanding to establish, represent one of the least expensive forms of study abroad. With sufficient promotion, they can yield a steady stream of exchange students while providing opportunities for Bush students opportunities to study abroad.

Several other initiatives emerged. Faculty began to offer courses that involved a field experience to a designated country with the travel component scheduled at the end of or between semesters. In cooperation with other departments at Texas A&M, the Bush School constructed a graduate Certificate in Chinese Studies, drawing on faculty expertise and their courses offered across the university. Drawing on international expertise elsewhere in the university—as in the Chinese studies certificate—will remain a valuable asset. In the longer term, the MPIA itself needs to acquire more of its own faculty with expertise in various regions of the world.

The Certificate in Chinese Studies became one of two additional graduate certificate programs at the Bush School. A twelve-credit-hour graduate Certificate in Homeland Security developed under the leadership of a new lecturer hired by the school—David McIntyre, a retired US Army colonel. McIntyre had been in the forefront of designing and implementing a homeland security field of study and training in our nation's capital. He started the study in response to the Oklahoma City bombing and accelerated the effort after 9/11. In 2003 he found it necessary to return to College Station from the Washington area as a result of his father's illness. The Bush School invited him to teach a pilot course on homeland security. The strong response led to the development of a multicourse Certificate in Homeland Security.[4]

Another experienced professional joined the Bush School's international affairs faculty in 2007. Ronald Sievert became a senior lecturer in the Bush School after a law career in the US Department of Justice. In 1990 Sievert began working as an international and national security coordinator in that department and worked with the FBI and intelligence agencies on national security–related cases and related matters. In addition to teaching and doing research on both national security and international law, he assumed directorship of the Certificate in Advanced International Affairs after Olson stepped down.

At the same time, a cadre of new assistant professors soon joined the faculty and began to provide some of the needed area expertise: in 2004 Antonio Madrid (Europe); in 2005 Rola el Hussini (Middle East); in 2007 Ren Mu (China) and Gabriela Marin Thornton (Europe). These new hires—together with several adjunct faculty teaching part-time in the Bush School (Adel Varghese and Klaus Aurisch)—helped build capability in the regional dimensions of the MPIA in its early years. They added another dimension to the construction of a blended faculty. So did Jasen Castillo, who worked for RAND and the office of the US secretary of defense before joining the Bush School in 2007.

With the additional faculty, the Master's Program in International Affairs quickly moved to a full two-year, forty-eight-credit-hour master's degree program. In parallel, the sister Master of Public Service and Administration reduced its required credit hours to forty-eight. As noted previously, both programs required noncredit summer internships for most students.

National Recognition and Expansion of the Master of Public Service and Administration

By the fall of 2006 the Bush School's Master of Public Service and Administration had graduated seven classes from its two-year program, had reworked its curriculum after the school became independent, and had twelve full-time faculty and several others part-time. From its beginning, the Bush School had been a participating member of the National Association of Schools of Public Affairs and Administration (NASPAA).[5] In 2006 the school sought this society's accreditation of its Master of Public Service and Administration. The move fit well with Chilcoat's objective of increasing the national visibility of the Bush School.

The association's accreditation is a protracted and demanding process requiring a structured self-study and a site inspection by designated outside evaluators. The undertaking fell substantially on Bill West, the program director. He and his colleagues succeeded, and the Bush School's program obtained accreditation. That process also fulfilled Texas A&M University's own requirement for periodic review and evaluation of every degree-granting program. West had successfully balanced that accreditation task with the overall program management as well as his own teaching and research. When John and Sara Lindsey gave their second endowed chair to the Bush School—the Sara H. Lindsey Chair—West clearly became the appropriate recipient.

Table 2 shows the year-by-year growth in applications and enrollment of both of the master's degree programs between the opening of the Bush School in 1997 and 2006. It reveals the steady increase in the MPSA Program across most of that first decade with a slight bump when the MPIA started in 2002 and the older program dropped its concentration in international affairs.

Table 2

Bush School student applications and enrollment, 1997–2006

	Public Administration		International Affairs	
Year	Applied	Enrolled	Applied	Enrolled
1997	58	18		
1998	68	20		
1999	58	22		
2000	84	23		
2001	99	31		
2002	83	34	85	20
2003	79	28	99	24
2004	71	33	112	30
2005	68	35	123	37
2006	66	30	121	40

Note: Bush School degree programs are two years in length. Total enrollment in any one year therefore is the sum of the entering students in that year plus the students who entered the previous year (minus any withdrawals).

Although the overall enrollment of the Bush School increased, the pause in enrollment growth in the MPSA Program precipitated initiatives to increase its attractiveness. The program sought to diversify and deepen its curriculum through hiring junior faculty with the positions created by the Gates faculty expansion program. In 2005, the program hired two new assistant professors: Domonic Bearfield (PhD, political science, Rutgers University) and Gina Reinhardt (PhD, political science, Washington University). Bearfield assumed responsibility for the program's required leadership course. The school's leadership program remained one of Chilcoat's principal objectives, and he urged Domonic Bearfield to participate in the summer leadership program at Harvard University's Kennedy School. In fact, not only did the dean insist that Bearfield pursue that Harvard program, but he also decided to attend as well. Few young assistant professors have their dean join them as co-seminar participants for the summer.

A year later for the fall semester of 2006, the MPSA Program hired Joanna Lahey as an assistant professor. She had won a national award for her MIT PhD research focus on labor policies. After joining the Bush School, Lahey continued to pursue her research and expertise on age discrimination and employment.

In 2007 the MPSA Program hired Danny Davis, a retired US Army officer, as a senior lecturer to strengthen its offerings on homeland security. In same year Sharon Caudle, who previously served as an assistant director in the US Government Accountability Office, joined the faculty as the Younger-Carter Policy Maker in Residence. Earlier the Younger-Carter resources had been used to bring policy makers (e.g., John Kasich, Ohio congressman and later governor) in for shorter periods of residency. Caudle agreed to a year-long appointment. Joining Davis in providing both resident and online courses in homeland security as well as financial management, Caudle subsequently accepted the invitation to stay on at the Bush School as a senior lecturer. The program thus continued to build strength in homeland security.

MPSA also began to create substantial capability in another area. In the fall of 2006 William Brown was hired as associate professor. He brought expertise and experience from leading a nonprofit management program in Arizona. Under his leadership nonprofit management has gradually evolved into a major component of the MPSA Program at the Bush School.

Many equate public-service careers with employment in government. It is reasonable to make that association. A multitude of governments at the local, regional, state, national, and international levels all require talented and dedicated personnel. Beyond governments, however, enormous arrays of organizations provide a service or promote the interests of some segment of society. They are neither for-profit enterprises nor an element of public government. Such organizations are the backbone of civil society and are important to the successful functioning of democracy. In the United States nonprofit entities run the gamut from small groups to large, complex organizations. According to the website Independent Sector, "There are many kinds of nonprofits—the Internal Revenue Code defines more than 25 categories of organizations that are exempt from federal income taxes."[6] The best-known nonprofit organizations are charitable enterprises that must benefit the broad public interest.

The larger a nonprofit organization and the more resources involved, the greater the need for professional leadership. William Brown developed this field of public service at the Bush School. Angela Bies, already on the faculty and having nonprofit experience, taught several related courses. Brown enlisted her help and that of other faculty to build a more comprehensive program. He envisioned educational opportunities through the Bush School for individuals at various stages in this career path. As a nonprofit focus evolved, Brown developed three sets of initiatives: (1) an online graduate Certificate in Nonprofit Management, (2) outreach to local and regional personnel engaged in nonprofit organizations, and (3) an expanded curriculum within the existing master's degree program. Like the Bush School's Certificate in Advanced International Affairs, the Certificate in Nonprofit Management requires twelve hours of graduate credit (four courses) and may be taken either in residence on the Texas A&M campus or online. The nonresidential component of the certificate is conducted by the school's Distance Education Program. Currently, the Certificate in Nonprofit Management has the largest enrollment of the school's three graduate distance education certificate programs. Brown supervises and teaches in both the online certificate program and the residential master's degree courses.

Until recently the community and regional outreach initiatives of the nonprofit program revolved around two activities. One was an annual nonprofit forum. It brought together area professionals in the field to participate in development workshops and acquire updated ideas and insights from recognized regional and national leaders. About one hundred participants registered annually. The Bush School launched and hosted the event for a number of years; however, most of the workshops associated with the forum have gradually been assumed by other area organizations.

The second outreach program continues: a three-day workshop titled "Emerging Leaders in Public Service." The workshop targets young professionals currently working in nonprofits who seek to move into more management responsibilities. "In addition to the three-day in-residence activities, the program includes three months of follow-up"[7]—including one-on-one coaching and networking initiatives. The workshop activities include some elements drawn from the Bush School's Leadership Program. Fifteen to twenty participants from across the state of Texas enroll each year. Subsidized in the first several years by a foundation, the program now runs on registration fees and a modest investment from the Bush School.

The third leg of the nonprofit program occurs in the resident Master of Public Service and Administration. With multiple faculty participating, this subject area has expanded to become a major focus of study within public administration. Two core courses provide the gateway to the nonprofit field followed by a series of elective seminars on subjects such as volunteer recruitment and fund-raising. In addition to classwork some students participate in the Board Fellows Program in which they are assigned for a year to be nonvoting members of a local nonprofit board. Overall a significant number of Bush School students in recent years have chosen nonprofit management as their career field. Matthew Upton, the assistant dean for career and student services, stated: "Over the past 5 years 20–30% of our graduates from the Public Administration program have started their post-graduate careers working for non-profit organizations."[8]

Students Synthesize Their Bush School Experience

From the outset, the Bush School's Master of Public Service and Administration required a concluding capstone seminar. When the

Master's Program in International Affairs expanded to a full two-year program, it established a similar requirement. Although many professional graduate programs have some form of integrating seminar near the completion of the degree, the Bush School capstone projects quickly developed a distinctive character that has become one of the defining attributes of both degree programs.

The basic structure of every Bush School capstone involves a group of students (typically six to nine) working under the supervision of a faculty member on a problem or policy issue specified by a government agency or nonprofit organization. The supervising faculty member will have interacted with the client entity in advance to establish the problem or issue to be investigated. Either the client organization or, more often, the Bush School will allocate a modest research budget for the project. The student team refines the task, engages in the necessary research, writes a report, and submits the report together with an oral briefing to the client. Occasionally the oral briefing occurs via closed-circuit conferencing. Increasingly a capstone team will conduct a formal rehearsal at the Bush School open to all before their final presentation to the client. The oral briefing, as well as the research report, is graded by the faculty member and evaluated by the client.

In some respects the Bush School capstones represent a distinctive group master's thesis. A core assumption underlying these projects is that most graduates will find their employment experience involves problem-solving tasks working as part of a group or team. The capstone requires students to bring together research skills and substantive knowledge that they acquired in the degree program. The students need to apply the skills in writing, team building, conflict resolution, and problem solving, which are integral parts of the school's Leadership Program.

After the Leadership Program structure was fully in place in 2007, capstone teams could incorporate some of the leadership capabilities to enhance their skills. The school's Leadership Program's staffer (Lindsey Pavelka and subsequently Holly Kasperbauer) are trained administrators of the Myers Briggs Type Indicator Instrument Personality Test as well as several other diagnostic tools. A capstone team can request the leadership staff to administer and guide them through ways of assessing skill sets or areas of potential conflict in problem management. For example, if all the members of a capstone team agree to complete and share information on each individual's preferred style of work, the staff can help them recognize potential pitfalls and develop strategies for working effectively together.[9] The school's writing lecturer also provides guidance as each team prepares its report. Each year teams elect to work and rework their draft reports in consultation with the in-house writing adviser. All of these resources enhance the educational experience of the capstone and better prepare students for success in the workplace.

During Chilcoat's second term as dean, the capstone experience became fully institutionalized within the school. It remains so to the present. Among the twenty-seven capstones completed between spring semester 2006 and spring 2007, the following illustrate the range of topics and clients:

Barriers to Childhood Immunization Rates (San Antonio Metro Health District), 2006

Finance for Low-Income Communities (Grameen Capital India), 2006

Election Technology and Risk Perception (Congressional Research Service), 2006

US Policy and the Future of Uzbekistan (Department of State), 2007

The Board's Role for Credit Union Mergers (Filene Institute for Credit Union Research), 2007

Nonprofit Capacity-Building "Industry" in Minnesota (Minnesota Council of Nonprofits), 2007

Effective Intelligence Operations during Counterinsurgency Campaigns (Rand Corp), 2008

Combating Child Labor through DESTINO (Department of Labor), 2008

Evaluating the Consequences of Texas' Dropout Rate (United Way of Texas), 2008

None of these projects use classified data, and all are conducted in conformity with the university's requirements for such inquiry. Increasing student awareness of the protection of individual data, operations with large data sets, intensive case studies, the task of forming and assessing inferences—come into play in capstone research. In capstones, previous classroom drills and exercises become applicable to a real-world policy problem whose value is determined by the client as well as the Bush School instructor.

School Leadership Changes

Midway through Chilcoat's second term the Bush School experienced significant leadership changes. It began when both Hank Jenkins-Smith and Larry Lynn independently received and accepted major offers from other universities. Although their visions for the program occasionally varied, Lynn and Jenkins-Smith provided the senior leadership, with Bill West, in shaping the MPSA after the Bush School became an independent academic unit. They were catalysts for attracting and guiding strong junior faculty. In the spring of 2007, they helped President Bush and the faculty and staffs in both master's degree programs celebrate the school's tenth anniversary. After the celebration, however, both scholars moved to their new institutions.

Earlier, Bill West had signaled that he would like to step down as program director of the MPSA at the conclusion of spring semester 2007. A search for his successor had thus been under way, and Jeryl Mumpower accepted the role as program director and as the Joe R. and Teresa Lozano Long Chair in Business and Government. Prior to coming to the Bush School, Mumpower had been at the Nelson Rockefeller College of Public Affairs and Policy at the State University of New York at Albany. There he held a number of administrative positions and engaged in research on negotiation and bargaining and the use of expertise in policy making. In effect, Mumpower filled one of the senior positions vacated by Jenkins-Smith and Lynn. The Bush School gained an important additional benefit when Edwina Dorch, Mumpower's spouse, accepted an appointment as a visiting associate professor in the MPSA.

Ann Bowman filled the other senior faculty position, serving as the Hazel Davis and Robert Kennedy Endowed Chair. Bowman's coauthored *State and Local Government* continues to be a highly regarded text that was published in its ninth edition in 2014. Her strong teaching and scholarship in state and urban politics have had an impact not only among Bush School students and colleagues but also within several professional organizations where she has held a series of major positions. In 2014 Bowman became president-elect of the Southern Political Science Association and, while serving as president the following year, was inducted as a fellow of the National Academy of Public Administration. In 2016 the Federalism and Intergovernmental Relations Section of the American Political Science Association presented her with a Distinguished Scholar Award.

The summer of 2007 seemed like a logical time to celebrate the momentum of the Bush School. Bush invited Chilcoat, the school's senior administrative leadership, and the school's Advisory Board to join him and Mrs. Bush at Kennebunkport, Maine.[10] There was much to celebrate. *U.S. News and World Report* planned to rank the young Bush School twenty-third among the 201 public affairs programs in the United States.[11] Both master's programs not only experienced continued growth in their enrollments, but also their graduates gained successful employment after graduation. In addition, the dean informed the Advisory Committee that the Bush School in collaboration with the Texas A&M Department of Nuclear Engineering had just initiated a new multiyear contract with Lawrence Livermore National Laboratory. Under the contract the MPIA would offer a special graduate credit program on national security affairs and policy making for selected Livermore employees. In sum, things were going well in 2007. But Richard Chilcoat soon faced a severe personal challenge.

After returning home from Kennebunkport, Chilcoat received a diagnosis of cancer. During fall semester 2007, Chilcoat began an extensive round of treatments. Sam Kirkpatrick assumed an increasing portion of the dean's responsibilities. The previous year, in response to reduced state support to higher education, all units of the Texas A&M University were required to reduce their budgets by a fixed percentage. Kirkpatrick, working with the school's fiscal officer, Joe Dillard, engineered the Bush School response. They managed the necessary cuts in the school budget without any reduction in personnel. Implementing that budget plan still required attention. Partially influenced by the reduced state support, Chilcoat planned a revamped endowment campaign. He hired a consultant who designed a possible campaign strategy. A Bush School development committee was appointed. Now all plans were to be placed on hold. By the end of fall semester 2008 Richard Chilcoat resigned from the deanship.[12]

The school was extremely fortunate in the appointment of its interim dean. Benton Cocanougher, who had recently stepped down as the highly regarded dean of the Mays Business School, agreed to serve temporarily. Bush School personnel who worked with Cocanougher marveled at the quickness with which he recognized administrative challenges and opportunities for the school. As interim dean, however, he focused on holding the school in a steady state as the search for a new permanent dean got under way.

As it happened, one of the guest speakers scheduled to address the Bush School in the spring of 2009 was Ryan Crocker, a distinguished career ambassador in the US Foreign Service.[13] Crocker was widely regarded as one of the country's top Middle East experts. At one time or another, he had served as the US ambassador to Pakistan, Syria, Kuwait, and Lebanon. He had just completed serving as US ambassador to Iraq at the critical time of the "surge," working closely with General David Petraeus as well as the Iraqi government. He was now retiring from the US Foreign Service.

During his visit to the Bush School, Crocker made a very positive impression on faculty and students. He not only visited the school but also talked to the Texas A&M Corps of Cadets. He acknowledged that the spirit of service quite evident among students at both places made a powerful impression on him.[14] Subsequently, the university asked if he would apply for the deanship of the Bush School. He returned to the campus as one of the candidates and received the offer. Later he reported receiving a call from Robert Gates, at that time serving as the US secretary of defense. Gates urged Crocker to accept the position but cautioned that if he received a call from Brent Scowcroft telling him that the job could be done one or two days a month to completely reject that statement. Crocker did receive a call from Scowcroft, encouraging him to accept the post. Crocker immediately informed Scowcroft that he had been warned. Scowcroft reportedly was quick to acknowledge that his earlier estimate to Gates of the time needed to run the Bush School might have been his biggest fib ever. Thus, fully informed, Ryan Crocker accepted the position as the new Bush School dean.

7

A Robust School in a New Decade

Public Service Creates a Revolving Door for Bush Dean

Having retired from the Foreign Service, Ryan Crocker began serving as the dean of the Bush School at the outset of the spring semester of 2010. Upon arrival, he discovered the university had mandated that the school prepare a formal strategic plan—a periodic requirement of all units in the university. Sam Kirkpatrick led a strategic planning committee. The committee met with various constituent groups seeking to identify goals, priorities, and means of achievement. Crocker attended nearly every session as a way to immerse himself in the school.[1] As Crocker became acquainted with the current condition of the Bush School and its future aspirations, he realized the school faced a financial challenge.

Over the years, a group of dedicated donors had been remarkably generous to the Bush School, but an organized capital campaign had stalled. One constraint resulted from the eight years marking the presidency of George W. Bush. His father and his associates wished to exercise great caution that requests for school support would not be interpreted as having any kind of connection to the current political administration in Washington. Indeed, occasionally potential donors—as well as prospective students—seemed uncertain as for which President Bush the school was named.

Crocker's predecessor, Richard Chilcoat, had taken some initial steps toward a financial campaign, but various challenges existed. The Bush School's Advisory Board, established early in the school's history, had been assured they would not be expected to engage in development efforts. A financial campaign required a separate structure committed to fund-raising. When the Texas A&M Foundation assigned Jerome Rektorik to work with the Bush School, he and Chilcoat decided to create an independent Development Council under Frank Muller, a very active A&M former student who was quite interested in the Bush School. That committee focused primarily on alumni of the university in a low-key fashion to minimize any confusion with national politics.

In 2010 with a new Bush School dean and a different administration in Washington, a new game plan became possible. Crocker used his considerable diplomatic skills to negotiate an understanding between the Bush Presidential Library Foundation and the Texas A&M Foundation. Both previously had generated donors for the Bush School but had different concerns and priorities. The Bush Library Foundation had been working with David B. Jones, a principal in the fund-raising consulting firm of Dini Spheris.[2] Ryan Crocker established a working relationship with Jones as well as the leadership of the Texas A&M Foundation. Jones helped Crocker develop a priority list of individuals and firms that might be attracted to the Bush School mission. Crocker initiated a full schedule of meetings and visits with prospects.

One of the early sessions involved meeting a group of prospects on April 26, 2011. Drayton McLane, a member of the school's Advisory Board and owner of the Houston Astros, invited guests to meet Crocker in the owner's suite at Minute Maid Park. As Crocker readied to speak, the Bush School's director of communications received a call from the media. The query was not about the Bush School capital campaign. Instead, they sought confirmation that President Obama had just asked Crocker to come out of retirement and become the US ambassador to Afghanistan.[3]

Back in College Station, Crocker posed the dilemma as a rhetorical question: How can one be the head of a professional school of public service and not answer the request of the president of the United States? He was the second Bush School dean called back to public service. Robert Gates, who subsequently became president of Texas A&M University, had been asked by President George W. Bush to be secretary of defense, a position he continued to hold in the Obama administration.

The Bush School also had current faculty called back to government service as the wars in Iraq and Afghanistan continued. In 2008 Larry Napper was asked to serve as cochair of the Iraq Governance Assessment Team. In that role Napper and his group made repeated visits to Iraq to make recommendations to General Petraeus and the American ambassador to Iraq at the time, Ryan Crocker. (That contact between Napper and Crocker triggered the initial invitation to Crocker to speak at the Bush School after he retired.)

Another incident involved the British government. In the year Napper began working with his team in Iraq, a part-time Bush School lecturer returned to a full-time job in Washington. She had been teaching a course on terrorism and had occasionally used a guest speaker, who had been extremely well received. He was a retired British military officer, Richard MacNamee. A graduate of the Royal Military Academy at Sandhurst, MacNamee had been commissioned as a British army officer. Later in British Special Forces he conducted operations for the UK's counterintelligence and security agency MI5 and been awarded the Queen's Commendation for Valuable Service. After he retired, MacNamee came to the United States and at that time gave guest lectures at the Bush School. He displayed excellent instructional talent, particularly in the areas of terrorism and counterterrorism. In need of a replacement instructor, the Bush School quickly hired him as a full-time lecturer.[4] Soon after he began his teaching assignment, the British government recalled MacNamee to serve in a Special Operations Task Force in Afghanistan. After completing that mission, he returned to the Bush School as a faculty member.

Ryan Crocker arranged a two-year leave of absence from the university. Although understandably distracted, he remained at the Bush School until his appointment as ambassador was approved by the US Senate in June 2011.[5] Crocker had been dean for less than two years.

As the Bush School capital campaign was taking shape under Crocker's leadership, Andrew Card had signaled his willingness to help. Card had a long association with President and Mrs. Bush, beginning as his campaign manager in Massachusetts when Bush ran for president in 1980. Later he served as the deputy chief of staff during the first part of Bush's administration; he then became the secretary of transportation. He returned to be the chief of staff for President George W. Bush and became the second-longest-serving chief of staff in the nation's history. With Crocker's recall, the Texas A&M University leadership already knew of Card's willingness to help with the Bush School capital campaign. They asked if he would play a larger role and use his administrative skills to serve as the Bush School's acting dean. He agreed. Card and his wife, Kathleene, moved to College Station prior to the start of the fall semester 2011.

As acting dean, Andrew Card played a vigorous role. Card intended to pursue Crocker's mission for the school, including the financial campaign. He described himself as a "student-centric dean," promoting the opportunities for public service.[6] In part, Card practiced leadership by walking around and interacting with everyone in the organization. When on campus, he would routinely drop in on faculty members and students, inquiring about their work and challenges. A number of students developed a personal relationship with Card, who worked with them on their career plans and employment. Card, however, usually divided each week between tasks on campus and road trips. He was tireless in speaking and soliciting prospective donors for the Bush School. He proved quite successful in establishing a strong start for the school's capital campaign. Between 2011 and 2013, the Bush School gained over twenty-three million dollars from donations. Some of that amount had been triggered by Ryan Crocker's initiative, but most of it resulted from Andrew Card's efforts. Additionally, like Crocker, Card made frequent media appearances and routinely made his identification with the Bush School clear.

Near the end of Card's two years as acting dean, Karan Watson, the university provost, asked Card to implement a plan to organize the Bush School into two academic departments. From the beginning of the school's establishment as a separate academic unit in the university organization, no department structure existed. There were two degree-granting programs (MPSA and MPIA), multiple certificate programs, and several research institutes. Despite these various components, the Bush School had one faculty who collectively made decisions recommending new hiring, promotions, and so on. All support activities (finance, recruitment, student services, technical support, communications, and external relations) reported directly to the dean or executive associate dean. The university administration recognized that the Bush School had grown to the point where a differentiated structure, parallel to that in other university colleges, would be beneficial. It also represented the kind of issue about which many faculty members have differing, but intense, views. It was a challenging task for an acting dean near the conclusion of his term. Andrew Card did it. The Bush School created two departments—Public Service and Administration and International Affairs—each with its own faculty, administration, bylaws, and so on.

After a two-year absence including time as US ambassador in Afghanistan, Ryan Crocker returned to his role as dean at the Bush School in August 2013. While Crocker was serving in Afghanistan, his security detail had quickly affixed an A&M logo to the back of his helmet. He commented that he was extremely glad to be back at the Bush School and operating without a helmet.[7]

Crocker quickly needed to address multiple new administrative appointments. Sam Kirkpatrick had retired after serving as executive associate dean since 2005. Crocker asked Arnie Vedlitz to become Kirkpatrick's successor. The dean also designated Larry Napper to be interim head of the new Department of International Affairs because Charles Hermann had been granted a year of professional leave. A major search for a permanent head of the Department of International Affairs successfully concluded with the selection of F. Gregory Gause III. He started in summer 2014 and received the John Lindsey Endowed Chair. A noted Middle East scholar, Gause had previously served as chair of the Political Science Department at the University of Vermont.

With Napper assuming departmental leadership for a year before Gause arrived, the school needed a new director of the Scowcroft Institute. Fortunately, Andrew Natsios had moved to the Bush School as an executive professor from his position on the faculty at Georgetown University. His long career in practical politics had culminated in his serving as the administrator of the US Agency for International Development from 2001 to 2006. After that assignment he was appointed US special envoy to Sudan in 2006–2007 before joining the faculty at Georgetown University. Now at the Bush School, Natsios became director of the Scowcroft Institute.

A year after appointing Arnie Vedlitz as executive associate dean in 2013, Crocker appointed three new assistant deans. Matthew Upton, who had led the school's career and student services since 2003, became assistant dean for career and student services with expanded oversight of recruitment and admissions activities. Leonard Bright, who had joined the faculty in the fall of 2011, became the assistant dean of graduate education. Cole Blease Graham Jr. became assistant dean of assessment and diversity initiatives. Graham had joined the faculty in 2009 as a visiting professor, offering courses on local government and politics. Subsequently, he became an executive professor at the Bush School. Bright and Graham balanced their part-time administrative responsibilities with teaching as members of the Department of Public Service and Administration faculty.

Upon his return in 2013, Crocker faced a whirlwind of activities beyond the demands of administrative appointments in the school. A seemingly endless stream of critical events arose in the Middle East—the Arab Spring, the emergence of ISIS, the effort to reach a nuclear agreement with Iran, the war in Syria, the violence in both Afghanistan and Iraq. These constituted only some of the critical developments unfolding in the Middle East. Of course, Crocker joined other Bush School faculty, such as Gause, in sharing their expertise and analysis with Bush School students and others. Crocker, however, because of his recent diplomatic mission in the region and his demonstrated expertise in the Middle East, became a major contact for the media. His administrative assistant, Mary Hein, estimated that in many weeks he would receive twenty to twenty-five media interview queries.[8] He undertook four to five per week. Additionally he engaged in written analysis and three to four speaking engagements each month without honoraria. He was relentless in insisting on his identity with the Bush School at Texas A&M and refused to do television spots without the Bush School/Texas A&M backdrop. Bush School students witnessed another dimension of public service at close range.

Growing Enrollment

Between 2010, when Crocker became dean, and the completion of his interrupted term in 2016, student enrollment grew steadily. As revealed in table 3, the number of master's degree candidates continued to increase in both departments. The combined enrollment of first- and second-year students exceeded three hundred in the fall of 2013 when Crocker returned.[9] That was more than one and a half times the total enrollment at the beginning of Chilcoat's last year.

Table 3 also shows a pattern of somewhat larger applications and enrollments in international affairs than public service and administration. The difference may well reflect the substantially greater number of professional graduate programs in public policy and administration than in international affairs. NASPAA has more than 160 accredited master's programs in North America. The Association of Professional Schools of International Affairs (APSIA)—to which the Bush School was admitted as a full member in 2012—has fewer than forty full members worldwide.

Table 3
Bush School student applications and enrollment, 2007–2016

	Public Administration		International Affairs	
Year	Applied	Enrolled	Applied	Enrolled
2007	87	45	186	49
2008	96	46	204	55
2009	109	52	207	58
2010	110	53	215	56
2011	121	63	244	73
2012	122	62	246	83
2013	122	65	226	92
2014	137	72	228	91
2015	161	78	257	90
2016	165	87	230	92

Note: Bush School degree programs are two years in length. Total enrollment in any one year is the sum of the entering students in that year plus the students who entered the previous year (minus any withdrawals).

One possible reason contributing to the growth of both degree programs occurred in 2011 when the Robertson Foundation for Government selected the Bush School as one of a small group of professional schools to which it annually awards significant scholarships to top students committed to careers in government. Furthermore, most Bush School students succeed in finding relevant employment after graduation, even in a period with reductions in new hiring at some levels of government service. Across the entire history of the Bush School, 70 percent of all graduates go into public-sector careers (state, local, federal, government contractors, and nonprofit/NGOs) within six months of graduation.[10]

A less visible reason for the continuing growth in enrollment at the Bush School is the school's administrative staff. A remarkable number of this small group have not only impressive years of service but also dedication to the success of the school. Consider this one example: When prospective students appear for the annual interview weekends, the talent and energy of the staff are dramatically visible. Kathryn Meyer, director of recruitment, likely will have had multiple individual communications with each visitor. Matthew Upton and his colleagues in student services supervise every detail of the weekend, which entails their arriving early and staying late into the night. The administrative assistants for each program/department (Kimberly Reeves for Public Service and Administration; Janeen Wood for International Affairs) will answer endless questions with patience and authority throughout the day. The same is true for the dean's staff, led by Mary Hein. The banks of computers for the required written exercises each visitor completes and the visuals for multiple presentations result from the overtime work of the computer staff. All this staff work is on weekends! For each of them, these events are only a minute portion of their overall responsibilities. Many of them have played significant and dedicated roles at the Bush School for much of the school's history.

Faculty Expansion

Ryan Crocker concurred with the university administration that the school would continue to increase its combined enrollment to a targeted number of four hundred graduate students in residence. To achieve that objective, both departments began planning for one-year executive master's degree programs for individuals (including military personnel) who already have multiple years of public service. In 2016, the Public Service and Administration Department launched its executive master's degree, which could be completed largely online with minimal residence at the university. When both departments establish such programs, they will enhance and sharpen the professional abilities of individuals already in public service and strengthen their career advancement. Additionally, the online graduate certificate programs continue their pattern of steady growth. Both of these initiatives will lead to increased student enrollment, which creates pressure for additional faculty. Also, an emphasis on seminar-size classes contributes pressure for faculty growth. As with most quality graduate instruction, Bush School classes usually take the form of seminars with lively dialogue between students and instructor. Such interaction with everyone engaged means a maximum class enrollment in the low twenties. The exceptions to the seminar format are the courses required of all students—usually taken near the beginning of their graduate experience. Furthermore, the physical constraints of classroom size in the Bush School reinforce the strong commitment to seminar learning. Among the classrooms currently available to the Bush School, one room seats slightly more than sixty, and another, forty. All the other classrooms are substantially smaller and designed for seminar-size classes.

Accordingly, as the student population grew during the Crocker/Card period from 2010 to 2016, so did the size and composition of the Bush School faculty. Some of the new members represented replacements for the inevitable number of colleagues who chose to move to other institutions or retire. Beyond that, the overall number of faculty members increased to expand the scope and depth of the curriculum and to accommodate the continued student growth.

In 2011 each Bush School program hired two additional faculty members. At the associate professor rank, the MPSA Program hired Leonard Bright. He brought added expertise on public-sector human resource management and became an assistant dean in 2014. The Bush School also hired three new assistant professors. Kalena Cortes (PhD, economics, University of California at Berkeley) was already recognized as expert on the economics of education and immigration policy. She joined the MPSA Program. Xiaobo Lu (PhD, political science, Yale), and William Norris (PhD, political science, MIT) both joined the MPIA and strengthened the examination of East Asia. Lu studies international political economy, and Norris examines Chinese foreign relations and economic statecraft. All four quickly became popular classroom instructors.

The growth in Bush School faculty continued and even accelerated over the next few years. In January 2012, Valerie Hudson joined the international affairs faculty and became recipient of the George H. W. Bush endowed chair previously held by Michael Desch. In 2009, *Foreign Policy* journal named her one of the one hundred most influential global thinkers for her demographic research on the implications of the enormous imbalance of males relative to females in China and elsewhere in Asia. At the Bush School, Hudson continued her pathbreaking research linking the security and status of women within countries to the international actions of countries. That work led to her selection as one of the first Carnegie Fellows in 2015.

In fall 2012 five more new faculty joined the Bush School. They included Andrew Natsios (previously director of the Scowcroft Institute) and four new assistant professors. Khaldoun AbouAsi (PhD, Maxwell School, Syracuse) and Laura Dague joined the public service and administration faculty. AbouAsi—a native of Lebanon—has extensive experience working with and studying NGOs. Dague specializes in health economics and immediately captured attention with her research on federal health-care reform.

One of the two new faculty in international affairs, Rekyo Huang (PhD, political science, Columbia University) had just completed a postdoctoral fellowship at Stanford. Her teaching and research on violent conflicts and the problem of political development bridged the two international affairs tracks on national security and development/economics. The other, Mohammad Tabaar (PhD, government, Georgetown University), had previous experience as a journalist for BBC World Service, where he applied his expertise on the Middle East, particularly Iran.

In 2013–2014 the MPSA Program added three more faculty. Laurie Paarlberg, an associate professor, arrived in 2013 to strengthen the rapidly expanding activities in nonprofit management. Her teaching and research give special attention to community philanthropy. A year later Kent Portney moved to the Bush School from Tufts University to assist in the leadership of the Institute of Science, Technology, and Public Policy when its director, Arnie Vedlitz, assumed major responsibilities as executive associate dean. Portney has conducted major research and teaching on urban politics and environmental policy, including the management of water resources. Also in 2014 Justin Bullock (PhD, political science, University of Georgia) joined as assistant professor and attracted attention with his research on the variable acceptance of patients based on their type of insurance.

The MPIA added five new faculty between 2013 and 2015. A surge of three new assistant professors began in the fall semester 2013. Jessica Gottlieb (PhD, political science, Stanford University) focuses on economic and political development involving cutting-edge experimental work in sub-Saharan Africa. Joshua Shifrinson (PhD, political science, MIT) has a keen eye for diplomatic history as well as military strategy and international power transitions. Erin Snider (PhD, politics and international studies, Cambridge University) studies Middle East politics and foreign assistance. Both Shifrinson and Snider joined the Bush School after postdoctoral fellowships at George Washington University and Princeton University, respectively.

In fall 2014 Andrew Ross arrived as a full professor from the University of New Mexico with earlier teaching experience at the US Naval War College. His ongoing research on national security issues and his administrative experience working on contracts with Department of Defense agencies positioned him well to take on leadership of the school's ongoing Certificate in National Security Affairs with Lawrence Livermore and Sandia National Laboratories.

After more than a decade directing the International Development and Economics Career Track in the school's MPIA, Kishore Gawande left for another distinguished academic position. Taking his place at the beginning of the 2015–2016 academic year was Raymond Robertson, an economist from Macalester College. Robertson also chaired the US Department of Labor's National Advisory Committee for Labor Provisions of the US Free Trade Agreement. He holds the Helen and Roy Ryu Chair in Economics and Government previously held by Gawande. That same year Mary Hilderbrand (PhD, political science, Harvard University) joined the Bush School faculty as a senior lecturer. Her research interests include the role of politics and governance in development and involves related field experience in programs dealing with Latin American countries and Indonesia.

The faculty enlargement continued in the newly established departments in 2016. Robert Greer and Ellie Heng Qu joined the Department of Public Service and Administration as assistant professors. Greer brings expertise in public budgeting and finance and examines state and local debt management. Heng Qu contributes to the department's focus on nonprofit management and philanthropy. The International Affairs Department welcomed John Schuessler as associate professor, who assumed responsibility for the Leadership Program after experience on the faculty of the Air War College. Emily Sellars arrived as an assistant professor in the International Affairs Department with expertise in comparative politics and developmental economics and with extensive fieldwork in Mexico and Central America.

During the six-and-a-half-year span between the arrival of Ryan Crocker through the interval Andrew Card served as acting dean until the completion of Crocker's term as dean in the summer of 2016, the faculty grew substantially. The newest faculty arrived simultaneously with the new dean for the beginning of the academic year 2016–2017. At that point, each of the two departments had twenty-two faculty. Given the turmoil in the national economy and the constraints on state funding for higher education during part of this period, the expansion is significant. And the school's student enrollment almost doubled as well. With all of the growth, the visibility and reputation of the school increased.

Jeryl Mumpower became head of the MPSA Program in 2007, but his leadership was interrupted. He took leave from the Bush School to serve as director in the Directorate for Social, Behavioral and Economic Sciences at the National Science Foundation. His absence from the Bush School between 2012 and 2015 resulted in long-serving William West returning as acting head of the MPSA Program. As luck would have it, during that time the program had to acquire reaccreditation from NASPAA. For the second time, West led the necessary self-study and hosted the required site-visit team. The team was impressed. After their visit to the Bush School, the head of the team of visitors from one of the widely recognized top programs wrote West: "I really appreciate programs like yours that emphasize academic quality. . . . Students will bring to and take from a program what they will, but your students have the opportunity for a world-class graduate education."[11]

The MPIA also gained recognition during that period. It achieved full membership in APSIA. It is one of twenty-two such schools in the United States and among the thirty-six worldwide. In 2014, a survey of more than sixteen hundred scholars in international affairs ranked the Bush School in the top twenty-five master's programs in the world for policy careers in international affairs.[12] Of those top twenty-five, the Bush School is only one of eight at public universities and is the youngest on the list.

Faculty Research: A Snapshot

Quality teaching and full engagement with students are an absolute necessity for any excellent university program. Faculty research represents another essential cornerstone of a top-flight school. Although a meaningful summary of research among a diverse faculty and across an extended period of time is problematic, enumeration of research under way by individual faculty members at a moment in time offers an alternative approach. What follows is a snapshot of the recent and ongoing research activities of Bush School faculty. We asked them to provide a research "selfie" of their work in 2016. A recurrent thread in what follows is the faculty member's attention to how the problem affects—or is related to—public or foreign policy.

> **Domonic A. Bearfield** coedited the *Encyclopedia of Public Administration and Public Policy* (2015).

> **Ann Bowman** coauthored *State and Local Government*, which will appear in its tenth edition in 2017.

> **Leonard A. Bright Jr.** coauthored with Cole Blease Graham Jr. "Why Does Interest in Government Careers Decline among Public Affairs Graduate Students?," published in *Journal of Public Affairs Education* (2015), and has a forthcoming article, "Are Individuals with High Levels of Public Service Motivation Satisfied with MPA Programs?" (Also see information for Cole Blease Graham Jr.)

William A. Brown coauthored two entries in *Voluntas* in 2015 ("Determinants of Nonprofit Sector Density" and "Dimensions of Capacity in Nonprofit Human Service Organizations") and has a forthcoming chapter, "Strategic Management," in *Handbook of Nonprofit Management & Leadership*.

Justin Bullock has coauthored "The Differential Effect of Compensation Structures on the Likelihood That Firms Accept New Patients by Insurance Type," accepted by the *International Journal of Health Economics and Management*.

Jasen Castillo authored *Endurance and War: The National Sources of Military Cohesion*, published by Stanford University Press in 2014.

Kalena E. Cortes coauthored "Efficacy vs. Equity: What Happens When States Tinker with College Admissions in a Race-Blind Era?," published in *Educational Evaluation and Policy Analysis* (2016).

Laura A. Dague published "The Effect of Medicaid Premiums on Enrollment" in the *Journal of Health Economics* (2014), and the article was named winner of the twenty-first annual NIHCM Foundation Health Care Research Award.

Danny Davis coauthored "The Constant Threat to Peace and Liberty: The Caliphate and Jihad," published in the *Journal of Human Security & Resilience* (2016), and coauthored "IT Disaster Recovery," published in *Homeland Security Today* (2015).

Lorraine Eden is completing an edited book on the economics of transfer pricing to be published by Edward Elgar Books.

F. Gregory Gause III authored "Revolution and Threat Perception: Iran and the Middle East," published in *International Politics* (2015), and is continuing work on international relations of the Middle East.

Jessica A. Gottlieb authored "Greater Expectations: A Field Experiment to Improve Accountability in Mali," published in *American Journal of Political Science* (2016).

Cole Blease Graham Jr. co-authored with Leonard Bright "The Predictors of Student Satisfaction in Public Administration Graduate Degree Programs," published in the *Journal of Public Affairs Education* (2016). (Also see information for Leonard Bright.)

James M. Griffin published "The Futile Search for Energy Security" in *Energy Journal* (2015).

Charles F. Hermann continues research on the response of US presidents when a foreign policy initiative to which they are committed appears in jeopardy.

Reyko Huang has a forthcoming book, *The Wartime Origins of Democratization: Civil War, Rebel Governance, and Political Regimes*, to be published by Cambridge University Press.

Valerie M. Hudson authored *The Hillary Doctrine: Sex and American Foreign Policy*, published by Columbia University Press (2015), and has received a Carnegie Corporation grant to continue her research.

Joanna Lahey is working on how employment discrimination changes over the life cycle in a project funded by the Sloan Foundation.

Christopher Layne authored "America Has to Wake-Up to the New Normal," published in the *National Interest* (June 2016).

Xinsheng Liu coauthored "Public Problem Characterization, Policy Solution Generation, and Intra-agenda Connectivity," published in *Policy Studies Journal* (2016), and is working on a survey on China governance and policy.

Richard C. MacNamee presented a paper on nonstate terrorism and intelligence collection efforts at a 2016 symposium of the Tokyo Institute of Technology and continues his work on nuclear terrorism.

David McIntyre is preparing a two-volume set of short essays on fundamental issues in homeland security (tentatively titled *Connecting the Dots*).

Ren Mu is investigating whether land tenure insecurity in China affects farmers' rural-to-urban migration decisions and is coauthor of a forthcoming article, "Migration and Young Child Nutrition," to be published in the *World Bank Economic Review*.

Jeryl L. Mumpower coauthored articles on the risk perceptions of terrorist events in *Journal of Risk Research* (2015) and received an NSF grant in 2016 to continue this research.

Andrew S. Natsios wrote "The Lords of the Tribes: The Real Roots of the Conflict in South Sudan," published in *Foreign Affairs Online* (2015), and is completing a book tentatively titled *Thinking about Foreign Aid*.

William J. Norris authored *Chinese Economic Statecraft*, published by Cornell University Press (2016), and is examining the potential foreign and security policy ramifications of China's recent economic slowdown.

James Olson is currently working on a book on counter-intelligence.

Kent E. Portney coauthored "The Impact of Local Environmental Advocacy Groups on City Sustainability Policies and Programs," published in *Policy Studies Journal* (2016), and coauthored "A Question Driven Socio-Hydrological Modeling Process," published in *Hydrology and Earth System Sciences* (2016).

Raymond Robertson coauthored "Stitches to Riches? Apparel Employment, Trade and Economic Development in South Asia," published in *Directions in Development-Poverty* by the World Bank (2016).

Andrew L. Ross wrote "New, Emerging and Over-the-Horizon Technologies," published in Richard Bitzinger's *Emerging Critical Technologies and Their Impact on Asian-Pacific Security* (2016).

John Schuessler wrote *Deceit on the Road to War*, published by Cornell University Press (2015), and is now working on an article with Joshua Shifrinson on geography and grand strategy.

Emily A. Sellars currently is working on two projects. The first is on political impacts of emigration in the migrants' home country. The second addresses determinants of poverty and inequality in Mexico and Central America.

Joshua R. Itzkowitz Shifrinson is completing a book, *Falling Giants: Rising States and the Fate of Declining Great Powers*, and writing several papers on the foreign policies of Ronald Reagan and George H. W. Bush.

Ronald J. Sievert authored "The Foreign Intelligence Surveillance Act Compared with the Law of Electronic Surveillance in Europe," to be published in the *American Journal of Criminal Law*.

Erin A. Snider is finishing a book on the political economy of US democracy aid in the Middle East and completing research on the impact of transitional aid after the 2011 Arab world uprisings.

Mohammad Ayatollahi Tabaar has just completed a book manuscript, "Womb to Tomb: The Politics of Religion in Iran."

Lori L. Taylor is working on a project evaluating the efficacy of teacher incentive pay in Tennessee and in 2015 published a coauthored article, "School District Consolidation," in the *Southern Economic Journal*.

Gabriela Marin Thornton wrote an article, "Lean Forward and Pull Back Options for US Grand Strategy," accepted for publication in *Oxford Bibliographies in International Relations*, and is working on an article on the juxtaposition of constructivism and classical realism.

Arnold Vedlitz coauthored "Public Problem Characterization, Policy Solution Generation, and Intra-agenda Connectivity," published in *Policy Studies Journal* (2016).

William West coauthored the article "Dynamic Rulemaking," forthcoming in the *New York Law Review*, and currently is engaged in projects on rulemaking and presidential bureaucracy management.

The Bush School Institutes

Research centers or institutes provide another instrument for pursuing and disseminating knowledge about policy issues.[13] As Crocker began his term as dean of the Bush School, the Texas A&M University System regents had recently approved a third institute at the school. The Mosbacher Institute for Trade, Economics, and Public Policy carries the name of the late Robert A. Mosbacher, secretary of commerce in President Bush's administration. The school continues as the home of the Scowcroft Institute of International Affairs and the Institute for Science, Technology, and Public Policy. The three institutes represent the continued evolution of research structures at the Bush School.

In 1990 the original Texas A&M proposal to President Bush for his library featured research centers as well as a school of public affairs. In fact, the original proposal devoted as much space to the characterization of each of the centers as to the school itself. Subsequently, the envisioned funding strategy for those centers experienced difficulties and forced changes. Nonetheless, as the school evolved, the broader concept of policy-oriented research units as an integral feature remained highly desirable elements. Each of the Bush School's current institutes pursues different approaches to knowledge generation. Each also features a somewhat distinctive mode of interaction among scholars and publics. Although the school provides some staff support for each institute, all three must pursue their own funding strategy.

Institute for Science, Technology, and Public Policy. ISTPP is the oldest and most established research unit in the Bush School, and its origins have been described earlier. The institute evolved from the original Center for Public Leadership with Arnold Vedlitz working with Robert Gates to obtain approval for the transformation to the institute in 2000. From its inception until mid-2016, Vedlitz served as the institute director. He refined the research strategy he initially developed in the Center for Public Leadership Studies involving cross-campus collaborative research. Vedlitz and his associates in ISTPP join with researchers in other parts of the campus to bid on competitive grants and contracts.

Their collaboration often includes technical, engineering, or science partners in the university and beyond. Examples of partners include the Texas Engineering Extension Service, Texas Transportation Institute, Energy Institute, Texas Sea Grant Program, Texas A&M Health Science Center, and Texas AgriLife Extension Service. This Bush School institute also forms partnerships with researchers at other universities and research organizations. In such collaborations the school's ISTPP provides research on the public policy dimensions of technical problems. More specifically, it primarily has focused on policy dimensions manifested in four areas: environment and natural resources, policy implications of emerging technologies, health policy and management, and infrastructure and the built environment.

ISTPP maintains a permanent staff of two or three research scientists in addition to the director. For a number of years Eric Linquist served as the associate director. Every year that team is augmented by Bush School students who become research assistants. When their own research interests intersect, Bush School faculty join in specific projects. In addition ISTPP has hired postdoctoral associates. At any given time, ISTPP typically will be involved in active research on two to four projects while pursuing new research grants in collaboration with other entities. In 2011, ISTPP estimated that it had submitted an average of ten major proposals annually for the past five years.[14] By the fall of 2013, ISTPP had accrued over fifteen million dollars in externally funded research grants and contracts since its inception.[15]

In addition to technical reports and presentations to their clients, ISTPP investigators generate a steady stream of publications in academic journals and books emerging from their research.[16] For example, Xinsheng Liu, Arnold Vedlitz, and Liu Shi used data from one contract to publish an article in *Environmental Science and Policy* on the factors that determine public concern with the environment. In 2014, Scott Robinson and Vedlitz received the best paper award from the American Political Science Association's Public Administration Section for their research on trust in the EPA and opposition to fracking.[17] Both Xinsheng Liu and Scott Robinson (now at the University of Oklahoma) have been long-term research scientists in ISTPP. Kent Portney assumed the directorship in the fall of 2016 as long-serving institute director Arnie Vedlitz took the opportunity for professional leave.

Scowcroft Institute of International Affairs. Earlier it was mentioned that the Bush School's second institute began operation in 2007. Its mission and primary funding method differs from those of ISTPP. The Scowcroft Institute sprang from the initiative of Michael Desch, who became the initial director for a brief period. Upon Desch's departure, Jeff Engel served as interim director in 2008–2009. The following year Larry Napper became Scowcroft director and led its operation for the next four years. In 2012, Napper appointed Don Bailey, a retired colonel, to replace retiring Peggy Holzweiss as assistant director. He continues to the present in that position.

The Scowcroft Institute operates primarily from endowment gifts and grants, including some transferred from the Bush Presidential Library Foundation. Part of the Scowcroft Institute financial support is designated for specific purposes such as speakers or conferences. Thus, these events have become a visible hallmark of the institute with an array of speakers and conferences throughout each year. Before he left, Desch had worked with the LBJ School at the University of Texas and the Tower Center for Political Studies at Southern Methodist University to establish an annual Lone Star National Security Forum that brings together scholars from the three institutions and invited guests to examine new scholarship in national security.

Under Napper's leadership, the Scowcroft Institute began providing grants for faculty research and assistance to junior faculty preparing book manuscripts. It provides each emerging author a working seminar with invited experts to provide feedback on the work in progress. Other university faculty members compete on an annual basis for research grants. Competitive awards also are made to student capstone research projects dealing with topics related to the institute's mission.[18] A special fund supports researchers from anywhere in the world seeking to do research in the Bush Presidential Library.

Napper negotiated with the US Army War College for the institute to be designated as one of the schools serving as an alternative site for midcareer army officers (colonels and lieutenant colonels) selected for a year of advanced study. Although most of the Army Fellows spend their year of study at the Army War College in Carlisle, Pennsylvania, two or three come to the Scowcroft Institute. Their year-long study and class participation have become a valued feature at the Bush School.

In the summer of 2013 another leadership transition occurred in the Scowcroft Institute. Larry Napper assumed the responsibility as the interim director of the MPIA at the request of Ryan Crocker. Andrew

Natsios, the new executive professor who had joined the Bush School from Georgetown University, assumed leadership of the Scowcroft Institute. At approximately the same time, the institute received $650,000 in three new grants, including a Texas A&M Systems research award. Natsios has increased the speaker and conference schedule and linked some of the resulting papers into a new monthly online series of research and policy papers. He also created Postdoctoral Fellows in the institute. Another new undertaking has been the introduction of released time from some teaching to allow junior faculty to concentrate on completion of their research.[19] Natsios has announced his institute will undertake research on the threat and response to future global pandemics. In that initiative, the Scowcroft Institute intends to follow the model of ISTPP and seek partners elsewhere in the university and beyond.

Mosbacher Institute for Trade, Economics, and Public Policy. In September 2009 the Board of Regents approved the school's third research unit with a clear economic policy focus. From its beginning the Bush School economists have urged the creation of an organization to investigate economic public policy issues. At the school's beginnings in 1997 Donald Deere, the first associate director of the school, had advocated such an initiative. The early effort to initiate a modest research program was jointly funded by the Department of Economics and the Bush School but collapsed when the school became an independent academic unit.

A decade later a new opportunity emerged. Robert A. Mosbacher, a close friend of President George H. W. Bush, had a distinguished career in public service and private practice. He served as secretary of commerce in the Bush administration, where he had been the chief US negotiator for NAFTA. In 2009 Mosbacher was diagnosed with a terminal illness. The former president spearheaded a campaign to find some way to recognize Mosbacher's distinguished career of public service while he could know of its creation. The Bush School responded by proposing the Mosbacher Institute for Trade, Economics, and Public Policy. When approved, James Griffin became its first director.

As with the Scowcroft Institute, the principal source of funding for the Mosbacher Institute in its first years of operation consisted primarily of financial gifts and endowments. Limited resources, however, influenced its agenda. Griffin initiated summer internship support for students engaged with an international trade organization. Another feature has been the management of four speaker series: the McLane Leadership in Business Award, the ConocoPhillips White House Lecture Series, the Bank of America Address on Volunteerism, and the Mosbacher Conversations in Public Policy. The McLane Leadership in Business Award honors a successful business executive who also engages in significant public service and/or philanthropy.

One of the distinctive initiatives of the Mosbacher Institute has been the publication of the *Takeaway*. Each short paper consists of a brief examination of a specific policy problem or current event featuring nontechnical analysis and usually specific recommendations. Typically authored by Bush School faculty with refinement by the Mosbacher staff, each *Takeaway* covers a broad range of issues. Among the topics examined have been environmental regulations, insolvency in the highway trust fund, gender bias in US import taxes, unintended consequences of US ethanol policy, maximizing return on investment in preschooling, and trade in oil and natural gas. In another recent *Takeaway*, Domonic Bearfield and Ann Bowman examine the degree of local government transparency as revealed in the websites of local government entities.[20]

In 2014, Lori Taylor, who received the Verlin and Howard Kruse Founders Associate Professorship, became the new director of the Mosbacher Institute. She has furthered the engagement of other faculty in three major research and training programs and designated one faculty member as the coordinator of each. Raymond Robertson serves as coordinator for the Integration of Global Markets Program. James Griffin heads the Energy in a Global Economy Program, and Domonic Bearfield leads the Governance and Public Service Program. Taylor views the three programs as having important interconnections in examining policy solutions. She notes that energy policy and trade policy need to be examined together in any analysis of China, Russia, India, or Brazil. Working with her deputies, Jennifer Moore and Cynthia Gause, Taylor intends to engage more faculty in each of the institute's programs and at their intersections.[21]

A New Dean Comes on Board

In the summer of 2016, Ryan Crocker completed his interrupted tour as dean of the Bush School. He had inspired students and faculty alike with his dramatic demonstration of a life of public service and his expertise on a critical area of the world. The Texas A&M System Board of Regents approved the university's recommendation for his successor, General Mark A. Welsh—another exemplar of a life of public service. Prior to joining the Bush School as dean, Welsh had been the chief of staff of the US Air Force. That appointment capped an outstanding career that began when he graduated from the US Air Force Academy. A native of Texas, Welsh will lead the Bush School as it completes its first two decades and starts its third.

Continued Engagement of President Bush

The Bush School has had one unmatched presence in its first twenty years. President and Mrs. Bush frequented the Texas A&M campus, making use of their apartment in the Bush Library complex. In her memoirs of life after the White House, Barbara Bush makes a revealing statement. She reports that her husband told her that if anything happened to her, their apartment at the library in College Station is "where he would live."[22] The entire campus and community encountered them regularly. They made themselves part of the community by attending home football weekends, hosting speakers the president had invited, dining at local restaurants, or walking their dogs around the complex. Both George and Barbara Bush unfailingly greeted friends and strangers warmly and posed tirelessly for photographs.

The president's activities at his library complex provided numerous distinctive opportunities for Bush School faculty, students, and staff. He continued to host and participate in an array of conferences and speaking engagements, many of which the Bush School's institutes organized or cosponsored with the Bush Presidential Library

Foundation. He maintained the practice of encouraging speakers to join him in a classroom for "Q&A" sessions with Bush students.

President Bush participated in several classes each year when he was well into his eighties and even when a form of Parkinson's disease confined him to a scooter or wheelchair. For a number of years he regularly participated in a class simulation on international politics conducted by Chuck Hermann. President Bush assumed the role of president. He cross-examined the student National Security Council team that briefed him on their recommendations pertaining to the issue of the simulation. In earlier years he would occasionally invite a group of students to join him for a meal and conversation, but as the school's enrollment grew, that form of interaction gradually ended.

President Bush's engagement with the school is powerfully evident in another way. His keen interest has generated strong financial support from his vast network of friends and admirers. Many graduates of Texas A&M count themselves among his fans, and that reinforces their tradition of giving back to their university. Bush himself remains unswerving in never asking for money for the Bush School or any of the other undertakings close to his heart (e.g., the Points of Light Foundation, MD Anderson Cancer Center, or the Barbara Bush Foundation for Family Literacy). Nonetheless, he is quick with his appreciation and an enthusiastic supporter of those who do seek donations.

The impact on the Bush School has been substantial. The student scholarship endowment fund exceeded twenty-nine million dollars in 2016. It is the engine that drives the fundamental commitment of the Bush School: Every person who seeks a career in public or international service obtains a top-flight professional master's degree without incurring additional student loan debt. The three-million-dollar Bush School Scholarship Fund established by the 104th Congress in honor of President Bush triggered the continuing commitment. Many have contributed to further that goal. From the day the Bush School opened, every student planning a public-service career has received some scholarship assistance.

The Bush School endowment—inspired by the president's evident interest—has also made possible the creation of seventeen endowed faculty chairs and eight professorships by 2016. At Texas A&M endowed faculty chair resources do not typically cover salary but provide substantial research funds. This kind of faculty support has enabled a very young school to attract and retain productive faculty. In addition to student and faculty support, the Bush School endowment has funds earmarked for the research institutes and for the promotion of excellence.[23]

There is another tradition between President Bush and his school that has continued past his ninety-first birthday—a photograph with the graduating Bush School students. In the later years, when Parkinson's disease obliged him to be seated in the photograph, the president always displayed his extremely colorful socks.

Bush School dean Ryan Crocker moderates a forum during celebration of the twentieth anniversary of the First Gulf War. From left to right: Brent Scowcroft, Ryan Crocker (back to camera), James Baker, Richard Cheney, Walter E. Boomer, and Colin Powell. Photo used with permission of Lorraine Eden.

Ryan Crocker is greeted by President Bush as the new Bush School dean before being recalled to active service as US ambassador to Afghanistan. Courtesy of George Bush Presidential Library Foundation. Photo by Chandler Arden.

President Bush welcomes Robert Gates, secretary of defense, back to Texas A&M, where he previously had served as Bush School dean and university president. Courtesy of Texas A&M University.

The fishing pond between the Presidential Library and the Bush School proved a good place for casual encounters with President Bush. Courtesy of George Bush Presidential Library Foundation. Photo by Chandler Arden.

The sign atop the adjacent Bush School building prepared by students had been removed by the Secret Service before President Bush made his parachute jump in front of the Presidential Library. Photo used with permission of Lorraine Eden.

Thomas Brandt, class of 2001, shows President Bush the students' method of seeking good luck on exams and other activities. They are also mindful of the quote below the President's bust. Courtesy of George Bush Presidential Library Foundation. Photo by Chandler Arden.

Andrew Card, Bush School acting dean, interviews President George W. Bush on his new book, *41*, about his father. Photo used with permission of Lorraine Eden.

Helping the Bush School recruit prospective students, President Bush joins Ryan Crocker in talking with applicants attending the school's interview weekend. Courtesy of Bush School of Government and Public Service. Photo by Chandler Arden.

President Bush responds to questions in a Bush School class. Courtesy of Bush School of Government and Public Service. Photo by of Chandler Arden.

Playing the role of president in a class simulation, President Bush receives a briefing from his student "national security adviser," Nick Reves. Courtesy of Bush School of Government and Public Service. Photo by Chandler Arden.

Chancellor Helmut Kohl of Germany and President Bush gather with Bush School students for a group photo following classroom discussion. Photo by Daniel Biskup.

President Bush and President Mikhail Gorbachev engage students during a classroom visit. Courtesy of George Bush Presidential Library Foundation. Photo by Chandler Arden.

Barbara Bush joins her husband participating in a Bush School class taught by Sharon Caudle, sitting at head of table. Courtesy of Bush School of Government and Public Service. Photo by Chandler Arden.

At a local restaurant President Bush and Richard Chilcoat listen to a student's comments. Courtesy of Bush School of Government and Public Service. Photo by Chandler Arden.

Domonic Bearfield receives from Jennifer Harris the annual "best teacher award" from the 2013 public service and administration graduates. Observing the event are Chuck Hermann; Andrew Card, acting dean; Kimberly Reeves; and Jeanne Wood. Photo used with permission of Lorraine Eden.

The 2015–2016 annual softball game between Bush School and LBJ School (University of Texas) students involved replacement of the old armadillo trophy with a more innocuous victory cup. Victorious Bush School team members show their new dean both trophies. Left to right: Sean Danielson (with old armadillo trophy), David Fujimoto (with new trophy), Samantha Ray, Mark Welsh, and Drew Domel. Photo used with permission of Jennifer Parks.

The 2015–2016 Bush School student championship winners of the Texas A&M competitive intramural co-ed soccer league present their dean, Ryan Crocker, with their victory cup. Photo used with permission of Sean Danielson.

President and Mrs. Bush volunteer to join in a project of the Bush School students' Public Service Organization that involved teams of students regularly reading at an early learning school in Bryan, Texas. Courtesy of Bush School of Government and Public Service. Photo by Chandler Arden.

8

Continuing Education

Certificate Programs

Online courses at the Bush School are not correspondence courses. They are rigorous, academic, graduate-level courses that require a commitment to learning, a desire to enhance employment credentials, an extraordinary command of time management, analytical thinking skills, strong written communications skills, and the ability to conduct and incorporate research into online discussions. Most of the time online students must integrate these skills with a full-time profession and a family.

Online courses at the Bush School frequently have identical content as their corresponding residence course, although the mode of presentation and interaction may be remarkably different. Students seeking an online certificate or the new Executive Master of Public Service and Administration must meet deadlines for academic readings and for posting responses to discussion questions. Students must also respond to their classmates' reactions to the readings. Often the responses become intense as classmates challenge one another's analysis and conclusions about the assigned readings. No superficial responses are allowed. They must document, according to the American Political Science Association (APSA) style, any references to academic sources and communicate their analysis clearly, concisely, and correctly. The students interact with professors through discussion boards and receive feedback for their discussions. In short, the online courses at the Bush School Distance Education Program require diligence and discipline.

In 2001, the Bush School administration sought ways to grow the program. A new Master's Program in International Affairs had just been approved, but it would take a year to recruit a first class. It was decided to develop a certificate program for in-residence graduate students at Texas A&M to get a quicker start in offering more graduate instruction in international affairs. With the concurrence of Chilcoat, Chuck Hermann asked Jim Olson to explore the possibility of creating a graduate certificate program. The program, Certificate in Advanced International Affairs (AIA), required four courses or twelve semester credits. Furthermore, the administration realized that additional students could be reached through online courses. In 2002, Olson contacted Elizabeth Tebeaux, director of distance education for the university, to discuss an online program. Tebeaux directed him to Nancy Small, who had been teaching online technical writing courses through the Department of English. Small agreed to set up the program and to run it as distance education coordinator.

Olson had specific requirements for the online courses: He did not want correspondence courses. He wanted interaction with the students, either live or in chat rooms. The discussion topics were to be posted and required prompt responses. The student-professor interaction needed to be intellectually stimulating and freewheeling and have intense give and take of ideas and theories.

At the end of the spring 2003 semester, twenty-five students enrolled in the online program. A survey of distance education student demographics from 2003 showed that the average age was 32.5 years: 75 percent were from Texas, 23 percent were from out of state, and 2 percent were international students. The students had an average of 7.6 years' professional experience; the professions included military officers, financial service providers, law enforcement professionals, a journalist, and a librarian. Of the group, 69 percent intended to complete a master's degree.

Like the residence AIA Certificate, the online AIA Certificate required at least twelve credit hours, which meant a minimum of four courses. Jim Olson, Chuck Hermann, Lorraine Eden, and Joe Cerami taught the original courses. The instructors quickly found that they had to adjust their expectations. Lecture scripts had to be written verbatim; slide preparation for the course offered challenges. Through trial and error, they learned that it was impossible to totally coordinate their day-to-day residence courses with distance classes. Residence and distance courses may have the same content, but each type of course had its own identity. Small's ability to know what and how to teach and how to structure courses built on a template contributed to the strength of the program.

As the program expanded, more online professors were needed. Olson assisted with recruiting and brought in mostly nonresident professionals in national security. Both the faculty and the workload for the coordinator increased. With professors in different locations, Small had to record their lectures and their visual material on her local computer and transfer the material to the online site. She also faced technology limitations. In his international affairs course, Hermann wanted to demonstrate how power and motion affect nation-states. The technology for filming a video and putting it online was not available. Small came up with the idea of layering. To demonstrate the concept, she and Hermann moved to the Dixie Chicken, a favorite watering hole for Texas A&M students, and placed billiard balls randomly on a pool table. She recorded the background chatter and took still shots of each ball knocking the others out of place. She arranged the still shots in rapid motion, and behold—the students had a Texas A&M/Dixie Chicken experience in the power of nation-states.

Small also assumed the role of problem solver for students who had questions, ranging from financial issues to course problems. She became the face of the Bush School Distance Education Program. In the first year the program had twenty-five students and four courses; by the summer of 2004, there were one hundred students and seven courses, with five more courses in the development stage. In January 2005, the Certificate in Homeland Security was added to the program under the leadership of David McIntyre. By the end of the fall semester 2006, there were 225 students in twenty sections with two certificate programs.

Nancy Small left the leadership position in 2006, and the program continued under the direction of Joanne Wheeler, followed by Jenny Jopling. In 2007, a third certificate program, Certificate in Nonprofit

Management, began with Will Brown as certificate director. The program name changed from Distance Education to Extended Education.

In 2013, Lisa Brown became director of extended education. In addition to her responsibility for overseeing the online courses, she is involved in marketing the program. She and her team promote the program through the efforts of the instructional team, resident Bush School faculty, and former students; they follow online leads and market through the *NonProfit Times* publication. All these efforts increase potential students' awareness of the program; however, the most effective recruiting tool is the reputation of the school. She attributes the excellent reputation of the faculty, the programs, and the placement services to the success in growing the program.

As of 2016, the program, with its three certificates, has grown to include twenty advanced international affairs courses, fourteen homeland security courses, and twenty-two nonprofit management courses. From the beginning with 30 seats, the program had 794 seats in 2015.[1]

Beginning in the summer semester of 2016, the newest program, the Executive Master of Public Service and Administration, will offer a master's degree to full-time working professionals who have at least five years' professional or executive-level experience and a bachelor's degree. This program combines residency with online instruction. During the two-year program, students will be in residence in College Station one week each year. The residency requirement offers students an opportunity to forge relationships with one another, to share experiences and expectations, and to experience the Texas A&M and Bush School culture. The program includes thirty-nine graduate-level credit hours and two available tracks: Homeland Security and Nonprofit Management. It also includes a collaborative capstone project at the end of the program. All of the program faculty members have strong academic credentials along with extensive in-field professional experience. The program combines foundational knowledge with practical experience.

Certificate in Advanced International Affairs

The AIA Certificate is a twelve-credit-hour program offered either online or in residence. Both programs follow a fifteen-week semester that includes core courses in American foreign policy and national security policy. Students who enroll in this program may select an emphasis area: diplomacy, defense policy and military affairs, intelligence, or counterterrorism. Electives, based on the emphasis area, include diplomacy, defense policy and military affairs, intelligence, and counterterrorism. Resident students may choose electives in global economy, energy policy, the European Union, and transnational security issues.

Jim Olson designed and directed the program from 2000 until July 2011. Ron Sievert became director of the program in September 2011. Sievert's first job was to add courses and to have backup instructors for the online program in case one of the instructors was not able to teach during a session. A requirement of the Bush School mandates that instructors have a PhD or significant practical experience in their field. As of 2016, there are eleven online faculty members, most of whom are recruited by recommendation from the Department of International Affairs in-house faculty.

The majority of the students in the AIA Certificate Program are from all over the world; many are government and military personnel who want to enhance their résumés and consider an AIA Certificate as a bonus for job promotion. They are generally Type A personalities who are eager to expand their knowledge.

Future plans include area-specific courses. Currently, the courses focus on broad topics such as American diplomacy, principles of international law, and military strategy. Sievert would like to add courses on the Middle East and China.

John Holloway

The AIA Certificate Program changed John Holloway's life. He served in the US Navy for twenty years and another twelve years with a government agency. In 2013, he learned about the program and, since he had spent his career in Middle East intelligence and enjoyed academic challenges, he signed up for the program. Little did he know what an impact it would have. The more he studied, the more he wanted to learn. He discovered how culture, language, and religion are intertwined and affect actions. He learned how intelligence helps drive foreign policy. He enjoyed all of the readings associated with each course and found his experience in the field enhanced his appreciation for the course material. He looked forward to developing the responses to his assignments, and his professors encouraged his writing efforts. Three years after his retirement in February 2014, Holloway returned to Washington and to work. He took with him new insights, a new more confident attitude, and a stronger background in his field. He also took with him all of the responses he had written for the certificate program, and now he is writing his own book on US policy in the Middle East.

Certificate in Homeland Security

The Oklahoma City bombing of April 19, 1995, gave the term "homeland security" a new and personal meaning. America faced the crisis of "homegrown" terrorists. Homeland security became a top priority for the nation and its citizens, but there was little information on how to train and educate responders and how to prevent a future attack. David McIntyre was the dean of the Army War College in Carlisle, Pennsylvania; Richard Chilcoat was the commandant. Chilcoat moved to the National Defense University in Washington, DC, and invited McIntyre to develop a course in homeland security for the university. In 2001, Chilcoat became the first dean of the Bush School, and in 2003 McIntyre visited Chilcoat in College Station and offered to teach a residence course in homeland security through the MPIA. A week later he began.

In the summer of 2004, the Bush School agreed to add an online Homeland Security Certificate Program. In spring semester 2005, the program began offering courses in foundations of homeland security, critical infrastructure, cyber security, and business continuity. By the fall, the program had grown to include seven faculty members and thirty students.

In 2007 Danny Davis began working in the program. With twenty years' experience in army infantry Special Forces, Davis was serving in Army North, located at Fort Sam Houston, San Antonio, Texas. There he was battalion commander and worked with General Dynamics as a defense support officer. His expertise concerned the ways the Department of Defense supports other nonmilitary agencies in times of crisis. McIntyre knew of Davis's qualifications and asked him to design a Homeland Security Certificate course: defense support for civil authorities, which became the first specialized course in the program. Davis assumed the position of director of the certificate program in 2010.

The Homeland Security Certificate Program offers emphasis options in national security policy and management, emergency management and crisis preparedness, critical infrastructure protection, and border security. There are currently thirteen instructors for the courses. These instructors must allow six hours a week for work online and participate in the discussion board at least three times a week. With the inability for real-time encounters, Davis constantly seeks new ways to engage students and faculty; he would like to bring professors who teach in the program to the Texas A&M campus for three days each year.

Brian Smith

Brian Smith has been with Texas A&M Engineering Extension (TEEX) Services for twelve years. He serves as training coordinator for the Urban Search and Rescue (US&R) Program at Disaster City. He is a member of Texas Task Force 1; he designed and developed the US&R Specialist Certificate Program; and he is the contract manager for a five-year nine-million-dollar Federal Emergency Management Agency (FEMA) national US&R training contract. He also earned a Certificate in Homeland Security from the Bush School. Smith joined the certificate program because he knew that with his full-time position at TEEX, he would have a difficult time balancing all of the on-campus courses with his job demands. His goal was to receive a master's degree, and he knew that the courses from the certificate program would count toward that goal. What he found was that the program was closely linked with his work at TEEX. Often the material covered in a section would coordinate with a situation that he faced at work. He said that the challenging curriculum of the program made him a better project manager.

He needed those skills when Hurricane Ike hit the Gulf Coast. Reliant Center in Houston was packed with teams in the Response Control

Command Center when the hurricane literally passed over the top of the center. All operations among all state and national agencies were run out of that location. Smith, as the public information officer, had to keep the message on point and manage political landmines for five days with very little sleep.

Smith benefited from the certificate program and decided to work on a Certificate in Nonprofit Management. Then he completed his master's degree in public policy at the Bush School. His ability to manage people, policy, and contracts attracted the attention of FEMA headquarters in Washington, DC. Once again, the Bush School prepared him for the interview. Deborah Kerr always assigned her students readings and then required the students to write a two-page response. In his interview, he was given a reading and asked to write a two-page response. Brian Smith is moving to Washington.

Certificate in Nonprofit Management

As noted previously, William Brown was recruited from Arizona State University in 2006 to join the Bush School faculty and develop a nonprofit management program. Brown began to develop a twelve-credit-hour graduate certificate program that would be taught to MPSA residence students at the Bush School and online to certificate students. The new program would have two core courses: foundations of the nonprofit sector and management and leadership of nonprofits. Then students could select an area of emphasis for the remaining credit hours: fund-raising and philanthropy, fiscal and performance management, leadership and management, health and human service policy, and international nongovernmental organizations.

One of the challenges Brown faced the first semester was to recruit faculty for the program. Angela Bies, a professor in the program, was already offering one or two courses in nonprofit management. To augment her classes, Brown pulled heavily from his colleagues' expertise at the Bush School: Lori Taylor, Leonard Bright, and Edwina Dorch. Then, through his extensive network of colleagues, he began to add eight to ten more faculty members. In spring semester 2009, the program had an enrollment of 74; in spring 2016 enrollment was 130. Brown's goals for the program are to enrich each student's learning experience and connect the students to the nonprofit profession for consistency in employment.

Stephanie Wehring

Stephanie Wehring found the certificate program the right fit for her. Professors not only provided theory and principles of nonprofit organizations but also offered practical application and assistance with employment. Today she is a regional director for The Rose, a nonprofit breast health provider in Houston, Texas. Her training from the Bush School has taught her to be resourceful, and she applies those principles to her work. Her mission at The Rose is to help the whole woman. Women often need more than a mammogram; they may need help finding a medical home or other organizations that can assist them with job skills training, transportation, and food. In response to a questionnaire in March 2016, Wehring commented, "Without nonprofits, many segments in society would go without goods and services they need." For Stephanie Wehring, nonprofits fulfill a deep need to serve and help others.

9

What Are the Graduates Doing?

Estimating Bush School Success

Public service embraces all facets of life: local, state, and national government; nonprofit organizations; volunteering; the military; even the private sector as it intersects with the public sector. With such broad reach, how can the success of a school whose name includes "Public Service" be measured? Of course, one can look at the curriculum: Do the courses taught include principles of effective government and nonprofit management? Look at the professors: Are they well qualified in their specific areas of expertise? Look at the research being produced: Is it making a meaningful contribution to the discipline? Look at the service organizations: Do they focus on giving back to the community? All of these criteria are important, but a significant measure of success is the graduates. Are they pursuing challenging and satisfying careers? Did the Bush School experience contribute to their ability to find positions and to be effective in some form of public service? Each year students come to the Bush School from all parts of the world. They are capable, optimistic, and ready to prepare for careers in public service. What happens when they graduate? How these men and women move from an academic experience to perform in the world may arguably be the best measure of the success of the school.

Since the first class completed the program in 1999, the Bush School has graduated 1,372 students from the MPIA and the MPSA Program. These former students now serve around the world. To determine what our graduates are doing and how they are contributing, we contacted a large number of them to see if they would be interested in our project. Most replied immediately that they would be happy to help in any way possible. From that group we selected students from both programs to interview. We faced a daunting dilemma in selecting a representative group from that number of graduates. We wanted a wide spectrum of years as well as experiences. We sought the advice of the faculty, staff, and administration in the selection process. Their suggestions and assistance were invaluable. For over a year, we interviewed a large number of graduates, all of whom represent the ideals and mission of the Bush School. We selected fifteen students who have moved into national, state, and local government service; nonprofit management; and the private sector where it intersects with the public sector.

These are bright, talented men and women. They could achieve success in any field, yet they chose public service. They realized when they embarked on the Bush School experience that they were not preparing for the highest-paying careers, but they enrolled anyway. Why? The common element is that each person wants to make a difference. Each wants to make life better for his or her fellow human beings. Esther Larson works with the homeless in Manhattan. Meaghan and Jerry Kenny served refugees in South Sudan. Catherine Muller and Griffin Rozell represent the United States through the Department of State. Corby Alexander helps the City of La Porte, Texas, provide the services its citizens need. Classmates Lauren Dangelmayr and Courtney Weigand, one in the public sector and one in the private sector, negotiate with foreign countries to ensure ethical treatment of American business interests. River Stuckey and Roman Napoli, also classmates, left their first jobs in Korea and the Caribbean to volunteer to aid evacuees from Hurricanes Katrina and Rita. Jeff Benson is protecting our security by serving in the US Navy in the South China Sea. The stories that follow offer a snapshot of the job that the Bush School is doing to prepare its students and a vision of the future with these former students in leadership roles.

Corby Alexander (1999)
City Manager, La Porte, Texas

Corby Alexander grew up in the small East Texas town of Henderson. He was one of six children reared by his mother, grandmother, and three aunts. His family had little financially, but they grew up with a strong sense of family, a strong work ethic, and a desire to serve. Corby excelled in his school work, and in the eighth grade he began to think about what he would like to pursue as a profession. The husband of his math teacher that year was the city manager of Henderson. Through that association, Corby learned how the city manager ensured that the citizens of Henderson had the services they needed and an organized government. Corby decided that being a city manager might be a good profession.

After high school, Corby attended Texas A&M on a Presidential Achievement Scholarship. During his undergraduate years he wavered between a profession in law or in city government; he decided he could cover both options with a degree in political science. In 1997, when Corby graduated from Texas A&M, the Bush School was organizing its first class. "Why not apply?" Corby thought. He made an excellent decision.

Corby joined the first class of eighteen students at the Bush School. He quickly became aware of the quality of the faculty and the staff, and they came to appreciate him. He was invited to give the invocation at the dedication of the school. His Bush School years strongly impacted his life and his decisions. His course work in local government confirmed his decision to pursue city management. His appreciation for national and international affairs grew as he listened to and visited with the dignitaries who often lectured at the Bush School.

Following graduation, Corby remained at Texas A&M in the Center for Public Leadership Studies. In 2000 he became the assistant to the city manager of College Station. There he applied the principles he had learned in graduate school. He helped prepared a $163 million budget, designed and conducted management reviews, and assisted with strategic plans for the community with a citywide Continuous Improvement Program. He was an integral part of a thriving, progressive city government and was prepared to move into more responsibility.

The tiny East Texas town of Jefferson, population 2,024, invited Corby to become its city manager. There is an old saying that there are no wasted experiences. This proved true for Corby because his understanding of East Texas culture from his years growing up in Henderson proved important; he knew that as an outsider to the community, he had to adapt to their expectations. He joined the community in celebrating birthdays; he kept his office open for those wanted to stop by, have a cup of coffee, and chat; his schedule did not always include appointments. He also learned that he needed to adapt his expectations to the capabilities of his staff; he learned to identify and encourage the strengths of his community. After four years in Jefferson, he accepted the city manager position in Bonham.

Bonham, a bit larger than Jefferson, had a median household income of $27,277 according to the 2001 census. When Corby arrived in Bonham, he had a list of projects that he wanted to address, but he encountered a "can't do" mind-set: no money available; accept things as they are. Corby, however, wanted to help people who could not help themselves. He sought available money from the Department of Housing and Urban Development (HUD) for renovating homes of low-income citizens. Some of these dilapidated homes had been lived in forty or fifty years and had leaky roofs, no heating, and rodents living on the premises. One house had had no running water for two years. The people who lived in these homes accepted a life of poverty. Corby demolished five homes and had new ones built that were clean, safe, and energy efficient. Before he left, Bonham was able to build a new city hall, renovate the Senior Citizens Center and the Police Department, and provide a new animal shelter.

Corby continued his goal of helping others with his move to La Porte as city manager. Again, his skill at adapting proved essential; the culture of La Porte differed dramatically from the culture of Bonham. La Porte is a "meat and potatoes" community: no frills, a short list of needs, no wasted money. Corby had to prove that city government, working with the private sector, could make a difference. As in Bonham, he attacked an impoverished area of the community. With

HUD funds, he had dilapidated homes remodeled instead of demolishing them as in Bonham. The endeavor proved so successful that private developers noticed and saw an opportunity for development. The private sector is now renewing rundown areas of La Porte.

Corby also adjusted to the citizens' concerns about local government. He first sought to develop the trust of his staff; then he mandated that his office be as transparent and open as possible. He makes available to the council and to the news media any information that is legally possible. He is determined to prove trust and transparency are the trademarks of his organization and that his office will be efficiently and effectively run.

Nasir Andisha (2009)
Deputy Foreign Minister,
Afghanistan

On December 24, 1979, the Soviet Union organized a massive airlift, involving an estimated 280 transport aircraft, and sent thousands of troops into Afghanistan. Nasir Andisha was six weeks old at the time of the invasion, and for the next ten years, he and his family lived under Soviet domination.

Nasir's family left Kapisa Province in northeastern Afghanistan and moved to Kabul when he was one year old. Despite the presence of the Soviets, his early years were spent in a relatively well-off section of Kabul. There he attended primary school with professional teachers. In 1993, when Nasir was fourteen, his family moved back to their village in Kapisa, where his education became a problem. His school had no roof; he and other boys had to construct a roof from leaves to shelter themselves from the oppressive heat. One year his classroom was a tent. Despite the physical hardships, his sense of determination was greater. He was determined to succeed in his studies. He focused on math, science, language, and English literature; most of his classmates were in the resistance army. His efforts paid off—he scored second highest on the university entrance exam and was accepted at Balkh Medical College.

He moved to Mazar-i-Sharif, the provincial capital of the UN-recognized government of Afghanistan, to study medicine. There Nasir made a career decision: He did not want to spend seven years studying medicine. In 1997, Nasir first met Ahmed Shah Massoud, commander of the mujahidin, in the Panshjir Valley. In 1998, they met again when Massoud was attending a cultural program in the auditorium of an old German textile factory at the Alberuni University. From 1999 to 2001, Nasir worked for the International Committee of the Red Cross and became part of the resistance as a member of the media and public affairs team. He and his team documented the difference in the way of life under Taliban rule and under the exiled government, including the education and work opportunities for women. Nasir decided to further his education; he wanted to connect cities and communities through journalism.

He went to Osmania University in India, where he studied economics, public administration, and political science. He also received a distance education diploma in UN and international understanding. He returned to Afghanistan to serve in the Ministry of Foreign Affairs and teach international relations and economics. In 2007, he applied for a Fulbright Scholarship, had interviews with Larry Napper and Kishore Gawande, and decided to come to Texas. The prospect of learning from a former ambassador and an economist was exactly what he wanted.

Nasir relates that the Bush School offered a valuable experience because of its leadership training with Joe Cerami, its negotiation simulations with Napper, and its intelligence training from Jim Olson. During his time at the Bush School Nasir completed the Certificate in Leadership.

In 2009, Nasir returned to Afghanistan to serve in the Foreign Ministry, in the America and Australia Affairs division. He served as chairman of the Dubai Process, an Afghanistan-Pakistan Joint Working Group on Law Enforcement, Counter Narcotics, and Custom Cooperation. In 2011, Nasir was named ambassador of the Islamic Republic of Afghanistan to Australia, New Zealand, and Fiji. While in Australia, Nasir completed his PhD in diplomatic studies at the Australian National University.

Nasir is currently deputy foreign minister of Afghanistan. He is responsible for management of resources as he works with Parliament on budget issues. His duties extend to diplomatic issues, as he oversees passport centers in five major cities, manages the status of forces in Afghanistan, and works with the Institute of Diplomacy, a training center for diplomats. He still has fond memories of his time in the United States, and he has a constant reminder of the Bush School. His young son, when he is asked where he is from, smiles and says, "Texas."

Jeff Benson (2003)
Commander, US Navy

Jeff Benson was in Beijing, China, in 2012 for a symposium at China Foreign Affairs University. It was a small gathering that included Yao Yunzhu, a female major general of the People's Liberation Army as a speaker. Later that evening, Jeff had dinner with one of his Bush School classmates, Lisa Liang. He mentioned the symposium and Yao's speech. Lisa whipped out her phone and within minutes was talking to Yao. Jeff thought, "Of all of the billions of people in China, Lisa knows the person I heard today in the symposium." That was *guanxi*, the Chinese term for a network of relationships built on trust. Jeff also practices *guanxi*, not only in his professional career but also as a way of life. Trust in relationships is essential.

Jeff attended and graduated from Texas Christian University and joined the navy for a four-year commitment. In 2001, he was seven days from completing his obligation when his commanding officer asked him, "Jeff, is there anything that will keep you in the navy?" Jeff had his acceptance for the University of Houston's master's program in communication. He planned to serve in politics. "Well," Jeff replied, "if you could send me to Texas A&M, I would be willing to stay." Shortly after the conversation, Jeff headed to Texas A&M to teach naval history to the Corps of Cadets. He discovered the Bush School of Government and Public Service and quickly signed up for the Certificate in Advanced International Affairs Program and subsequently the master's program. Dick Chilcoat had just become the first dean of the Bush School, and Jeff found a mentor.

When Adm. David Jeremiah visited the Bush School in 2002, President Bush invited Jeff to join the two of them for breakfast. Jeremiah visited extensively with Jeff during the breakfast, and afterward Jeff sent a note of appreciation to the admiral. They corresponded and began what became a lasting relationship with Jeremiah as a mentor, director, and friend.

Jeff's focus on politics returned when, in the summer of 2003, he received a summer internship in the office of Don Evans, secretary of commerce. At the department, Jeff worked in the White House liaison division, where he saw the intersection of politics and process. He found all government process to be influenced by politics. Following his graduation in December, Jeff resigned from the navy. He had agreed to manage the congressional campaign for Charlie Stenholm, who served thirteen terms in the House of Representatives. Redistricting in Texas forced Stenholm into a tight race: incumbent versus incumbent. Stenholm lost by eighteen percentage points. The loss was particularly difficult for Jeff because he considered Stenholm to be the epitome of a public servant.

After the election, Jeremiah approached Jeff and asked if he would like to work with his consulting firm, Technology Strategies & Alliances. Jeff committed himself to his job and to learning; he joined several diverse outside study groups and organizations that focused on aspects of national security. He used his network of contacts to solve a major problem in the organization. The company needed additional staff to work on a project. Jeff suggested hiring Texas A&M interns to meet the needs. Jeff handled all of the communication and contacts with the university. The interns performed well, and Jeremiah was pleased with the results. Jeff loved his work and was happy that he had seized the opportunity to work in consulting, but he began to feel that his heart was elsewhere. In 2006, at the christening of the USS *George H. W. Bush*, Jeff visited with Jeremiah about the option of returning to the navy.

Jeff did not leap head first into the decision to return to the navy. He was engaged to be married, and Jeremiah counseled him to consider how the lifestyle of navy personnel affects the spouse. During long walks and long talks, he examined all of the possible options, but he said, "The call of the sea—and to a different kind of service—beckoned. For it was through my journey of helping others [who were] trying to achieve elected office to serve their constituents that I reaffirmed what my passion was—serving others and defending the nation that has given my family and me so much." Despite the inherent problems with moving back into the navy, Jeff rejoined and was stationed in Japan.

In his position as operations officer for Destroyer Squadron Fifteen stationed in Yokosuka, Jeff was involved in two major world events between 2009 and 2011. In 2009, the South Korean warship *Cheonan* sank. Amid the initial confusion over the incident, authorities thought the ship had run aground, but investigation later showed that North Korea had attacked the vessel. Following that event, US naval forces launched a training exercise with South Korean warships off the coast of Korea. Jeff was instrumental in planning for the warships involved in the exercise, "Invincible Spirit." During that exercise, he established several strong personal relationships with his Japanese counterparts.

Three months later, these relationships were revisited. On March 11, 2011, a magnitude 9 earthquake struck northeastern Japan and set off a tsunami. The earthquake was the fifth largest in history. The tsunami, which reached a peak height of 133 feet, resulted in a level 7 meltdown at the Fukushima Dalichi nuclear power plant. In that event, which lasted only minutes, 15,828 people lost their lives. The US Navy worked with the Japanese coast guard to search, rescue, and recover bodies and debris and to provide supplies ashore. Jeff had a major role in the planning of this effort, "Operation Tomodachi" (Friend). The logistics of the operation were overwhelming: Eighteen warships were involved, and helicopters were sent into areas without communication. The Japanese ships involved were in radiation areas. There was no land area free from contamination, so the helicopters used ships in the area as lily pads to refuel and reach the affected regions with supplies. For his part in planning the high-risk operations, Jeff received the Meritorious Service Medal for leadership, planning, high-risk recovery, and saving countless lives in a compromised environment.

Jeff says that his "experiences in Japan shaped my worldview by stressing the importance of relationship building, the importance of multinational military exercises for future operations, and the necessity of an allied force to prevent or win wars." It is all about building relationships through trust: *guanxi*. He will continue to use his leadership skills and his commitment to building relationships in a new way. In November 2016, he will assume command of the naval destroyer USS *Stethem*.

Lauren Dangelmayr (2007)
Transfer Pricing Manager,
Baker Hughes

Muenster, Texas, is on Route 82, just east of Nocona. The 2010 census lists the population as 1,544. Life is simple in this small German community that was founded in 1889 when the Missouri-Kansas-Texas Railroad constructed a line from Gainesville to Henrietta. In Muenster visitors and residents can enjoy the Oktoberfest Arts and Craft show; they can enjoy Mexican and German food at Rohmer's Restaurant; they can shop at the community garage sale; or they can hunt birds, hogs, or deer on local wild game ranches. Lauren Dangelmayr is the third generation of a ranching family in Muenster; her grandfather and her father are cattle ranchers, and her mother raises and shows quarter horses. Lauren still calls Muenster home.

She was the first in her family to attend Texas A&M, where she studied agricultural business because it offered applied economics with a business degree. Like many college graduates, she had an excellent undergraduate education, but she had not focused on a career path. She heard about the Bush School and thought that she would explore the options it offered. At the Bush School she found a flexible approach that allowed her to find her niche. After her first year, a summer internship in Johannesburg, South Africa, helped Lauren realize how business, universities, and governments could achieve significant goals through efficient cooperation.

In her second year at the Bush School, Lauren chose the International Economics and Development track and discovered transfer pricing, which she saw as the perfect blend of economics and business. Today's corporate world is not limited to one business in one location but is global. Multinational corporations sell not only to outside customers but also to subsidiaries within the multinational group that trade with the parent company and/or with each other. Selling goods from a subsidiary to a parent company requires the parent company to pay for the goods or services. That cost is transfer pricing and must be an "arms'-length" transaction that adheres strictly to the US corporate income tax code and other legal requirements. The Bush School's commitments to assisting students find the right place of service paid off.

Following graduation from the Bush School, Lauren accepted a position with Ernst & Young in Houston. Ernst & Young, primarily known for accounting, also offers transfer pricing services to its multinational clients. Lauren was hired as a transfer pricing tax consultant and economist. A major client of Lauren's was Baker Hughes, one of the world's largest oil field services companies. The company's 2014 annual report indicated revenue of more than twenty-four billion dollars. The multinational is headquartered in Houston but operates in ninety countries around the world, providing technology and service for the petroleum industry. Baker Hughes, in an effort to provide an extensive array of services to its customers, acquired a number of companies that offer complementary services. The Baker Hughes group is divided into several service categories: drilling, evaluation, and fluids; completion, production, and chemicals; pressure pumping; and reservoir development services. These divisions buy and sell products to each other, hence the need for expert transfer pricing. Baker Hughes created a job for Lauren that she could not resist: transfer pricing manager. It offered the opportunity to move up to the position she holds today, which she earned when she was only thirty-two years old: tax director, global transfer pricing.

Lauren's job requires working with all Baker Hughes's international divisions to ensure their in-house pricing is set up so the corporation complies with US and foreign corporation income tax laws. She ensures global pricing compliance for sixty countries. She negotiates global pricing transfer fees and manages the budget. So how does a young woman from Muenster, Texas, handle the intricacies of international business? She applies the life skills that she learned growing up on the ranch and at the Bush School to her everyday encounters. In the tiny town of Muenster she had to adapt to others' viewpoints and ambitions; in the Bush School she learned about the global economy and how culture affects business.

First, Lauren enjoys doing business in different cultures. What many would consider a challenge, she considers an opportunity. She has the opportunity to see how the decision-making process in various countries is different from decision making in the United States; she sees how different cultures prioritize life and work experiences; she sees how verbal and written communication convey messages differently. She enjoys the experience of adapting to each circumstance as she encounters it. She develops strategies for working with tax authorities, consultants, and in-company personnel.

Second, Lauren understands the importance of building and establishing a network. In one eighteen-month project, she traveled during a six-week period to fifteen countries and interviewed more than three hundred people. That project established her network. It did not stop there; she continues to work each day to maintain that international network. She spends approximately 25 percent of each day on the phone with international clients or officials. She adapts her approach to the culture of the country. When dealing with Latin American, African, or European clients, she seeks to know about their families; when dealing with Russia and Eastern Europe, she focuses on the issues and work; when dealing with Asian countries, she realizes she must share because businesspeople hesitate to ask about families.

Third, Lauren applies perception and common sense to every situation. In every business encounter she employs cultural awareness, even with something as simple as being aware and considerate of the time difference; teamwork—she always considers every project from a team perspective; priorities—she realizes each member of the project has different motivations, and she seeks to build a consensus; and motivation. Lauren said that the perception of tax experts is that they always say no. She strives to listen to each person to determine the real motivation and to work for a conclusion in which the objectives are reached and each member thinks that a reasonable response has been achieved.

Emily Gesing (2011)
Program Manager, United Way

The Gesing family believed in volunteering. Living in Cedar Rapids, Iowa, with no close relatives nearby, Emily's family created an extended family through volunteering: church, school, and community. Her mother, a local community college counselor, would remind the family not to forget what others were going through, and the Gesing family was always there to lend a hand. Emily's childhood experience with volunteering led to a life of giving and a career with the United Way of Houston, Texas.

On June 13, 2008, the Cedar River reached its highest level in history. Massive flooding hit the city of Cedar Rapids. The spreading water affected 14 percent of the city, impacting more than five thousand homes and dislocating more than eighteen thousand residents. The Cedar Rapids flood was the sixth-largest FEMA disaster declaration in the nation's history. Emily Gesing wanted to help. She, along with others, filled sandbags, but the water rose too quickly for the sandbags to have any effect. The damage was done. Although cleanup and change would take years, Emily saw how public organizations responded with both immediate and long-term relief. She saw how national, state, and local officials worked together to help rebuild the community. That cooperation made an impression.

At Bradley University, Emily became part of a leadership program for four years. Each semester the program required forty hours of service. Emily served with the American Red Cross in its back office and learned to appreciate the value of indirect service: the second layer of an organization that empowers social workers to make an impact on the community. While she was at Bradley, one of her professors suggested that she consider a graduate degree in public policy and mentioned applying to the Bush School of Government and Public Service. She attended interview weekend and left with a strong sense of the teamwork and support the school offered. She discovered an intellectual community where students explored and shared ideas with fellow students. She felt at home.

At the Bush School as a first-year student, she learned how to think like a public servant in Domonic Bearfield's class: "Is this what the community wants? They should have the best you can find." Her defining moment for selecting a career path was in Angela Bies's course on philanthropy and fund-raising. Following her first year, she held an internship with the Meadows Foundation in Dallas, where she participated in the entire grant process cycle. She discovered a facet of volunteerism that she had not known before, and she loved it. She returned for her second year and led the PSO.

Following her graduation in 2011, she began a career with the United Way of Houston. Today she is a senior program manager who oversees investment of more than twenty million dollars into community programs at more than twenty-five agencies. She implemented a Youth Program Quality Intervention network at more than one hundred sites to assess program training and reporting. She developed a peer-to-peer reading program in five schools and a peer-to-peer math program in fifteen schools. She trains volunteers in grant review and program assessment to determine future funding for agencies.

Her role as manager requires strong leadership skills, which she also attributes to her Bush School experience. She depends on a "You" approach to build trust and a strong relationship. She always wants to know "How can I learn more about you?" To many people, she is a face of United Way that carries a great deal of responsibility. Finally, her role requires tough analytical skills and decisions to be certain that the programs receiving funds are meeting their responsibilities and commitment to the high standards of United Way. Those decisions may affect the funding of an organization. Currently, she is moving into a new role: helping others set a vision for reaching their goals. Emily embraces the mission of United Way: mobilizing the caring power of communities to advance the common good.

Meaghan and Jerry Kenny (2011)
Foreign Aid Workers, World Vision

Armenia, Democratic Republic of the Congo, Liberia, Ghana, Afghanistan, Sierra Leone, and South Sudan are not places on most people's list of top vacation spots; however, Meaghan and Jerry Kenny have served in all of these countries through the Peace Corps, the Norman Borlaug Institute, the Center on Conflict and Development, and World Vision. Meaghan and Jerry do not just talk about helping the helpless; they have boots-on-the-ground involvement with providing aid to those in need.

Meaghan and Jerry grew up in Texas: she in Tyler and he in Mount Pleasant. She was a cheerleader, he was a football player, and they met in high school. Both came from families with a strong work ethic where academic excellence and community service were stressed through the home and through their church. They attended Austin College and majored in psychology. After college, they were determined to join the Peace Corps: "There are lots of ways to give, but we like going to the source of the need, trying to help people where they are." They were sent to Sevan, Armenia. After their two-year commitment, they decided that they needed master's degrees to accomplish the work that they wanted to do. They chose the Bush School to pursue degrees in international affairs.

The Bush School experience expanded their vision and enhanced their credentials. They knew that the school required an internship and that the Borlaug Institute had programs that would be a good fit. Jerry volunteered to help four dozen Iraqi scholars who were seeking master's degrees. Meaghan met Catherine Clement with the Borlaug Institute and offered to work for her as an unpaid intern. In their final semester at the Bush School, they received six-hours' credit for designing and implementing a food production analysis and policy recommendation report for the United Nations World Food Program in Sierra Leone. There they worked side by side with UN professionals. They also participated in three capstones with Kishore Gawande, Gabriela Thornton, and Ren Mu.

After graduating from the Bush School, they felt the calling of the field and left for South Africa to work with the Borlaug Institute and later the Center on Conflict and Development. Projects with these organizations took them to the Democratic Republic of the Congo, Afghanistan, and South Sudan; however, they wanted to work full time in South Sudan, and that opportunity came in 2014 through World Vision.

"South Sudan is a cesspool of human suffering," says Rich Stearns, president of World Vision. The brutal civil conflict that began in 2013 has displaced 1.5 million people inside South Sudan, including more than 800,000 children.[1] More than one in three people require humanitarian assistance, and over 100,000 have sought refuge in Protection of Civilians (PoC) sites.[2] Yet, even in this nightmare of suffering, they found caring, honest, even hospitable people who managed to maintain a sense of hope and optimism while trying to keep their families together and safe.

Based in Juba, the capital, Meaghan and Jerry lived in a single compound with all the other aid workers. They shared a ten- by fifteen-foot living facility with a broken bed and a kitchen that served thirty other people. They ate tuna from a can. The only water was cold water from the Nile River, and water pressure was unreliable. They knew to shower with their mouths closed. Periodically, they would hear AK-47 gunfire at night, but if it did not seem close, then they went back to sleep. Their greatest danger came from the threat of hijacked vehicles. All of the workers traveled in large Toyota vehicles, and the temptation to steal one was often too great for some of the rebels. They lived and worked in that facility about 70 percent of their time in South Sudan. The rest of the time was spent living apart in different sections of the country.

Meaghan spent most of her time outside the city of Malakai in a PoC camp. Because the city of Malakai was too dangerous for aid workers, the camp was built on a plain, about two miles from city center. Unfortunately, the camp was built during the dry season. In the rainy season, the plain turned into a marsh, and floods brought raw sewage into the streets. Over one thousand makeshift shelters were filled with sewage-contaminated water. Meaghan and three other female aid workers lived in a cargo container. They slept on the floor, had no circulating air in the building, and had to walk a mile to the nearest sanitary facility. The intensive heat made showers twice a day a necessity.

Each morning Meaghan woke early. She checked her computer to see if there was violence in the area and then reported to the project site. Projects varied from something as simple as delivering water or dispensing needed supplies, but whatever the project, chaos and frustration reigned. World Vision ordered supplies, but they would arrive with supplies for all other aid agencies and nothing would be labeled. Workers had to open all of the containers to find what they needed. No order was ever completely filled, so the bartering system became the norm: "I have this and need that. I will trade one of mine for one of yours." One of the more exasperating projects involved building latrines. Initially, the team built thirty latrines for the camp population. However, the next day the camp population had increased, and the latrines were filled. That meant new latrines, but there was never sufficient material.

Jerry served as a policy and advocacy adviser and in program development for World Vision. He coordinated partnerships with UN agencies and other international organizations. His major project involved field research for a child advocacy report that World Vision wanted written to provide a clear record of the impact the violence had on the children of South Sudan. Jerry and his two coauthors interviewed 160 children in Central Equatoria and the Upper Nile states. Their mission was to determine their living conditions and the risks they faced daily. World Vision had published a report on the condition of the children in May 2014, but six months later the conditions had worsened: More children were displaced or separated from their families, and more children were recruited into armed groups. The findings were grim: The children said that they lived in fear that armed rebels will attack them and their families. One twelve-year-old girl said, "I am afraid that if war comes again to Juba, the tanks will come to the Protection of Civilians site and crush us." They also found that child labor had replaced child education. More than 50 percent of the boys interviewed in Malakai work to support the family, and children as young as seven work in the marketplace.

Still not everything was despair. In the midst of misery, Jerry and Meaghan found that hope still abounded. The children displayed remarkable resiliency to their living conditions. In the camp outside Malakai, the children had no toys; they had only mud, a lot of mud. One young boy made toy figures from the mud and shared them with his friends. He did not need G. I. Joe; he had mud figures. The children all had hope for a better future: "I want to be the president to bring peace"; "I want to be a doctor"; and the most universal response, "I want to go to school so that I become a better person and in the future do something good for myself and my parents." Each child wanted to be in school, each child wanted the violence to end, and each child wanted life in a stable environment.

Esther Larson (2006)
Senior Manager, Hope for New York

On October 29, 2012, Hurricane Sandy slammed into New York City, causing approximately nineteen billion dollars in damage. The storm, with wind gusts up to ninety miles per hour and a storm surge of fourteen feet, flooded tunnels, damaged or destroyed 305,000 housing units, and left thousands of residents of Manhattan without electricity for several days. Esther Larson was one of the residents. For five days, she wore the same clothes and never knew what she would have to eat. For the first time in her life, she fully understood the plight of the homeless street people in New York. These were the people she served.

Esther's path to service began when she was eight years old, peeling potatoes in a soup kitchen in downtown Phoenix. Committed to serving the underprivileged, her parents instilled in their children the idea that serving others was a responsibility. Her mother said, "They may look different and dress different, but they are human beings that we should care for. There is no noblesse oblige. Whatever we have been given, we have a responsibility to give back to others."

After high school, Esther and her two sisters, Marsha and Leslie, chose to study at Vanderbilt University. A chance encounter with Arnie Vedlitz opened the door to the Bush School. Leslie heard Vedlitz speak to a class. She was impressed and told Marsha about the Bush School. Marsha applied, was accepted, and was the first of the three sisters to attend the Bush School; Esther followed Marsha. Esther had always considered volunteerism to be something everyone should do to help a community, but when she served as a White House intern, she saw firsthand how government and nonprofits can work together to accomplish goals. In her second year at the Bush School she focused on nonprofit management and grant writing with Carol Holtzapple. Her first attempt at grant writing was a PSO project for the Children's Museum of Bryan. It was funded by the Barbara Bush Foundation.

During her second year at the Bush School, Esther received a Presidential Management Fellowship appointment. She thought she would head to Washington and pursue public service. However, as she interviewed with different agencies, she realized she did not want to be part of budget cutting; she wanted to be part of budget expanding. Washington was not the place for Esther; New York offered the best opportunities. Within a month of moving to New York, she began working with the Metropolitan Council on Jewish Poverty. There she honed her communication and development skills and then moved to the New York City Coalition against Hunger, where she served as director of development for four years. Then came Hope for New York, a faith-based, nonprofit agency that mobilizes volunteers and financial resources to support forty nonprofit affiliates who serve poor and marginalized people in New York City.

Hurricane Sandy created pandemonium, and Hope for New York sprang into action. Most of the forty programs that Hope for New York support are in downtown Manhattan, and several are residential programs for the homeless and addicts. Hope for New York worked quickly to create a plan to meet the emergency needs. They faced two crucial issues: How do they coordinate their response with the government, and how do they mobilize volunteers most effectively? They needed to enhance what the city was doing. Hope for New York partnered with organizations that had electricity and could provide shelter. They raised more than $270,000 to support recovery work and mobilized volunteers to get food, water, and clothing to those in need.

Today, Esther is using her Bush School experience as the senior manager of affiliate development at Hope for New York. A major part of her work is obtaining financial grants, which provide $1.4 million to the forty nonprofits. A capacity-building aspect of these nonprofits is that they provide people who want to serve as volunteers. Volunteerism is core to the future of the nonprofit sector. According to Esther, "It's not just a nice touchy-feely thing to do. Volunteerism is a key way to help nonprofits to be more effective and efficient."

As a senior member of the management team, Esther seeks to develop long-term partnerships with their nonprofit affiliates. They give financial resources and volunteers only to their established network of forty nonprofits. They do, however, remain on the lookout for organizations that align with their faith-based mission and who serve a demographic sector currently not reached by Hope for New York. They are committed to long-term success of their affiliates.

As part of their commitment to success, Hope for New York measures the effectiveness of organizations and programs to determine their proven, and potential, ability to effect real change in the lives of those who are poor and marginalized in New York City. They have a core-capacity assessment through the TCC consulting group that offers strategic planning, program development, capacity building and grant management to nonprofit organizations. She says, "Our grantees provide us with an interim and a final report so we have an idea of the outcomes the organization has successfully completed as well as the challenges the organization may have faced in the grant term."

Hope for New York does not rely solely on assessment reports; the staff also know and visit with the directors and staff of the affiliate programs four times a year. They view their relationships with nonprofits as a transparent partnership. Each nonprofit knows Hope for New York has resources to help, and they want access to those resources. Transparency is the key to a successful relationship.

Lisa Liang (2004)
Business-Government Relations Manager,
J. P. Morgan, China

In May 2002, Chuck Hermann and Lorraine Eden were visiting professors for a month at the Foreign Affairs College in Beijing, China. Hermann taught a course in US foreign policy, and Lorraine gave occasional guest lectures. In Eden's first guest lecture to an undergraduate economics class, a student raised her hand and asked a question. Then she left her seat, moved to the front of the classroom, and began to diagram her question on the blackboard and to comment. For a student, even in the United States, to get up in class and draw on the blackboard was highly unusual. That unusual student was Lisa Liang. Lisa was a senior economics major at Foreign Affairs College who had an internship with China Central Television (CCTV). Lisa's position as assistant producer was to search newspapers and periodicals for interesting topics and speakers that were appropriate for *Dialogue*, a CCTV news program. This position allowed her to interact with well-known Chinese and foreign dignitaries, including the US ambassador to China, Henry Kissinger, and other professionals. She was establishing a professional network and was not shy about asking questions of foreign visitors, including the professors from Texas A&M. Lisa stayed after class, visited with Eden and Hermann, and learned about the Bush School.

Lisa applied to the Bush School and was accepted in the fall 2002 class; however, her student visa had not been processed by the time classes began. Fortunately, the head of Texas A&M International Programs, Emily Ashworth, intervened with the US embassy in Beijing. On a Friday afternoon, Lisa received a call telling her to come to the visa office immediately. When she arrived at the embassy, she was the only person there besides a diplomat waiting to interview her and to process her application. The next day Lisa bought an airline ticket to College Station, packed her belongings, and flew from Beijing to the United States. She landed at Easterwood Airport, exhausted after a long overseas flight. The first thing she remembered smelling was grass. At the airport, she was met by a student and taken to the Bush School, where she met Richard Chilcoat.

At the Bush School, Lisa found the curriculum challenging. She encountered a culture totally different from what she had experienced at home. At first, she was upset because the other students challenged her ideas and questioned her about China. She thought the students did not like her, but she gradually discovered that the students engaged in the same types of discussions with each other, questioning their positions and views, not just hers. She had not come from a culture of debate but often she found herself debating Chinese foreign policy with the other students, and she learned from the exchanges and discussions.

In October 2002, Jiang Zemin, president of China, visited the Bush School. Lisa, as the only student from China, met Presidents Bush and Jiang. Today a picture of the three of them has a prominent place on her desk.

After her first year, Lisa accepted a summer internship with the Nixon Center in Washington, DC, where she worked on a research project on China–North Korea relations.

After she graduated in 2004, she accepted an internship with the United Nations Conference on Trade and Development (UNCTAD), in Geneva, Switzerland. On her second day there, she fell and broke her arm. Her insurance was not yet set up with UNCTAD, and the Human Resources Department representative suggested that "maybe Lisa should consider going home." Lisa convinced the woman that she should stay. She stayed, performed research for the group's annual *World Investment Report*, and enjoyed and learned from the other interns, all of whom came from different cultures. At the end of the internship, UNCTAD officials offered her a position to remain there; she chose to return to China.

In September 2004, she returned to Beijing, where she accepted a position with Burson-Marsteller, a public relations firm, and underwent an excellent training program. Long hours on the job helped her master the thought process for public relations, the importance of building and delivering key messages, and the best ways for the company to interact with the media. Her clients included Accenture, Reuters, BHP, and J. P. Morgan. In 2006 she moved to J. P. Morgan, her client for a year and a half. The firm had never had a public relations employee in China and was looking for a senior-level person with at least ten years' experience to fill the new position. Lisa had only two years' experience; the company made an exception and hired her. Today she is the firm's head of marketing and communications for all of China.

In 2008 a massive (7.9) earthquake occurred in the Sichuan Province of southwestern China, a remote and mountainous area. The epicenter was about fifty miles from the provincial capital of Chengdu. The quake flattened about four-fifths of the structures in the area. Almost 90,000 people were dead or missing, including 5,300 children, and nearly 375,000 people were injured. Mudslides killed two hundred relief workers. The quake was so strong that Lisa felt it in Beijing on the twentieth floor of her building.

Lisa, who was responsible for corporate philanthropy, knew that J. P. Morgan had to take an active role in the response. The media clamored for international companies to be involved. Everyone in China and the world was watching the response of corporations. The question was, were the foreign multinationals in China to be partners, or were they in China just for the profits? Lisa and her team explored options and settled on what the population needed the most—basic necessities, such as water and food: instant noodles and bottled water. The team had to move quickly. Lisa found large warehouses that could hold supplies, but they had only two days to get the food and water to those who needed it. Lisa located fourteen large trucks with containers. They had to travel to three different sites to deliver the supplies. Lisa traveled on each of the trucks to ensure the food and water went where they were needed. Very few multinational companies immediately sent an employee to the disaster area where the danger of aftershocks remained a constant threat. She and her trucks made the dangerous journey to Chengdu. She also spoke to media and created positive press for J. P. Morgan on its support to the local community. She had a successful public relations event, but more important, she made an important humanitarian impact where it was needed.

Lisa continues her role in corporate responsibility through public relations and marketing. Five years ago, J. P. Morgan launched its thirty-five-year-old global initiative Corporate Challenge in Shanghai, China. It is a 5.6-kilometer running race to encourage a healthy lifestyle, team building, and camaraderie among the business community. Each year, thousands of runners from the Shanghai business community participate in the initiative.

Tony Maffei (2002)
Special Agent, Fraud Investigation,
US Department of Health and Human Services

American taxpayers foot the bill for Medicare and Medicaid fraud, which adds an additional ninety-eight billion dollars each year to the legitimate costs of the programs. In 2013 federal prosecutors handled more than two thousand health-fraud cases.[3] At the forefront in the fight against fraud are the special agents in the US Department of Health and Human Services (HHS). As a special agent, Tony Maffei investigates allegations of waste and fraud in Medicare and Medicaid funds, including kickbacks, money laundering, and billing irregularities. Trafficking in illegal prescription drugs is another area of responsibility. Tony serves search warrants, conducts undercover investigations, participates in surveillance operations, and makes arrests. He is also a former Bush School student.

At the University of Dayton, Tony Maffei majored in political science, considering a possible career in law. One day, while walking through the halls of the political science building, he saw a flyer. It was just a flyer, easily overlooked with other flyers clustered on the bulletin board. "Bush School" it read; "This is public service." Tony decided to investigate. He gradually became attracted to the idea of public service and discovered that the Bush School students and faculty believed in professional preparation for such vital careers. He decided that a master's degree from the Bush School offered the best opportunity for service in the federal government. In retrospect, Tony says that simple flyer changed the direction of his life.

During his first year he explored various career options, but he was drawn to law enforcement. He accepted an internship at the Federal Law Enforcement Training Center in Brunswick, Georgia, where he received intensive training in self-defense, firearms, defensive driving, and law enforcement techniques. "Training is serious. We are fighting for our lives and must have the skills we need to be able to go home at night," said Tony. Following graduation, he accepted a special agent position in HHS. In 2011 Tony was the lead HHS-OIG (Office of Inspector General) agent for an investigation that resulted in the largest civil fraud recovery by the US Attorney's Office for the Eastern

District of Tennessee. The investigative team included members from the HHS, Federal Bureau of Investigation, Railroad Retirement Board Office of Inspector General, US Attorney's Offices for the Eastern District of Tennessee and the District of South Carolina, US Department of Justice, and five assistant US attorneys.[4]

Hill-Rom was one of the nation's largest suppliers of durable medical equipment. It supplied specialized bed support for patients who suffered from pressure ulcers or bed sores. In 2005, Lisa Brocco and Laurie Salmon, employees of Hill-Rom, filed a whistle-blower suit claiming that the company knowingly filed false claims to Medicare. The investigation team found that for almost ten years Hill-Rom had submitted claims for patients who no longer required or were no longer using their product. In fact, some of these patients had died. Hill-Rom automatically billed Medicare for the equipment and had not made a reasonable effort to determine if the patients met Medicare requirements. There were hundreds of thousands of patients involved, and the false claims by Hill-Rom cost taxpayers millions of dollars. Hill-Rom agreed to a $41.8 million settlement to resolve the investigation. Following the settlement, Bill Killian, US attorney, "commended the dedication and diligence of all who played a role in this complex investigation, in particular lead HHS-OIG Special Agent Tony Maffei."[5] Working effectively with this many experts required all of Tony's team-building skills, which he learned in the classroom and developed in his career.

Reflecting on the case, Tony commented that the cornerstone for the operation was trust. He trusted that his fellow agents were following leads, checking facts, connecting the dots. The Bush School encouraged this principle of trust, and Tony applied it in all of his team projects. He trusted that his partner for a case study would carry his share of the work; he trusted that his capstone teammates were following through with their research and writing in a thorough and timely manner. Trust, a simple principle, but it affected every aspect of Tony's profession. He said, "I never know what I will find behind a front door. What I do have to know is that my partner has my back and that I can count on him."

Are we winning the war on fraud? Tony commented, "Criminals are smart. The lure of easy money will always be there. We may not eliminate fraud, but we are making good progress in eliminating corrupt practitioners. We have found that those who engage in corrupt financial practices generally engage in corrupt treatment practices." If he looked only at the big picture, he would get discouraged. Instead, he goes to work every day focusing on what he can accomplish that day and grateful for the opportunity to serve.

Daniel Morales (2000)
Business–Government Relations Manager, Walmart

Daniel Morales first learned of the Bush School during his internship in the office of Kay Bailey Hutchison, Republican senator from Texas. At the time he was a student at University of the Incarnate Word in San Antonio, majoring in political science, and he found that his internship reinforced the value of public service to him. He also met Elizabeth McKee, vice president of the Texas A&M student body. She encouraged him to pursue his interests in public service and apply to the Bush School. He was accepted in the MPSA Program. At the Bush School he learned about the "systems that allow people to govern and the ways those systems can be used to improve people's lives." He learned the importance of economics and how the intersection of public and private entities can be beneficial for the American public. He realized the ways that good policies benefit America by generating opportunities in communities. He developed a passion for economic development.

After his graduation, he accepted a position in the Harris County Tax Assessor-Collector's Office. Daniel began as a policy analyst; however, the organization had no Spanish media spokesperson. He spoke fluent Spanish. He began working with the Spanish broadcast outlets and found he enjoyed the work. In 2009, the George W. Bush administration needed Spanish-speaking spokespeople to work with cabinet-level officials. His work with media relations took a giant leap forward as he moved to the US Department of Labor. In that position he organized meetings between the secretary of labor and Hispanic business leaders to discuss laws that would be beneficial to Hispanic small businesses. He sought to develop positive relationships between the department and the Hispanic business community.

Two years later, he joined the US Department of Health and Human Services as the acting communications director. In that position, he enforced stringent external communication policies for twelve different HHS departments. His job was to ensure that each department consistently adhered to the administration's policy in their messages to the media. He moved in 2005 to the US Department of Energy, where he was the strategic communications adviser. In the Department of Energy he oversaw the flow of sensitive and confidential communication to the assistant secretary for policy and international affairs. He also served as an aide to the assistant secretary when he testified before Congress, gave public addresses, or worked with the White House. Daniel's positions in the federal government bought him extensive experience with the ways government seeks to coordinate and communicate public policy. In 2007 a new administration was elected; it was time for Daniel to move in a different direction: linking the private sector with the public sector as the community relations director for Walmart. Community relations are not always easy, but they can be rewarding.

Cibolo, Texas, is located on the corridor between Austin and San Antonio. This rapidly developing community had a population of 3,035 in 2000 but grew to 25,280 in 2014. It is largely made up of homes and has little commercial growth and low tax revenue. Walmart decided to put a store in Cibolo. All of the community political and bureaucratic leaders were in favor, but, as often happens, not all of the citizens were enthusiastic about Walmart coming to their community. When citizens protest, elected officials listen. They dropped their support for the store. Daniel was dispatched to the scene to see if he could salvage the project. He said, "I had to employ communication skills, negotiation skills, diplomacy, coalition building, project management, as well as managing attorneys, engineers, and consultants." He also had to understand how local governments work and how local politicians think. After exhaustive efforts and negotiations, they opened the Walmart store with massive fanfare. The local men and women lined up to see the new store in their neighborhood and ended up welcoming it enthusiastically. Today that Walmart employs three hundred local people and contributes millions of dollars in tax revenue.

As the liaison between a private enterprise and public organizations, Daniel knows that cooperation makes the difference in times of disaster. On April 20, 2016, Houston, Texas, received more than twelve inches of rain in twenty-four hours. More than one thousand homes were flooded, seven people died, and the city was shut down. Some of the first responders were Sylvester Turner (mayor), Senfronia Thompson (state representative), Armando Walle (state representative), and Sylvia Garcia (state senator). They reached out to Walmart for in-kind donations. Daniel worked with Walmart operations and the Walmart Foundation to meet the requests for life-sustaining items. One shelter needed undergarments, diapers, and toiletries as well as over-the-counter medication. People who were still in flooded apartments had no electricity or water. Daniel arranged for Walmart to put together small care packages that would sustain people for a couple of days. He worked with the City of Houston to put together and distribute cleaning kits to those whose homes had flooded. They worked with suppliers to provide cleaning agents, brooms, and mops. In the first three days, the legislators and Daniel's team went door to door handing out supplies. The company donated approximately fifty thousand dollars' worth of products, and the Walmart Foundation donated four hundred thousand dollars, which was split between the Red Cross, Salvation Army, Mayor's Disaster Fund, and neighborhood centers. Private-sector and government cooperation can make a difference, a big difference.

Catherine Ford Muller (2008)
Foreign Service Officer,
US Department of State

When Catherine Ford boarded a plane in Texas in the summer of 2007, she had no idea that the next twenty-four hours would impact the rest of her life. Catherine, a first-year Bush School student, was headed to Athens, Greece, for an internship with the State Department. After the long flight, she took a cab to her new apartment and met her new roommate, who said, "Hi, let's go to a barbecue." Catherine looked at her in total dismay and replied, "But I just got off a plane from Texas." Her roommate quickly got on the phone and called her supervisor at the embassy. "Is it all right if my roommate goes with us to the barbecue?" she asked. The supervisor assured her that Catherine was welcome. Catherine, not wanting to begin with a bad impression, agreed to go along. The supervisor was Lonny Muller. Catherine and Lonny married eighteen months later.

In 2007 Catherine's career plans were not well defined, but she knew two things: She wanted to work overseas, and she wanted to have a positive impact on people. Because her father was in the military, Catherine spent her childhood living across the United States. She attended high school in Izmir, Turkey, and went to the University of New Mexico, where she majored in Russian and had concentrations in Spanish, French, Mandarin Chinese, and Italian. At a graduate program fair at New Mexico, she saw Bush School brochures. She stopped, read about the program, and said, "This is where I want to be." At the end of her first year, she applied and was accepted for an internship with the State Department. By the beginning of her second year she knew that a career in the State Department and a marriage with Lonny were right for her. They were determined to serve the United States and to serve together.

One word describes Catherine's approach to her position in public diplomacy: *creative*. Her first consular tour was in Vienna, Austria. At the time of her tour, Belarus, a former Soviet Republic known for its repressive government, expelled all of the diplomats who worked at the US embassy in Minsk. Angry exchanges occurred, but the United States, wanting to keep options open, declared that there were no plans to close the embassy in Minsk or to order Belarus to close its embassy in Washington. Wanting Catherine to have experiences outside the consular section in Vienna, her supervisor sent her to Belarus. The controversy between the two countries left only four American diplomats in Belarus.

With such a small embassy staff, Catherine served as consular office and public diplomacy officer, and she and her fellow officers were expected to attend all diplomatic and cultural events. At a reception, Catherine met two American choreographers who were in Belarus through the Arts Envoy Program to stage an adaptation of *West Side Story* at the Belarus State Musical Theater. It was the first time American choreographers had been allowed to work with Belarusian performers. Catherine had long been interested in dance, so the choreographers invited her to take their warm-up classes with the Belarusian dancers. Catherine used her "rusty" Russian from her undergraduate days to visit with the dancers, many of whom had never spoken to an American before. They wanted her to come back to the classes and to attend the premier of the play. Catherine said that there is "power with one person being able to share American ideals, traits, and to dispel stereotypes of America."

She continued her creative approach to diplomacy during her second tour in Hong Kong. One area of outreach was lagging behind: social media. Catherine began with the Facebook page that had been republishing articles with few visuals; it was not very successful in connecting with the Hong Kong population. At the time she assumed control, the consulate had eighteen hundred Facebook friends. Catherine first established an editorial calendar so publishing was predictable. She wanted their Facebook page to be strategic: covering issues that were important to the United States and to Hong Kong and to get people's attention. She targeted the demographic of fifteen- to thirty-five-year-olds. She wanted to "draw people in with candy but get them to stay for the vegetables." After Catherine revamped the Facebook page, they had twenty-five thousand friends.

Her creativity extended to the position of consul general. Hong Kong was to get a new consul general, and the people needed to know him before he arrived. They wanted him to be perceived as a real person, not merely someone behind a desk. She began by issuing direct posts from the new consul general. He would write short pieces, only one or two sentences, in his own words. People felt as though he were speaking directly to them. It had an immediate positive effect; it humanized the US government and put a face on it. They were able to connect with people whom they would never have reached otherwise.

She did not stop with Facebook; she moved to YouTube. They needed a message for the Lunar New Year, but a speech did not have much appeal. It was the Year of the Snake. Catherine placed a stuffed snake with the staff of the consulate, and they sang a well-known, popular song in Cantonese. The next year was Year of the Horse. Catherine knew they could not stand around a horse and sing, but they could have a horse puppet who was applying for a job in the motor pool at the consulate. To be considered for the job, the horse puppet had to interview all of the staff of the consulate, including the consul general, who told the horse in Cantonese: "I would love for you to be in my motor pool and to drive me around!" The entire video was lighthearted, but it carried important messages. The horse was green, so it did not have a big carbon footprint; it made the people who worked at the consulate human and caring. The horse was a huge success. It received one hundred thousand hits on YouTube and more than five hundred thousand on Sina Weibo, the Chinese version of Twitter.

Catherine said that understanding the audience she is working with and adapting to their needs and values are an important part of diplomacy. "I like to do things that are a little bit different, not stick with the standard 'this is what we have always done.' I want to reach people we haven't reached before. Of course, that doesn't mean doing everything differently. Some things need to remain the same." She thinks that there is room to find new ways to interact with people and to project the United States overseas. "At the end of the day, we are all just people who are different and have different ways of doing things. Personal interaction through social media or in person can be much more effective than giving a speech." One person at a time, Catherine Ford Muller seeks to win the world.

Roman Napoli (2003)
Administrative Officer,
US Agency for International Development (USAID)

Roman Napoli has a suitcase that he takes wherever he goes. His unique suitcase does not contain the usual items one would expect to find. Instead, it is packed with analytical skills, consensus-building skills, communications skills, and the burning desire to serve people. Roman's hypothetical suitcase has served him well as he has served with the Drug Enforcement Administration (DEA), USAID, FEMA, and the Department of State.

Roman came to Texas A&M to earn a PhD in psychology. Someone suggested that he should consider taking Jim Olson's course in crisis management. That course changed Roman's career path. He recalls thinking, "This is fun. I think I would like to do this for a living." He was hooked; he wanted a career in public service. Following his graduation from the Bush School in 2003, he was awarded a Presidential Management Internship. He chose two rotations with the DEA. In his second year he was assigned as a staffer to a congressman. Roman was testifying before a congressional committee when he met Andrew Natsios, who was with USAID. Roman was so impressed with the work Natsios was doing that at the end of his rotation, he took a job with USAID in the Strategic Planning Office for Central America and the Caribbean.

He served throughout the Caribbean region, assisting with program planning, grant proposal review, and budget planning. On August 29, 2005, Hurricane Katrina devastated the Louisiana coast. Roman was from Eunice, Louisiana, a small town about an hour from Lafayette. Roman and his wife agreed that they needed to be there. They took a month's leave from their jobs, moved back to Louisiana, and worked in a shelter where they did what needed to be done to help evacuees: mopping floors and working with the Red Cross. They were so moved by the relief effort that they decided to seek work in recovery. Roman accepted a job with FEMA as special assistant to the director of Louisiana Recovery, became the youngest person in senior management, and worked mandatory seventy-two-hour workweeks. He coordinated the field budget, developed the first strategic plan linking support functions to outcomes, and served as acting deputy director to the temporary housing program, which served more than ninety thousand households. Later, as liaison for the state of Louisiana to the federal coordinator's office, he became the eyes and ears on the ground for the White House. Roman's suitcase was gathering valuable skills.

In 2008, Roman accepted a position with USAID as the principal budget analyst in the office of the director of foreign assistance, with responsibilities for the Near East region: Israel, West Bank, Lebanon, and Yemen. This area constituted 7 percent of the USAID aid budget. Barack Obama was elected president on November 4, 2008; on December 27, 2008, war began between Israel and the Palestinians in the Gaza Strip. The United States had to respond, but there was little staff in place for the new administration. Roman served as coordinator for Palestinian assistance for the director of foreign assistance. As the Arab Spring began in 2011 and spread through Egypt, Libya, and much of the Middle East, Roman moved to the Department of State, where he served as the financial management officer to ensure that budget formulation, execution, and evaluation processes were in place for a more than $450 million aid package to promote democratic and economic growth in the region.

Today Roman is the administrative officer for the Office of Budget and Resource Management, USAID's corporate budget section. His experience with foreign assistance programs has given him a strong understanding of how internal processes work. These skills became essential during the Ebola crisis of 2014.

The need for aid in the Ebola crisis was urgent; however, funds were not available. The situation called for a supplemental budget, something that had not been done since 2011. Roman and three of his friends developed the budget, gathered the large team of expert witnesses, and took the budget to Congress in less than five weeks. Included in the group was a recent Bush School graduate: Brandon Pichanick. Congress approved the measure. Ebola victims and aid workers received the support they needed to abate the crisis.

Roman's suitcase of skills and attributes has served him well. Although he has served in different agencies and in different capacities, his guiding principles remain being considerate of coworkers, realizing that each situation is unique and there are no "one-size-fits-all" solutions, not trying to win every battle, and building relationships. The most important item in the suitcase is being willing to do what your country needs you to do.

Griffin Rozell (2008)
Foreign Service Officer,
US Department of State

In 2003, Griffin Rozell made an audacious decision. He had lived in Harlingen, Texas, all of his life; had followed his family members to Abilene Christian University; and had planned to study law like his father. In 2003, he applied for a study abroad program in Russia. He could have chosen Oxford, England; instead, he chose Russia—big, totally foreign, unlike any place he or his friends at home would have experienced. He wanted to see the world. While he was studying in

Russia, Harley Wegler, a mentor, suggested that he consider a career in the Foreign Service. Why not see the world in the Foreign Service?

Griffin returned to Abilene, completed his undergraduate degree, and went back to Russia for a year of language training. During that year, his parents visited. As they rode the train from Moscow to Nizhni Novgorod, Griffin told his parents that he wanted to join the Foreign Service; they encouraged his decision.

He began studying for the Foreign Service exam and realized he needed a stronger background in international affairs to pass the test. He researched graduate programs and was attracted to the Bush School. The other programs he considered cost three to four times more than those at the Bush School. Although his decision was driven by practicality, he found a rigorous course of study that prepared him for a Foreign Service career, a faculty that offered not only instruction but also guidance, a proven record of significant job placement after graduation, and a culture that focused on service. Today he proudly wears his Aggie ring and tells people that he went to Texas A&M. He entered the Foreign Service after his graduation from the Bush School.

One of Griffin's most meaningful experiences from the Bush School was his position as assistant director of the Scowcroft Institute of International Affairs. In that position he managed the budget, daily operations, and special events, but more important, he learned how to manage employees. Through example and day-to-day experience, Jeff Engel, director of the Scowcroft Institute, taught Griffin to be straightforward and to trust and empower his employees. Griffin tries to apply these principles with his staff today.

From College Station, Griffin moved to the US embassy in Warsaw, Poland, where he served as vice consul, processing visas and overseeing a team of Polish and American staff. Griffin had the responsibility of upholding US immigration laws while being the face of the United States to those he worked with and to those who were applying for visas. It was an opportunity to show the best and most gracious side of the United States. Protection of American citizens was also a serious part of his responsibility. He says, "We have to remember that routine work like replacing a lost or stolen passport is incredibly important to the person standing in front of you asking for the service. For that citizen, it may be his or her first time overseas; we want our citizens to have a positive impression of government workers."

In July 2013, Griffin and his family moved to Tashkent, Uzbekistan. His new positon was to serve as the human resources officer for the embassy. Uzbekistan is on few bucket lists. If you can locate the country on a map, then a lack of flights in and out of the city, border restrictions, extremely expensive travel arrangements, and no convenient neighboring countries make Uzbekistan less than user-friendly. As Griffin commented, "Once you are there, you are there." In Tashkent, Griffin expanded his administrative skills in management. Griffin's job was to build consensus on issues and required using all of the diplomatic skills in his arsenal: negotiation, proposals, and counter-proposals.

For the past two years, Griffin has served in Karachi, Pakistan, where he is the assistant cultural affairs officer. His responsibilities include English-language programming and educational and cultural exchanges.

A Foreign Service officer faces language challenges and cultural challenges with the frequent moves. In Poland, Griffin had a year of Polish-language and cultural training before he arrived; nevertheless, he says that you know the country only by living there. In Uzbekistan, he had no cultural training. Although his knowledge of the Russian language was helpful, many of the people there speak only Uzbek, which he did not know. In Pakistan, some segments of society speak English extremely well; in other segments, English comprehension or conversation is nonexistent. Language is a challenge every day. Griffin and his family are on the move again. Their next stop after language training in Washington is Bratislava, Slovakia.

Murray Stockinger (2002)
Deputy Director, President's Daily Brief,
Federal Bureau of Investigation

On December 25, 2009, Northwest Airlines flight 253 was en route from Amsterdam to Detroit with 290 people aboard. A passenger, Umar Farouk Abdulmutullab, attempted to set off plastic explosives that had been sewn in his underwear. The explosives failed to detonate, but if the terrorist had succeeded, it would have been the deadliest aviation tragedy on US soil. Authorities learned that Abdulmutullab had ties to

Houston; thus, Houston could be at risk for a terrorist attack. The FBI moved quickly to assess the situation. Murray Stockinger had recently moved to Houston as the supervisory intelligence analyst for the FBI; he had work to do and little time to do it. Murray needed an assessment plan, and he needed it quickly.

Abdulmutullab attended a conference in 2008 in Houston that included almost one hundred people. All of the participants in the conference had to be checked as possible associates of Abdulmutullab. Murray's team assembled a list of people at the conference and developed a checklist for each person. Then, using agency specialists who had access to various databases in the Houston office, they began a methodical analysis of the conference attendees. Within two hours, they had checked every person who attended the same conference as Abdulmutullab.

When Murray arrived at Texas A&M as a freshman, he had no plans to join the FBI. He explored several options of study but discovered that he enjoyed history and political science. This interest was reinforced through the James Earl Rudder Normandy Study Abroad Program. There he studied D-Day, walked along the beaches of Normandy, and gazed up at the cliffs at Pointe du Hoc. He realized the massive coordination for such an endeavor and the sacrifice made. Most important, he saw what an impact our involvement in international affairs made. Fifty years after the battle, the influence was still apparent. He knew the field of study he wanted to follow: international affairs. Following his undergraduate program, he chose the Bush School. He appreciated that the Bush School offered students access to world leaders, to see them as real people and to listen to their views on international affairs.

After his first year, Murray and another Bush School student served an internship with the Scowcroft Group in Washington, DC. Each Friday the two interns were invited to Scowcroft's office for an hour and allowed to ask any questions they wanted—no filter. Scowcroft told them exactly what was going on in the world, what the political atmosphere was, and how decisions were actually made—rarely systematic and often messy. At the Bush School, he learned when the unexpected happens, you are the person who makes things right. You are the person who has to protect the community. You are in the driver's seat: Accept the challenge and "move the ball forward."

Murray's move to the FBI was a result of being in the right place at the right time. He became a Presidential Management Fellow in 2002. After visiting with FBI representatives at a national hiring conference, he was interested in them and they were interested in him. September 11 had rocked the nation. The FBI realized it needed a more robust information-sharing capability. At the time of the attack, the FBI had no report officers. In August 2002, it established the report officer position to bolster information sharing. When Murray was hired, the FBI had only five report officers and needed more people with the right skill set. Murray applied for the job because he thought that his analytical and communications skills were a good fit with the FBI. In May 2003 he was the first analyst to go to Riyadh, Saudi Arabia, as part of a team investigating a terrorist attack in a residential neighborhood. The bombings left twenty-three people dead, including nine Americans.[6] In 2005 he was part of a cooperative intelligence effort between Great Britain and the United States that investigated the London Underground bombings. Murray arrived in London at the bombing site and found carnage. The team's number-one mission was to determine if another attack was to follow. Quickly, the team collected pocket litter—cards, tickets, phones, wallets—anything that could be connected to the bombers. Within hours, the team assembled large stacks of random documents and objects that had to be checked for information about a possible threat to the United States. The team, housed in the US embassy, worked for two weeks while under a bomb threat to the embassy.

In 2013 Murray moved to New York as the first tactical intelligence branch chief for FBI New York. There he faced a managerial dilemma. His job was to oversee and coordinate all of the intelligence programs and analysts in Manhattan: twelve supervisors and 185 diverse intelligence agents who were located across the city. Each program had different procedures and different supervision standards; embracing change was not welcome. Murray established standard policy and procedure for day-to-day operations and created training and auditing functions to ensure compliance. He secured additional financial resources from FBI headquarters, which enabled him to hire one hundred new intelligence personnel, doubling the intelligence staff in New York. He was fortunate to have supervisors who encouraged him to use his skills and initiative; he was a self-starter. He faced challenges and worked toward the goal of improving the intelligence process.

What is next? Murray will move to Washington, DC, for a two-year assignment as deputy director of the President's Daily Brief. He will be responsible for hiring the analysts and briefers, supervising the production of the brief, and providing any assistance to the president. The president's intelligence brief is in good hands.

River Burton Stuckey (2003)
Emergency Management Program Specialist, Federal Emergency Management Agency

Most people run from natural disasters: earthquakes, hurricanes, tornados. River Stuckey runs toward them. As a member of FEMA, River has been in the trenches of natural disasters since Hurricane Rita hit the Texas coast in 2005. She has aided people who lost family, homes, property, and everything important to them. As a child growing up in Southeast Texas, her lifelong dream was not to help clean up after hurricanes, but her education and experience pointed her in that direction.

After graduating with a degree in Spanish from Lamar University, River was uncertain of her next move. She was considering anthropology at Texas A&M when several students from the Bush School gave a presentation to her class. She was impressed by their knowledge and professionalism, and they were in a practical field of study. "I want to be like them," she said to herself. She applied to the Bush School and was accepted to the MPSA Program.

Following her first year, she served an internship in Honduras with the Pan American Health Organization. She was assigned to a remote village, accessible only by boat. The leaders of the village wanted help with the problems of severe flooding and health awareness programs. She was the only person in the village who could offer help, but she had to reach the people through humility, on their terms. She had to listen to their problems, adapt to their culture, understand their values, and help them meet their needs through workshops and community projects. She discovered that helping people brought great personal satisfaction. She graduated from the Bush School in 2005 and began teaching English in South Korea.

Disaster struck twice along the Gulf Coast in the summer of 2005 when Hurricane Katrina devastated Louisiana on August 29 and Hurricane Rita ripped through Southeast Texas ten days later on September 7. The coastal areas of Louisiana, Mississippi, and Alabama, as well as the entire upper Texas coast, dealt with apocalyptic damage from the two major, back-to-back storms. Evacuees from Mississippi, Alabama, and Louisiana joined thousands of displaced persons in the Texas area. River had grown up on the coast of Texas. She left Korea and hurried back to Southeast Texas to help her family, who had to relocate to Houston. FEMA, still responding to Hurricane Katrina, faced a shortage of workers. River's mother said, "Why don't you work for FEMA?" That was the beginning.

Southeast Texas was devastated by Hurricane Rita: no power, no water, trees down, homes destroyed. Some 4,526 single-family homes were destroyed in Orange and Jefferson Counties; nine counties were declared federal disaster areas. In addition to the physical problems, there were traumatized individuals who thought that they had no place to go for help. River, a volunteer, helped them register for assistance. As she worked with the FEMA team, she realized how the Bush School had prepared her for this type of work.

Her Bush School capstone was in emergency management; most of her Bush School projects included working in teams with people who may or may not have shared her perspective of the problem. She honed her listening and communication skills. Her internship taught her empathy; she saw problems through the eyes of others. River said that she owes much of her success with FEMA to the Bush School.

Hurricane damage is not cleaned up overnight. People have to be resettled, homes have to be rebuilt, and critical services have to be restored. FEMA had to have temporary housing for the victims—the portable trailers. River managed the Travel Trailer Recertification Program for Hurricane Rita and later for Hurricane Ike. She explained, "I think that the Temporary Housing Program is one of the crown jewels of FEMA's programs for the general public. We provide thousands of temporary housing units to families who have lost their homes; they have lost their personal property and in some cases they have lost loved ones. It's a great feeling to able to provide an essential need to those families in their time of crisis. It's a great feeling to be able to provide them with a roof over their head and someplace to be while they organize themselves and they make plans to rebuild or repair their homes."

Hurricane Ike visited the Texas coast in 2008. A hurricane victim explained, "We were told there was mandatory evacuation. I have been in floods, but I have never witnessed what we saw in this area. Houses washed into other houses; a boat washed over a six-foot fence, right in my backyard; debris was everywhere, and everywhere was mud and dirt and nothing, nothing left. FEMA came in and set up in a public park to provide relief and support to local victims." River supervised more than three hundred staff members who supported Ike recovery and coordinated operations with the FEMA Joint Area Field Office in Austin. River is grateful that no hurricanes have hit the Texas coast since then, but her responsibilities did not decrease; they increased. Currently, she is an emergency management program specialist who develops and updates plans for handling possible disasters, including medical emergencies, nuclear disasters, and travel disasters. She spent six months with the Paiute Indians of Utah coordinating emergency preparedness measures. Of her eleven years with FEMA, she has been deployed more than two thousand days (50 percent of her time with FEMA) to regions needing assistance. River's life work is dedicated to protecting the citizens of the United States. She said it best: "We are in the people business."

Tyson Voelkel (2007)
President, Texas A&M Foundation

Tyson Voelkel's path to public service has been circuitous: at times by choice, at other times the result of uncontrollable circumstances. Although the path and the circumstances have varied, the lessons from his childhood stayed with him. As the eldest son of parents from different cultures and different religions, he learned three core values:

> **Perspective matters:** Problems may seem simple when viewed through one set of lenses, but effective solutions come through the ability to see the issues from each party's perspective.

Service: Be grateful for what you have and do not waste time wishing for something else. We are to serve and give back where we are. Tyson's mother was the only person of her faith in the small community of Brenham; she gave back by going to churches, explaining her faith, and seeking to break barriers.

Respect: Each person, regardless of his or her station in life, deserves respect and courtesy. Treat each person equally.

Tyson applied, and continues to apply, these values to every endeavor. After spending the first seven years of his life traveling with his parents while his father served in USAID, Tyson and his family settled in Brenham, where he completed high school and headed for Texas A&M and the Corps of Cadets. His goal: a career in the US Army. Through his Corps experiences, Tyson learned that anything is possible if he worked hard enough and made sacrifices. He honed his leadership philosophy: Leaders have to earn respect; they have to collaborate to achieve goals and effect positive change. Being the leader in a situation does not come with entitlement. During his senior year at Texas A&M, he was selected commander. Following his graduation, he received his commission in the US Army and headed to Fort Benning, Georgia, and then Germany.

In Germany, Tyson worked side by side with German, Polish, and Danish military and served as the aide-de-camp to the general of the Seventh Army Training Command. Along the way, he realized that there were complex problems with no simple answers. He had to navigate cultural and political realities. He also realized that there is more than one effective leadership style. The most important aspect of leadership is to be true to one's self and not adopt a different style of leadership. Following his tour in Germany, he was assigned as company commander for the 325th Airborne Infantry Regiment and Operation Iraqi Freedom. The next stop: Baghdad, where he was in charge of a unit of 140 paratroopers. His assignment was to decrease attacks on his unit and establish a line of intelligence within the sector of 250,000 Iraqis. The first problem was that his unit was dysfunctional. They dehumanized the Iraqi population and had little respect for anyone different from themselves. Tyson decided to tackle the problem by engaging the population with US soldiers.

The sector was a cesspool of trash and filth. Areas of open land had three to four feet of trash stacked. Tyson went directly to the State Department and USAID for help. His proposal was to remove the trash and build soccer fields where the locals could participate in sports. Then he wanted to build markets for people to shop and meet their neighbors. He hired the local Iraqis for one dollar per day to help with the cleanup. The plan worked. The local men were proud to help; they were working and earning a wage. As a result, attacks on the company went down, there were fewer improvised explosive devices (IEDs), and local intelligence about the enemy improved. For his efforts, Tyson was awarded the MacArthur Award, given to a member of the US Army who demonstrates the ideals of General Douglas MacArthur: duty, honor, and country. In every command position Tyson held—Corps of Cadets, Texas A&M; brigade assistant operations officer, Fort Bragg; company commander, Iraq and Fort Bragg; academy instructor, West Point; operation and plans officer, Ellington Armed Forces Center—his performance was ranked number one.

In 2005, Tyson decided to pursue a master's degree. Richard Chilcoat encouraged him to attend the Bush School of Government and Public Service. Before school started, his brother Trevor noticed an article in the *Battalion* about a new position: student member of the Board of Regents. He encouraged Tyson to apply: "You are the best person for the job. Do you really want a sophomore in that position?" Tyson became the first student regent. In graduate school, Tyson found his worldview challenged and enlarged by his professors and experienced an education in mentorship through his work on the Board of Regents. Through the guidance of regents such as Gene Stallings and Wendy Gramm, he learned the depth and breadth of issues at Texas A&M. There were no simple problems with simple answers.

On June 23, 2009, the lives of Tyson and his wife, Christi, changed forever. Lily was born. They knew that she would have complications, but they were not prepared for what would follow: She was born blind and deaf (CHARGE syndrome); she had her first heart surgery when she was six days old. She weighed six pounds, two ounces. Lily stayed in the hospital four months with Tyson and Christi constantly by her crib. She came home for a week, then back to the hospital. Christi spent days at the hospital while Tyson tried to keep life normal for their three-year-old daughter, Eliana. Tyson spent nights at the hospital with Lily and studied his MBA course work from Rice. He called Lily his "study partner." For the first time in Tyson's life he had totally no control over the situation. All they could do was pray, love her, and support her as best they could. Lily lived three years; she knew love. In her memory they established the Lily Voelkel Foundation for children with CHARGE. They wanted to use their talents and resources to help those in need: "I value people. There is no point in being the richest person in the cemetery."

Tyson resigned from the military and remained in Houston in financial and foundation management. Erle Nye, a former Texas A&M regent, once told Tyson that public service takes many forms. Military service, volunteering in the community, and philanthropy are all forms of service. In 2016 Tyson's path to service returned him to Texas A&M as president of the Texas A&M Foundation, where he will lead a four-billion-dollar Lead by Example campaign.

Courtney Weigand (2007)
Transfer Pricing Senior Economist, US Internal Revenue Service

Courtney Weigand and Lauren Dangelmayr have striking similarities in their background and professional life. Courtney, like Lauren, grew up in a rural setting: Lauren in Texas; Courtney in Missouri. Courtney's father and grandfather were farmers, and her mother taught home economics. Her hometown, Centerview, Missouri, had a population of just over two hundred. Her graduating class in Chilhowee, with a population of approximately three hundred, had fourteen students. Courtney's life centered on the farm and sports—running, basketball, and volleyball.

Courtney and Lauren faced the challenge of adjusting to a large university. Lauren attended Texas A&M, and Courtney, the University of Missouri. Each university had student populations that far exceeded anything they had experienced. Courtney decided to major in parks and recreation because she thought that park projects would be fun to organize, but she minored in business with a focus on economics to have a practical background. At Missouri, she applied for and received a United States Navy Parks and Recreation internship at a naval base in Italy. She was in charge of nonalcoholic recreation programs for the young sailors. That internship became a turning point in her life; she discovered that she liked international life. She began searching for graduate programs that would offer an international focus; she found the Bush School International Economic Development Program. It was the perfect combination for her interests and academic background.

In her first year at the Bush School, she added a multinational enterprise course to the required course work. At the end of her first year, she accepted an internship with the Internal Revenue Service (IRS). She worked on research projects in the Washington, DC, headquarters. At the end of the internship, the IRS offered her a position, but she turned it down and returned to the Bush School. In her second year, she signed up for transfer pricing, the study of international taxation. After graduation, she accepted a position with the Ernst & Young accounting firm in its Transfer Pricing Division and moved to Manhattan. Courtney worked for Ernst & Young for four years, enjoying its excellent training program and open-door policy. Even though she worked long hours, she knew the experience was worthwhile. She was responsible for documentation that provided penalty protection for her clients. Her hard work paid off, and she was promoted to manager. Eventually, she wanted a change. She had remained in contact with her internship adviser at the IRS. He suggested she apply to the IRS. It was time to move from the private sector to the public sector and from New York City to Washington, DC.

At Ernst & Young Courtney had managed two or three clients that required constant attention. Much of her work involved necessary documentation but seldom seemed pivotal. At the IRS, she is a senior economist who works with lawyers and accountants on teams that deal with foreign governments. She finds her job extremely fulfilling. Often she ensures that US corporations are not double taxed, which is a serious issue. She has flexibility in her position. At one time, the team leader for two pending cases left the IRS. In those two cases, Courtney asked if she might assume two roles in the negotiations: economist and team leader. It worked.

Currently, Courtney has to balance work on more than twenty cases involving negotiations with foreign governments. As a young woman, she finds dealing at the senior level with foreign governments challenging. The tax world is male dominated. Although most countries have become accustomed to dealing with women, they often find Courtney's age a factor in negotiations. She is in her midthirties, and most in her field are well over fifty.

Negotiations are rarely, if ever, easy. She must be able to endure long days of constant debating, defend any position she promotes, think on her feet, and counterpoint any arguments presented, all while not showing frustration. She also has to adapt to each country's manner of negotiating: for example, Germany, Japan, Mexico, and Canada. The United States has tax treaties with more than fifty countries.

How does Courtney deal with the stress of international negotiations? She pulls from her days on the farm in Missouri when she ran and played volleyball and basketball. On weekends Courtney runs marathons and plays volleyball and basketball.

Zoe Zebra
Analyst, Central Intelligence Agency

Note: National security concerns require that we not identify the person in this profile and that we submit questions to the agency, hence the change in format from the other profiles. Zoe Zebra is a composite of four former Bush School students who work for the CIA.

Who was the most influential person(s) in your early life?

My mother offered a model of perseverance that kept me on the straight and narrow. She also taught me from a young age that I could do anything I determined to do and inspired me to do my best in all situations. She was adventurous as well. The summer before I started high school, she and I spent a month backpacking throughout Switzerland. We faced challenges hiking in a foreign country, but we came away with amazing memories and a sense of pride in our accomplishment. My grandfather also inspired me; his knowledge of international affairs fueled my interest in government service.

How did you become interested in public service, particularly foreign policy and national security?

My family instilled a love of country and a sense of right and wrong. That influence was critical to nudging me to government service. Also,

I did not want a career that was routine and boring; I wanted challenges and travel. My father was an airline pilot, and I grew up traveling the world. I loved visiting new countries, experiencing their foods and their culture, and learning about their histories. Today, I still feel the same way. I initially pursued my interest in international security policy in college. I was attracted to the complexities of national security decision making. Only when I came to the Bush School did I become totally committed to a career in national security. I have never regretted the decision I made to serve in the intelligence community. I count myself fortunate to have studied under the guidance of Hermann, Olson, and Gates and to have had the benefit of their mentoring and their confidence in my ability.

Why did you decide to come to the Bush School?

I was familiar with the Bush School and Library as an undergraduate student at Texas A&M. Although I applied to and was accepted by other well-established schools, I liked the unique combination of theory and practice that the Bush School offered. I was especially impressed by the professors, who advanced research in public service, political science, history, and economics, as well as professionals with long careers and excellent experience in government and national security.

What are your major recollections of the Bush School?

My memories of the stress associated with graduate school have faded over time. Now I mostly remember warm feelings: late nights working on assignments or studying in our offices, periodically punctuated by visits to friends' offices to unwind, or by playing a form of bocce ball in the halls while several different radio tunes filtered from the offices . . . listening to Bob Gates recount stories, such as how Margaret Thatcher like to refer to him and Lawrence Eagleburger as "Tweedle Dum and Tweedle Dee" . . . meeting former president George H. W. Bush . . . taking the Dillo from the LBJ School . . . walking the grounds of the Bush School campus in the early evening . . . bushwhackers' softball practice, while a small white dog scurried around the diamond . . . my summer internship in Washington . . . and, of course, the Dixie Chicken and Dry Bean. Most important, I remember the camaraderie and close friendships I built there. The Bush School was a family, and the togetherness and long hours yielded lifelong friendships.

How well did the Bush School prepare you for what you do now?

The Bush School's focus on honor and integrity continues to inspire me today. My course work stressed competencies that are absolutely critical to my work: how to sift through a lot of information to find the most important data points; how to identify the central tension between policy options; how to develop a well-structured, hard-hitting argument; how to boil a lot of information into a few finely crafted pages of text or a short briefing. In addition, the "other" education: Professional development and leadership have served me well.

In particular, Dr. Ken Ashworth's class taught me about executive presence and understanding my audience. Those skills have been invaluable when I am briefing Congress on complicated or thorny issues. The leadership experience offered self-awareness that has impacted my approach to leadership in my profession. I learned that while I was strong at being able to drive toward a solution or outcome, I would sometimes do so in a way that my teammates did not feel included. I took this feedback to heart and now am pleased to be recognized as having a consultative leadership style.

Can you describe any incident in which you played a significant role in preserving the safety of the country?

I can't speak about any specifics regarding my role, but I am very proud to have been part of the Bin Laden operation. To have been part of the team that brought him to justice was by far the most significant experience in my career. And, on a broader scale, I am proud of all the agency and government has done to combat Al-Qaeda and terrorist threats. Counterterrorism is not easy; it takes a mental and physical toll on those who work in it—long days and nights, time away from family and often in tough places, the constant pressure that "missing something" could cost lives. Despite the pressures, the commitment and dedication of this community are amazing, and I am proud to be part of the fight.

Was there an experience for you that was an aha moment and made you think about the impact you have?

One of the most enjoyable aspects of my position is being able to inform policy makers to help them make critical decisions about foreign policy and national security. My job is not to make policy but to ensure the president and the cabinet have the information and context they need from our analysis. One aha moment was my involvement in providing analysis to help the administration evaluate the future of our engagement with a certain country. The pieces my team and I wrote directly contributed to the president making the decision to alter previous policy. We had an impact, and we knew it.

How has your job affected your personal life and family?

I would say that the three "Fs" have sustained me over the course of an intense and stressful career: faith, family, and fitness.

My faith is a source of strength for me. Being grounded in a steadfast faith has given me a perspective during challenging times. Second, I could not do this job without the support of my husband. He has been a rock and is my greatest ally. He has supported me in very demanding times. During the entire month leading to the Bin Laden operation, I did not get home for dinner any night. He did not know any of the specifics of my work, but he never complained. Definitely my career has had an impact on him, and life is not easy, especially when I work long hours. So I ensure that I fully focus on my family when I am home, which is one of the nice things about working in a world of classified information—I can't take my work home with me. Finally, my daily fitness routine helps me start each day on a strong footing. I wake up at 4:45 each morning and workout for an hour—kickboxing, weightlifting, yoga. I believe this daily habit of exercise has helped increase my physical and mental durability.

What do you intend to do for the next twenty years?

I plan, as far as can be planned in such situations, to remain with the CIA until I am eligible to retire. I find the work extremely rewarding, have been fortunate to advance quickly into positions of leadership, and realize there are unlimited opportunities to gain new perspectives and experiences. After I retire, I envision a career in academia and the arts. One of my goals is to return to the Bush School and carry on Professor Olson's legacy and investment in the next generation of intelligence and national security professionals.

Postscript

This account of the Bush School history has been descriptive, not analytical. Certainly, merit exists for institutional analysis, including those of educational organizations such as professional schools.[1] We recognize the interest in hypotheses about organizational effectiveness, leadership, goal realization, and so on and their possible implications for the Bush School; however, that would be a different project from ours.

Nonetheless, it seems appropriate when describing the path of the Bush School for its first two decades, that we offer several observations about critical factors in the way the school has developed. Specifically, we call attention to four that have had profound effects.

Texas A&M Presidential Library Initiative. The first factor is the bold and creative initiative in proposing that President Bush locate his library at Texas A&M and incorporating professional education and research on public affairs as part of the proposal. In Texas A&M University lore, the story of the Aggie oil legend Michel Halbouty telling his friend, the president-elect, that he ought to put his library on the campus is significant. The follow-up and enthusiasm of a small cluster of other former students—some of whom also enjoyed close friendship with Bush—transformed an idea into a commitment. That might have remained a "back-burner" concept were it not for the proposal to invite the new president to make a commencement address at Texas A&M less than six months after taking office. That invitation compelled the university regents—the initiators of the concept—to create a concrete proposal within a matter of several months. The regents then discovered that the dean of the College of Liberal Arts college and several professors independently had been thinking that the university should seek the presidential library. That academic group conceptualized connecting the presidential library to specific educational endeavors.

Locating a presidential library within a university complex was uncommon. The Kennedy Library is in Boston, not on the Harvard University campus that is home to the Kennedy School of Government. The Ford Library and the Ford School are not in the same communities in Michigan. The Carter Library enjoys a relationship with Emory University in Atlanta, but the Carter Center operates independently in a separate location. The effort to place the Reagan Library at Stanford University failed. At the time of the proposal, the one clear example of a presidential library on a university campus was the LBJ Library at the University of Texas—archrival of Texas A&M.

Not only was locating a presidential library on a university campus not a common arrangement, but George H. W. Bush did not attend Texas A&M nor had he ever lived in College Station. He had limited prior visits to the campus. President Bush had campaigned there and given a commencement address as vice president. The creative courtship of President Bush by Texas A&M began with his return for the commencement address in May 1989. During that visit the university officials and faculty took the unusual step for Texas A&M of awarding him an honorary degree. Then, surrounded by Aggies who were his friends, they presented him and his party with a specific proposal that included the Bush School. One of the people, who worked at that time for the Texas A&M chancellor, recalls being told that Bush said, "My God, this is like old home week."[2]

The early Bush commencement visit to Texas A&M required getting a concrete library proposal prepared and presented. It was equally important in getting the presidential library selection on the president's agenda. Of course, Bush was not personally engaged with the issue until much later, but on the Air Force One flight from College Station he assigned a deputy (James Cicconi) to take charge of the library selection issue—likely at an earlier point in his presidency than would have otherwise occurred. The Texas A&M proposal became the reference point.

When the authors sat down with President Bush in the spring of 2015 to discuss the idea of this book, we asked him whether he ever entertained any other location for his library. "Never," he replied. Of course, George Hebert Walker Bush is a master politician, skilled at friendly exchanges, but James Cicconi confirms that at a minimum the A&M proposal was in a very favored position with the president from an early point. In sum, the Texas A&M initiative for the library appears masterful.

Involvement of President Bush with the School. The engagement of George H. W. Bush with the Bush School and Texas A&M in the years since he has left the presidency has had a powerful influence on the school's evolution. Bush did not simply loan his name to the Bush School. He has taken a strong personal, continuing interest. Several examples illustrate this observation.

The university's original plan for the Bush School drew on its own immediate experience—with one significant innovation. At the time the College of Liberal Arts team prepared their concept for a school as part of the university's proposal, they already had experience with a Master's Program in Public Administration in their Political Science Department. Their idea was essentially to move their current program from the Political Science Department to the new Bush School. The existing political science program attracted ten to fifteen students per year. They assumed that the new Bush School would attract roughly the same number of students. That guided the number and size of classrooms allocated for the new school when the academic building in the Bush Library complex was designed and built.

As an incentive to the College of Liberal Arts at Texas A&M, the proposed new school would draw on faculty expertise from across many departments in that college. Thus, the proposed Bush School would be part of their college and would provide new opportunities for a number of their faculty. The proposed school would enhance the College of Liberal Arts. This innovation—borrowing faculty from elsewhere in the university—was modeled on the structure of the Woodrow Wilson School at Princeton University. Don Wilson, assigned by President Bush to evaluate proposals for the library and later the first head of the Bush Presidential Library Foundation at Texas A&M, thought the school arrangement was flawed. He and others suggested to Bush that the design for the school's operation was too constrained. After seeing the Bush School in operation, President Bush appears to have recognized that assessment, which led to his conversation at

Kennebunkport with Ray Bowen, university president. Bowen visited the Kennedy School at Harvard and became convinced of a need for an independent school with its own faculty.

Would Texas A&M University have ultimately concluded that the Bush School had to be configured differently than in the original plan? Perhaps, but it happened when it happened because of the keen interest of President Bush and the favorable reception from a sympathetic state legislature for the necessary additional funds sought by the governor, George W. Bush, and the lieutenant governor, Bob Bullock. Chuck Hermann's recollection of the Kennebunkport meeting with Bowen is that President Bush went out of his way to stress that he was only sharing his observations and that Bowen was the academic expert and authority. But when Bowen decided that the Bush School needed to be an independent unit within the university, Bush certainly gave his support. From that decision flows the development of the Bush School, including acquiring its own faculty and creating a much larger student enrollment. That, in turn, has created the visibility, reputation, and impact the Bush School enjoys. A school as originally conceived with only twenty or thirty students and faculty committed to research back in their home departments would have been unlikely to create an equivalent effect.

Bush's impact also concerns the people who have associated with the school. Consider the initial deans—Robert Gates, Richard Chilcoat, Ryan Crocker, Andrew Card, and Mark Welsh. Each of them applied for the position and was vetted in the standard Texas A&M University process for selecting leadership for its colleges and schools. Nevertheless, few schools have a former president of the United States encouraging public leaders to consider applying for a deanship or, if offered a position by the university, receiving vigorous encouragement from a president to accept. The active engagement of Bush does not stop with candidates for leadership positions. For more than a decade, he gladly wrote letters to senior faculty who had been offered positions at the Bush School, urging them to accept. Regardless of an individual's political affiliation, the encouraging letters appeared and often had a significant impact. In fact, the "presidential treatment" has been applied to prospective students. On more than one occasion, when Bush was in College Station during interview weekend with Bush School student applicants, he would drop by and promote the degree programs. In sum, the Bush School has been successful in attracting talented people. The help of President Bush in such efforts has been substantial.

The relationship between the Bush School and President Bush in all probability has been reciprocal. He found things that attracted him to the school and university. The proposition of investing in an institution whose mission was to prepare future generations for careers in public service appears to have strongly resonated with him. Interacting with particular students was especially meaningful. In her own style, Barbara Bush captures something that her husband might also have appreciated. She noted, "At Texas A&M the person who asks the questions does so to learn something, not to embarrass the speaker."[3] The policy topics discussed and debated in presentations and conferences interested the president. Card, when he was acting dean, recalls the president asking if he might simply slip into some classes and watch student interaction from the back of the room.[4] Faculty members like Jeff Engel, who searched intensely into his library archives and encouraged him to review past decisions, provided a strong demonstration of the purpose of his presidential library archive.

Bush School Financial Campaign Success. Any organization is affected by its financial resources. The decision to shift the Bush School from a relatively small unit inside the College of Liberal Arts with no permanent faculty of its own to an independent school within the university had enormous budgetary implications. The state of Texas, together with the Texas A&M University System and the university itself, made the core commitments that provided basic funding. Nothing would have been possible without that. The amount of state funding remains essential—as it does for every other part of the university. The quid pro quo demands that the Bush School, like those of the other parts of any state university, demonstrate a strong and efficient return on the state's investment.

The inescapable fact remains that building excellence—particularly for a new start-up school—requires more financial resources than the state can provide. The Bush School has been exceptionally fortunate to attract the engagement of a substantial network of people who joined in helping to further its mission and vision. Some have been longtime friends and admirers of George and Barbara Bush. Others have been strong alumni who have become intensely engaged with the new school. Still others have been leaders in the local community and elsewhere in Texas who have been attracted to the idea of creating affordable, quality advanced education for those talented individuals wanting careers in public service. They have created student scholarships, speaker programs, research underwriting, and faculty support. In 2016 the Bush School had seventeen faculty endowed chairs, eight professorships, and four fellowships for junior faculty—all from the remarkable, ongoing commitment of this network of individuals who believe in the Bush School purpose: to pursue cutting-edge research on policy problems and to enable students keen on careers in public service to acquire top-flight professional education without incurring major student debt.

The Bush School recognized that its success would critically depend on offering a very high-quality professional education at an affordable price for those seeking public-service careers. In the current market this has been a significant challenge. Many talented students have incurred substantial student-loan debts in acquiring their undergraduate education. No matter how strong their original interest might have been in a public-service career, students who incur significant debt while acquiring an advanced degree find the higher salaries of the private sector compelling. This has been an acute problem for some of the best-known private schools of public and international affairs. The Bush School challenge has been to keep the students' costs down and deliver a top-quality educational preparation, a two-part challenge.

Texas A&M had some real advantages in containing costs. As a university it is recognized as a leader in efficient higher education. Furthermore, its location in a college town rather than a large metropolitan center curbs living expenses for students. The Bush School—with strong help from its network of supporters—seeks to build on these university advantages by providing scholarships for almost every student. Admission to both degree programs remains quite competitive; thus, the Bush School demonstrates that every admitted student is qualified for some financial assistance.

With expanding enrollment and rising student costs, sufficient funds for scholarships becomes an endless challenge. To date, however, the Bush School has done well for a young professional program. Several deans have made the endowment efforts a central part of their work at the school. Key Texas A&M Foundation officers assigned to the Bush School and directors of the Bush Presidential Library Foundation have provided critical help. All these efforts made an unmistakable impact on the evolution of the young Bush School. In 2016 the scholarship endowment exceeded twenty-six million dollars with some additional student support to assist with unpaid internships. The school's institutes and some faculty research grants provide other student support. Nonetheless, the road ahead looks steep unless the robust network of Bush School supporters is expanded.

Providing an excellent professional graduate education means attracting and retaining top-flight faculty. It also means maintaining major research endeavors that tackle critical policy problems. The Bush School has been remarkably successful in securing the resources for endowed faculty chairs as a means of attracting talented faculty. It also has created endowments for rotating professorships for younger faculty who have demonstrated excellence in teaching and research. It is difficult to imagine that a small, young professional school in a college town would have had the success it has enjoyed without this remarkable ability to attract strong faculty. Again, this achievement was made possible by Bush School donors.

Policy-Oriented Research Institutes. The creation of research organizations within the Bush School constitute the fourth "leg" of its success. With strong leadership and funding for collective, ongoing research endeavors, the institutes mobilize the faculty and students to investigate major problems facing our country and world.

The individuals who conceptualized the original plan for the creation of the Bush School recognized the critical role of research centers. The funding arrangement for those research units as initially conceptualized faltered. Nonetheless, the central mission of policy-focused research remained a core part of the school. During the first two decades the Bush School has gradually constructed three research institutes—the Institute for Science, Technology, and Public Policy; the Scowcroft Institute of International Affairs; and the Mosbacher Institute for Trade, Economics, and Public Policy. Each has become a vital element of the Bush School and a key to enabling its mission of promoting policy-oriented research.

Research grants, financial gifts, and endowment support have been essential for each institute. At this time their collective endowment is more than $7.5 million, which is relatively small and is uneven across the three units, but such funding has made them possible. Individuals and teams of faculty regularly compete and succeed in obtaining research grants and contracts for specific projects. All three institutes depend on such grant seeking by their participating faculty. However, core endowments and gifts have made their continued existence possible. All three of the Bush School's institutes use endowments and financial underwriting to serve as a bridge between individual grants and to initiate new ventures. For young faculty beginning their careers, the research funding that the institutes have been able to provide has been essential for encouraging them to address policy issues.

In short, the school's research institutes have enabled faculty to address some of the toughest issues facing our society and world. How can we sustain the water resources we will need in the decades ahead? How can we minimize the risk of global pandemics? How can we systematically enhance the quality of public education for all young people at a sustainable cost? Those are representative of the major questions faculty researchers in the Bush School institutes are investigating. Encouraging and enabling faculty and their students to explore such questions—and disseminate their findings—make the institutes key elements of the Bush School.

Notes

Chapter 1

1. See Robert L. Walker, "Michel T. Halbouty," in *Footprints in Aggieland: Memoirs of a Veteran Fundraiser* (College Station: Texas A&M University Press, 2015), 33–35.

2. Michel T. Halbouty, memorandum to Mary Stewart, Presidential Library at Texas A&M University, December 8, 1988, Bush Presidential Library Correspondence.

3. Ibid.

4. George H. W. Bush to Michel T. Halbouty, December 14, 1988, Bush Presidential Library Correspondence.

5. Daniel Fallon, interview with Charles Hermann, May 22, 2015.

6. George Edwards, memorandum to Bryan Jones, head, Political Science Department, Texas A&M University, January 18, 1989; and Bryan Jones to Daniel Fallon, January 19, 1989.

7. Interview with Shirley Joiner, June 14, 2015; and undated "Chronology" of the activities leading to securing the Bush President Library, Cushing Memorial Library and Archives, Texas A&M University.

8. "A Preliminary Proposal for George Bush Presidential Library & Museum, Texas A&M University," undated, presented to President Bush May 12, 1989, 11.

9. George Bush and Brent Scowcroft, *A World Transformed* (New York: Knopf, 1998), 53.

10. Interview with Bookman Peters, December 4, 2015.

11. James W. Cicconi, "Vision & Leadership of George Bush in Creation of the Bush Presidential Library Center," John Miles Rowlett Lecture Series, Bush Presidential Conference Center, February 10, 1998.

12. Kenneth Lay, letter to President George H. W. Bush, October 5, 1989, 1–2, Bush Presidential Library.

13. George H. W. Bush, note to James Cicconi, October 12, 1989, Bush Presidential Library Correspondence.

14. James Cicconi, memorandum to President Bush, October 13, 1989, Bush Presidential Library Correspondence.

15. "Dueling Libraries," Bob Tutt, *Houston Chronicle*, February 28, 1989, 1. The story quotes a *Newsweek* article indicating that Bush wanted his library in Texas. He had expressed the same idea earlier to Perry Adkisson, Texas A&M chancellor, but that preference had not been conveyed publicly until later. Bush, letter to Perry Adkisson, February 28, 1989, Bush Presidential Library Correspondence.

16. Material prepared for Don W. Wilson, Texas A&M University, April 20, 1990.

17. Don W. Wilson, memorandum to James W. Cicconi, meeting with Texas A&M officials, November 1, 1989. Cicconi passed the memo to President Bush, who wrote his long-hand response to Wilson, November 2, 1989, Bush Presidential Library Correspondence.

18. "Proposal for Location of George Bush Library and Museum, Texas A&M University," January 18, 1990, Cushing Memorial Library and Archives, Texas A&M University.

19. Ibid., 12.

20. "Proposal to Establish a School of Government and Public Service at Texas A&M University," in "Proposal for Location of George Bush Library and Museum, Texas A&M University," January 18, 1990, 30–48.

21. Ibid., 40, 43.

22. James W. Cicconi, "Meeting to Discuss the Presidential Library," White House, memorandum, January 17, 1990, Bush Presidential Library.

23. Cicconi, "Vision & Leadership," 11.

24. Greater Houston Partnership, letter to William McKenzie, March 2, 1990, Bush Presidential Library Correspondence.

25. James Cicconi to President Bush, accompanying letter from Greater Houston Partnership to William McKenzie, chairman, Texas A&M University System Board of Regents, March 9, 1990, Bush Presidential Library Correspondence.

26. Material prepared for Don W. Wilson.

27. Don W. Wilson, archivist of the United States, letter to the president of the United States, July 17, 1990, 1, Bush Presidential Library Correspondence.

28. Jane Ely, "Bush Could End Library Debate," *Houston Chronicle*, July 14, 1990, 2.

29. Dan Carney, "Bush Library Proposal Showcases New Computer Imaging Technology," *Houston Chronicle*, July 16, 1990, B1.

30. Todd Ackerman, "Bush Library Fight Turns into Subtle Game of Chess," *Houston Chronicle*, July 22, 1990, C5.

31. Todd Ackerman, "Library Recommendation on the President's Desk," *Houston Chronicle*, September 22, 1990, A29.

32. "Bush Library" (editorial), *Houston Chronicle*, April 2, 1991, C10.

33. Delia M. Rios, "Peering inside the Presidency," *Dallas Morning News*, April 16, 1991, C1.

34. Minutes, Steering Committee, Bush Presidential Library, Texas A&M University, May 2, 1991, Bush Presidential Library photocopy.

35. Todd Ackerman, "A&M Ready to Get to Work on Library," *Houston Chronicle*, May 4, 1991, A29.

36. President George H. W. Bush, letter to Ross D. Margraves Jr., May 3, 1991, 1, Bush Presidential Library Correspondence.

37. Karen Roebuck and John Gravois, "Texas A&M Wins Bush Library Sweepstakes," *Houston Post*, May 4, 1991, 1.

38. Jane Ely, "OK, Aggies, Now You Can Gloat," *Houston Chronicle*, May 5, 1991, 2.

39. President George H. W. Bush, letter to James Cicconi, August 28, 1991, Bush Presidential Library Correspondence.

40. Shirley A. Joiner, address to Delta Kappa Gamma, February 2, 1999.

41. Jon Meacham, *Destiny and Power* (New York: Random House, 2015), 466.

Chapter 2

1. Don W. Wilson, letter to William A. McKenzie, November 20, 1990, Bush Presidential Library Correspondence.

2. Rios, "Peering inside the Presidency."

3. Center for Public Leadership Studies Program Review, College of Liberal Arts, Texas A&M University, September 6, 1995.

4. Minutes, Steering Committee, 1.

5. Roebuck and Gravois, "Texas A&M Wins Bush Library Sweepstakes," 1.

6. Don W. Wilson, interview with Charles Hermann, April 19, 2016.

7. Texas A&M University press release, October 21, 1996.

8. Don Wilson, memorandum to William McKenzie, November 20, 1990; Don Wilson, memorandum to President Bush through James Cicconi, December 1, 1992, Bush Presidential Library Correspondence. Handwritten note at top of memorandum to President Bush: "Disc'd verbally not given to POTUS."

9. Perry L. Adkisson, memorandum to Robert Smith, November 30, 1992, Bush Presidential Library Correspondence.

10. Charles A. Johnson, personal letter to James Cicconi, July 28, 1994.

Chapter 3

1. Kenneth Ashworth, *Caught between the Dog and the Fireplug, or How to Survive Public Service* (Washington, DC: Georgetown University Press, 2001).

2. See "Ed F. Kruse, Class of 1949 and Howard Kruse, Class of 1952," in Walker, *Footprints in Aggieland*. The Kruse brothers later gave the Bush School a second endowed chair. They overwhelmed us by calling it the School's Founders Chair in honor of George Edwards, Arnie Vedlitz, and Charles Hermann.

3. See "Sara and John H. Lindsey, Class of 1944," in Walker, *Footprints in Aggieland*.

4. I (Charles Hermann) have the distinct honor of becoming the first Bush School faculty member to hold the Brent Scowcroft Chair in International Policy Studies. Barbara Bush noted that she and her husband were surprised when they learned of his endowment gift. She wrote: "That really touched us both as we are so grateful for his help in so many other ways." Barbara Bush, *Reflections: Life after the White House* (New York: Scribner, 2003), 273.

5. Ray Bowen, interview with Charles Hermann, March 4, 2016.

6. Donald E. Powell, a graduate of Texas A&M and successful Texas banker, served as chairman of the US Federal Deposit Insurance Corporation during the

latter part of the administration of George H. W. Bush. He has maintained a strong interest in the Bush School, linking the leadership of the university and his dedicated commitment to the Bush family.

7. George C. Edwards, "Center for Presidential Studies," in *The Bush School Status Report*, December 9, 1999, draft text of proposed brochure on Bush School, fall 1999.

8. Arnold Vedlitz, "Center for Public Leadership Studies," in *The Bush School Status Report*, December 9, 1999; and *Center for Public Leadership Annual Report, 1997–1998*.

9. Charles Hermann, e-mail to Ray Bowen, January 19, 1999.

10. Interview with Ray Bowen, March 4, 2016.

11. The Texas A&M University response to Wilson was developed in the document "The Development of Government and Public Service Program at Texas A&M: A Concept Paper," requested by William Mobley in a memorandum to Dean Gage, provost and vice president for academic affairs, December 3, 1990, Records of the Office of the President, Texas A&M University.

Chapter 4

1. Stuart Hutson, "Faculty Senate Oks Proposal for Independent Bush School," *The Battalion*, June 13, 1999, 1.

2. John Kirsch, "Redirected Course," *The Eagle*, January 30, 2000, 1.

3. Robert Gates, interview with the authors, February 23, 2016.

4. The material in this paragraph draws on the authors' interview with Robert Gates.

5. John LeBAS, "A&M Announces Chair Endowed in Recognition of Bullock," *The Eagle*, November 30, 2000, 1.

6. "Center for Public Leadership Studies."

7. This narrative account of the Center for Presidential Studies depends primarily on material prepared for the authors in the fall of 2015 by George C. Edwards, "Center for Presidential Studies and Research," and on interviews with Edwards.

8. Recall that the Master of Public Service and Administration at that time included international affairs as one of its areas of concentration. The Certificate in Advanced International Affairs used those existing courses as part of the arrangement for students taking the certificate on campus.

Chapter 5

1. The Bush School relationship with Ed and Howard Kruse and Blue Bell Creameries is described by Karla Strone, "Milk, Sugar, Honesty, Fairness," *A Noble Calling*, 2003 Annual Magazine of the Bush School of Government and Public Service, 8.

2. John LeBAS, "Bush School Dean Anticipates Success," *The Eagle*, December 1, 2001, 1.

3. This section draws on interviews by Charles Hermann with Joe Cerami and with Holly Kasperbauer, the current director of the Bush School Leadership Pro-

gram. It also draws on Christopher Causey, *The Bush School Public Service Leadership Program: Report on the Program Development, 2002–2008* (March 2009).

4. Joe Cerami, interview with Charles Hermann.

5. "Faculty Highlight," *A Noble Calling*, 2002 Annual Magazine of the Bush School of Government and Public Service, 3.

6. This section draws on an interview with William West and the "NASPAA Self-Study for Accreditation," Section 1.1.1 A, "Background and History" (2006), 2–3.

7. See Charles F. Hermann and Maurice A. East, "Assessing a Mediated Learning Joint Television Course: Foreign Policy Problem Management in the First Bush Administration," *International Studies Perspectives* 6 (2005): 462–476.

8. At the time of the International Affairs Self-Study in 2008, the program had three affiliated faculty teaching one course each from geography, agricultural economics, and management (all full professors). Two of the three continue in 2015–2016. The program also had five career practitioners (two with PhDs). Of the ten full-time PhDs on the international affairs faculty seven were from political science, two from economics, and one from history. Two others had law degrees. "Five-Year Self-Study of the Graduate Master's Program in International Affairs," prepared for the provost and academic vice president, Texas A&M University, December 2008.

9. "Q & A with President George H. W. Bush and Senator Edward M. Kennedy," *A Noble Calling*, 2003 Annual Magazine of the Bush School of Government and Public Service, 7.

10. One of this book's authors, Sally Dee Wade, was the writing lecturer at the Bush School from January 2006 through May 2014.

11. Robert Gates, interview with the authors.

12. Robert M. Gates, *A Passion for Leadership* (New York: Knopf, 2016), 19.

Chapter 6

1. Sam Kirkpatrick, interview with Charles Hermann.

2. Jeffrey A. Engel, ed., *The China Diary of George H. W. Bush* (Princeton, NJ: Princeton University Press, 2008).

3. The title of Engel's forthcoming book with Houghton Mifflin Harcourt is *When the World Seemed New: George H. W. Bush and the Surprisingly Peaceful End of the World War*. The volumes he edited from Scowcroft conferences are *The Fall of the Berlin Wall* (New York: Oxford University Press, 2009) and *Into the Desert* (New York: Oxford University Press, 2013).

4. Initially, Richard Ewing, vice president for research at Texas A&M, had supported McIntyre's leadership of a university-wide Integrative Center of Homeland Security. Support for that effort gradually faded after Ewing's sudden death. Interview with David McIntyre.

5. Although retaining the acronym NASPAA, that professional society now uses the more inclusive full name Network of Schools of Public Policy, Affairs, and Administration.

6. See "What Is a Nonprofit Organization?," Independent Sector, 2017, https://www.independentsector.org/nonprofit.
7. "Emerging Leaders Program," *Bush School News*, fall 2010, 1.
8. Matthew Upton, text message to Charles Hermann, May 24, 2016.
9. As described in the interview with the current Leadership Program director, Holly Kasperbauer.
10. Now called the Bush School Advisory Board, this group had added several new members, including Jean Becker, chief of staff for President George H. W. Bush; Jan Felts Bullock; Robert H. Allen of the Challenge Investment Partners; and Drayton McLane Jr. of the McLane Group. Condoleezza Rice had resigned after becoming secretary of state.
11. Ranking is among the public universities offering a master's degree in public policy or administration as reported in the *Bush School News*, summer 2008, 3.
12. Richard A. Chilcoat died in March 2010 and was buried in Arlington National Cemetery. As dean of the Bush School, Chilcoat regularly declared the school was quickly closing in on a goal of educational excellence. To illustrate his point, he tirelessly employed a visual that displayed a rapidly rising curve with major Bush School achievements denoted along a time line in the upward sweep toward excellence. Although colleagues repeatedly suggested to him many indicators of academic achievement, Chilcoat often chose to use the *US News & World Report*'s rankings of schools of public affairs as his preferred marker of excellence. Accordingly, it must have been with a real sense of achievement that he could report that the Bush School had made the top twenty-five schools on that rating a few months before his retirement.
13. In 2008, while Crocker was serving as US ambassador to Iraq, he had repeated interactions with Bush School faculty member Larry Napper, who was serving as the co-leader of the Iraq Governance Assessment Team. When Crocker retired, Napper invited him to speak at the Bush School.
14. Ryan Crocker, interview with Charles Hermann.

Chapter 7

1. Sam Kirkpatrick, interview with Charles Hermann.
2. David B. Jones became the chief executive officer of the George Bush Library Foundation in May 2016.
3. Sam Kirkpatrick and Susan Robertson, Bush School director of communications and external relations, interviews with Charles Hermann.
4. As an instructor in the Bush School, MacNamee replaced Sara A. Daley, who returned to the intelligence community.
5. Ryan Crocker, interview with Charles Hermann.
6. Andrew Card, interview with Charles Hermann.
7. Ryan Crocker, interview with Charles Hermann.
8. Mary Hein, administrative assistant to the dean, interview with Charles Hermann.

9. To the full-time residential student enrollment in the Bush School must be added the much larger number of graduate-level students enrolled online in the Extended Education Program.

10. Matthew Upton, interview with Charles Hermann.

11. Member of NASPAA accreditation team, letter to William West, April 18, 2014.

12. Daniel Maliniak, Susan Peterson, Ryan Powers, and Michael J. Tierney, "The Best International Relations Schools in the World," *Foreign Policy*, January–February 2015.

13. At Texas A&M, "institutes" seek to engage research across multiple university departments and require approval by the regents, whereas "centers" tend to focus on the research within one department.

14. *Institute for Science, Technology, and Public Policy Five-Year Review, September 1, 2006 to August 31, 2011*, prepared for the Office of the Vice President for Research, Texas A&M University.

15. *Bush School News*, fall 2013, 3.

16. In 2011 ISTPP reported: "Over the last five years, Institute researchers have produced approximately 39 peer-reviewed journal articles and 2 books." *Institute for Science Technology and Public Policy Five-Year Review, September 1, 2006 to August 31, 2011*, 7.

17. *Bush School News*, fall 2014, 2, 8.

18. The Scowcroft Institute awarded more than ninety-six thousand dollars in faculty grants between 2008 and 2015 and eighty thousand dollars in student capstone support. These totals do not include funding for junior faculty book preparation seminars or support for conferences and speakers undertaken with individual faculty. *Scowcroft Institute of International Affairs Five-Year Review and Evaluation, November 10, 2007–August 31, 2012*, report to the vice president for research, Texas A&M University; *Scowcroft Institute of International Affairs Three-Year Report to Dean of the Bush School, 2013–2016*.

19. Under the released time program, the Scowcroft Institute provides funding for the Bush School to hire a temporary teaching replacement for a junior faculty member for a semester, thereby allowing the tenure-seeking faculty member to concentrate during that time on completion of research. As of April 2016, the Scowcroft Institute has spent $134,246 to help junior faculty. *Scowcroft Institute of International Affairs Three-Year Report*, 9.

20. Domonic A. Bearfield and Ann O'M. Bowman, "Texas Cities in the Era of Government Transparency," *The Takeaway* 5, no. 4 (2014), http://bush.tamu.edu/mosbacher/takeaway/Takeaway%20-%20Era%20of%20Transparency.pdf.

21. Lori Taylor, interview with Charles Hermann.

22. B. Bush, *Reflections*, 201.

23. Information on the current state of the Bush School endowment has been provided by Derek Dictson, a graduate of the Bush School in 2000 and now a member of the Texas A&M Foundation assigned as director of development to the Bush School.

Chapter 8

1. *Seats* refer to the number of students in each class. A student may be enrolled in more than one class.

Chapter 9

1. "South Sudan Crisis," World Vision, 2016, www.wvi.org/south-sudan-crisis.
2. Jessica Bousquette, Jerry Kenney, and John Eldebo, *Fear and Want: Children Living in Crisis in South Sudan*, World Vision International, 2014, http://www.wvi.org/south-sudan/publication/fear-and-want-children-living-crisis-south-sudan.
3. "Why Thieves Love America's Health-Care System," *The Economist*, May 31, 2014, http://www.economist.com/news/united-states/21603078-why-thieves-love-americas-health-care-system.
4. "Hill-Rom Company, Inc. Will Pay $41.8 Million to Resolve Federal Health Care Fraud Investigation," The FBI Columbia Division, press release, September 27, 2011, https://archives.fbi.gov/archives/columbia/press-releases/2011/hill-rom-company-inc.-will-pay-41.8-million-to-resolve-federal-health-care-fraud-investigation.
5. "Hill-Rom Company, Inc. Will Pay $41.8 Million to Resolve Federal Health Care Fraud Investigation," United States Attorney's Office, Eastern District of Tennessee, press release, September 27, 2011, https://www.justice.gov/archive/usao/tne/news/2011/September/092711A%20Hill-Rom%20Settlement.html.
6. "Saudi Official Blames Riyadh Attacks on al Qaeda," CNN News International Edition, November 9, 2003, http://www.cnn.com/2003/US/11/08/saudi.explosion/.

Postscript

1. Several studies of professional schools of public and international affairs were located in the preparation of this manuscript, including Lynn Cooksey, "The Development of a Public Institution: The LBJ School of Public Affairs," master's thesis, Lyndon B. Johnson School of Public Affairs, University of Texas, 1977; Robert B. Stewart, *History of the Fletcher School of Law and Diplomacy* (Fletcher School of Law and Diplomacy, 1975, photocopy); Seth P. Tillman, *Georgetown's School of Foreign Service: The First 75 Years*, (Washington, DC: Edmund A. Walsh School of Foreign Service,1994).
2. Michel O'Quinn, graduate assistant to the university chancellor at the time and now vice president for government relations in the Texas A&M University System, interview with Sally Dee Wade and Charles Hermann.
3. B. Bush, *Reflections*, 202.
4. Andrew Card, interview with Charles Hermann.

Index

Abell-Hanger Foundation, 41, 43
AbouAsi, Khaldoun, 99
Academic Planning Committee, 6–7, 9, 20
Adkisson, Perry, 2, 4, 9, 14, 29, 181n9
Advisory Board, Bush School, 45–46, 49, 88. *See also* Board of Counselors, Bush School
Afghanistan, 91–92, 94–95, 128–29, 137–38
Agricultural Economics, Department of, 26, 39t, 183n8
Agricultural Education, Department of, 26, 38t, 64
Agriculture, College of, 21, 24
Alexander, Corby, 30, 50, 125–27
Allen, Robert, 43, 73, 184n10
Alpern, Sara, 38t
American Political Science Association, 88, 108, 115
American Red Cross, 129, 136, 150, 154
Anderson, James E., 38t
Anderson, Richard Kenneth, 38t
Andisha, Nasir, 128–30
Annenberg Presidential Conference Center, 14–15, 43, 45, 61, 74
Arab Spring, 95, 154
architectural subcommittee, 6, 9
Army fellows-in-residence, 43, 109
Arthur, Winfred, 23, 28
Ashworth, Emily, 143
Ashworth, Kenneth, 36, 38t, 56, 169, 181n1
Association of Professional Schools of International Affairs (APSIA), 96, 102
Aurisch, Klaus, 80
Austin, Texas, 52, 62–63, 70, 149, 162

Bailey, Don W., 109
Baker Hughes, 133–34
Bame, Sherry, 38t
Barbara Bush Foundation for Family Literacy, 113, 141
Barton, Joe, 22
Bearfield, Dominic, 82, 102, 111, 136, 185n20
Becker, Jean, 29, 46, 184n10
Beijing, China, 71, 130, 143–44, 155
Belarus, 151–52
Benson, Jeff, 125, 130–32
Bertelli, Anthony, 67
Beschloss, Michael, 70
Bierman, Leonard, 38t
Bies, Angela, 66, 83, 122, 136
Bin Laden, Osama, 169–70. *See also* terrorism
Blair, Tony, 70
Blue Bell Creameries, 41, 63, 182
Board of Counselors, Bush School, 45, 49. *See also* Advisory Board, Bush School
Board of Regents, Texas A&M University System, 2, 4–5, 10, 13, 20, 52, 110–11, 164, 171
Bob Bullock Chair in Government and Public Policy, 43, 56
Bond, James, 2
Bowen, Ray, 30, 32–33, 40, 42, 44, 46, 49–50, 174, 181n5, 182n9–10
Bowman, Ann, 87–88, 102, 111, 185n20
Brands, H. W. (Bill), 23, 47, 59
Bright, Leonard, 95, 98, 102, 104, 122
Brown, Lisa, 118

Brown, William A., 82, 103, 118
Bryan, Texas, 2, 10, 13–14
Bullock, Bob, 43, 56, 174
Bullock, Jan, 56, 184n10
Bullock, Justin, 100, 103
Bush School of Government and Public Service: as unit of university, 19, 24, 26, 29, 50–52, 54–55, 57, 76, 88, 93–94, 110, 173–74; construction of, 18, 28, 60–61; in proposal for presidential library, 7–8, 10, 15, 171–73
Bush, Barbara, 9, 14–16, 29–30, 41, 43–46, 61, 72, 88, 93, 112, 175, 181n4, 185n22, 186n3
Bush Congressional Scholarships, 22–23
Bush, George H. W.: bust of, 30, 41; involvement with school, 7, 8, 13, 17–18, 29–30, 41, 44–45, 54, 88, 171, 174–75; involvement with students, 30–31, 44–45, 48, 50, 70–72, 87, 144, 168, 174; commencement, 3–4, 6–7, 172. *See also* Barbara Bush; Bush Congressional Fellowships
Bush, George W., 16, 30, 43, 90, 92–93, 148, 174, 184
Bush, Jeb, 43
Bush, Laura, 70
Bush, Neil, 45
bylaws, 19, 23–24, 70–71, 94

Caldera, Louis, 42
Canada, 11, 16, 79, 167
Canion, Rod, 9
capital campaign, 37, 40, 43, 88–89, 90–93, 175–77. *See also* endowment
capstone seminars, 34, 66, 84–87, 109, 118, 138, 147, 161, 185
Card, Andrew, 92–94, 98, 101, 174–175, 186n4
Carter Presidential Library, 172
Castillo, Jasen, 80, 103
Caudle, Sharon, 82
Center for Presidential Studies, 8, 13, 19–22, 38, 41, 54, 57–58, 182
Center for Public Leadership Studies, 9, 16, 19–21, 39, 47, 54–55, 57–58, 64, 107, 126, 181–82
Center on Conflict and Development, 137–38

Central Intelligence Agency, 27, 30, 36, 52–53, 56, 167, 170
Cerami, Joe, 65–66, 69, 116, 129, 182n3, 183n4
Certificate in Advanced International Affairs, 59–60, 68, 81, 83, 116, 118, 130, 182
Certificate in Chinese Studies, 79
Certificate in Homeland Security, 64, 79, 117, 120–21
Certificate in National Security Affairs, 88, 100
Certificate in Nonprofit Management, 83, 117–18, 181
Charlie Rose (television program), 41
Chao, Elaine, 70
Cheney, Lynne, 45
Cheney, Richard, 30
Chilcoat, Richard, 19, 63–66, 68, 71, 73, 75–77, 80, 82, 86–89, 91, 96, 116, 120, 130, 143, 164, 174, 184n12
China. *See* People's Republic of China
Cicconi, James W., 5–7, 9–10, 12–14, 20–21, 28–29, 172–73, 179n11, 179n13–14, 180n17, n22–23, 180n25–181n39, 181n8, n10 (chap. 2)
Cisneros, Marc, 45
Clement, Catherine, 138
Clinton, Bill, 23, 43
Cocanougher, Benton, 89
College Station, Texas: Bush presence in, 4–5, 112, 171, 174; library bid support, 2, 10, 128; living in, 59, 73, 76, 79, 91, 93, 112, 118, 143, 172
commencement address, 3, 4, 7, 171–72
Communications, Department of, 26, 39, 55
congressional scholarships. *See* Bush Congressional Scholarships
ConocoPhillips White House Lecture Series, 111
Conoley, Jane, 18
Cooksey, Lynn, 186n1
Continuing education. *See* Distance Education Program at Bush School. *See also* Certificate in Advanced International Affairs; Certificate in Homeland Security; Certificate in Nonprofit Management

Index

Corps of Cadets, 44, 89, 130, 163–64
Cortes, Kalena, 98, 103
counterterrorism, 64, 92, 119, 169. *See also* terrorism
course concentrations, 34, 67–68, 151
credit hours, 34, 59, 61, 68–69, 80, 116, 118, 122
Crocker, Ryan C., 89–98, 101, 107, 109, 112, 174, 184n13, 14, 184n5, 184n7 (chap. 7)
Crouch, Ben, 16
CRS Sirrine, 6, 9, 14
Cullen Trust, 41
Cummins, Richard L., 38t
Cunningham, Lavern, 27
curriculum, 8, 19, 23–26, 28, 34, 60, 64, 67, 80, 82–83, 98, 121, 124, 144

Dague, Laura, 99, 103
Dangelmayr, Lauren, 125, 133–35, 164–65
Davis, Danny W., 82, 87, 103, 120–21
dean, Bush School, 19, 50–51, 53, 59–60, 63, 73–75, 89–94, 107, 112, 120, 130, 182, 184–85
Dean's Leadership Certificate, 66
dedication, Bush School, 28–30, 97, 126
Deere, Donald, 25, 28, 38t, 47, 49, 51, 110
Desch, Michael, 76–78, 99, 109
development campaign. *See* capital campaign; endowment
Dillard, Joe, 88
Dini Spheris, 91
Distance Education Program, 60, 68, 83, 116–17, 129
Donaldson, Sam, 70
Doolen, Tim, 7
Dorch, Edwina, 87, 122
Douglas, Ronald, 48–50
Drug Enforcement Administration, 153–54
Dunn, Allison, 65
Durant, Robert, 35, 38t, 51, 57

Eagleburger, Lawrence, 69, 168
earthquake, 132, 145, 160
Ebola crisis, 155
Economics, Department of, 25–26, 29, 35, 38–39, 48, 51, 56, 61, 110
Eden, Lorraine, 38t, 48, 60, 103, 116, 143

Education and Human Development, College of, 18, 24
Edwards, George C., III, 3, 7, 9–10, 13, 15–16, 20–22, 38t41–42, 47, 58, 179n6, 182n7 (chap. 3), 182n7 (chap. 4)
Eisenhower Leadership Program, 21
el Hussini, Rola, 80
Elliott School of International Affairs, joint course with, 69
Ely, Jan, 13, 180–181
Edward and Howard Kruse Endowed Chair, 63
Emory University, 172
endowed faculty chairs, 43, 56, 113, 176–77
endowed professorships, 176
endowment, 13, 73, 88, 111, 177–78. *See also* capital campaign
Engel, Jeffery, 76–77, 109, 156, 175, 183n2–3
Engineering, College of, 6, 21, 24
English, Department of, 116
enrollment. *See* student enrollment
Ernst & Young, 134, 166
Evans, Don, 131
executive associate dean, Bush School, 75, 94–95, 100
Executive Master of Public Service and Administration, 98, 115, 118
Extended Education Program, 185n9; *See also* Distance Education Program

Faculty Senate, Texas A&M, 52
Fallon, Daniel, 3, 6, 9–10, 13, 15, 20, 179n5–6
Federal Bureau of Investigation (FBI), 27, 80, 147, 157–59, 186
Federal Emergency Management Agency (FEMA), 121–22, 136, 153–54, 160–62
Ford Presidential Library and School, 6, 172
Foreign Service Officer, 150, 155, 157
foreign language proficiency, 69, 78–79
Fulbright Scholarship, 129

Gallup Organization, 22
Garcia, Sylvia, 150
Garcia, Tony, 45
Gage, Dean, 182n11

Gates, Becky, 53
Gates, Robert M., 45, 51–62, 66, 68, 73–76, 78, 82, 89, 92, 107, 148, 168, 174, 182n3, 183n11–12
Gause, Cynthia, 112
Gause, F. Gregory, III, 94–95, 103, 112
Gawande, Kishore, 69, 100, 129, 138
George Bush Presidential Library: bid by Texas A&M for, 2–4, 9–11, 13, 19, 27, 34, 57; construction and dedication, 14–16, 29, 43; other bids for, 9–12; parachute jump in front of, 44; research in, 76, 109. *See also* George Bush Presidential Library Foundation
George Bush Presidential Library Foundation, 14–15, 19–21, 26, 41, 51, 71, 77, 91, 109, 112–13, 173, 177, 184
George H. W. Bush endowed chair, 67, 99
Georgetown University, 53, 94–95, 99, 110, 181, 186
Geosciences, College of, 24, 48
Geren, Preston, 2–4, 9, 14
Germany, 11, 31, 79, 163, 167
Gesing, Emily, 135–137
Giscard d'Estaing, Valéry, 45
Gorbachev, Mikhail, 4, 69–70
Gottlieb, Jessica, 100, 103
government and political leaders, Texas, 16, 22, 30, 36, 43, 49–50, 60, 131, 148, 175
Graham, Cole Blease, Jr., 94, 102, 104
Gramm, Wendy, 164
Greater Houston Partnership, 10, 12
Greer, John, 6
Greer, Robert, 101
Griffin, James, 38t, 48, 56, 104, 110–111
Gronberg, Timothy, 38t

Halbouty, Michel T., 1–4, 9, 20, 171, 179n1–4
Hancher, Donn, 6
Harvard University, 45–46, 50, 65, 82, 100, 172, 174
Hazel Davis and Robert Kennedy Endowed Chair, 87
Hazelton, Jared, 7
Health and Human Services, Department of, 27, 122, 146, 149

health policy, 21, 108
Hein, Mary, 95, 97, 184n8
Helen and Roy Ryu Chair in Economics and Government, 100
Hermann, Charles (Chuck), 16–19, 23–26, 29, 32–33, 36, 38t, 40–43, 46, 49–51, 55–56, 59–60, 65, 68–69, 75, 77, 94, 104, 113, 116–17, 143, 168, 174, 179n5, 181n2
Hewlett Foundation, 57
Hilderbrand, Mary, 100
Hill, Kim, 9, 23–24, 38t
Hill, Larry, 7
Hines, Charles, 45
History, Department of, 7, 26, 38
Hoadley, Irene, 7
Holland, Lee Ann, 51
Holloway, John, 119–20
Holtzapple, Carol, 141
Holzweiss, Peggy, 109
Homeland Security, Department of, 79, 82, 104, 118, 120
Hope for New York, 140–42
Huang, Reyko, 99, 104
Hudson, Valerie, 99, 104
Hugill, Peter, 38t
hurricanes, 121, 126, 140–41, 154, 160–62
Hutchison, Kay Bailey, 148

India, 79, 111, 129
Institute for Science, Technology, and Public Policy (ISTPP), 58, 60, 100, 107–10, 185n13–14, 185n16
Internal Revenue Service (IRS), 165–66
International Affairs, Department of, 94, 101, 119
international affairs, master's degree in, 29, 48, 51, 59–60, 68–69, 78
internships, 34, 61, 65, 80, 111, 131, 133, 136, 138, 143–44, 148, 150–51, 158, 160–61, 165–66, 168, 177
interview weekend, 33, 97, 136, 174
Iran, 95, 99, 103, 106
Iraq, 89, 92, 95, 138, 163–64, 184
Isett, Kim, 67

J. P. Morgan, 143–44
Japan, 11, 131–32, 167
Jenkins-Smith, Hank, 57, 66–67, 87

Jeremiah, David, 29, 130, 131
Joe R. and Teresa Lozano Long Endowed Chair, 57, 87
Johnson, Charles A., 9, 16, 29, 181
Johnson, Fredrick (Rick), 18–19, 25, 29, 51
Joiner, Shirley, 3, 14, 179n7, 186n40
Jones, David B., 91, 184n2
Jones, Shirley, 2, 7
Jones, Woodrow, 16–18, 23
Jones, Bryan, 3, 7, 9, 15–16, 20, 179
Jopling, Jenny, 117
Jordan, George and Julia, 22, 41
Journalism, Department of, 7

Kaplan, Howard, 50
Kasich, John, 82
Kasperbauer, Holly, 85, 182n3, 184n9
Kennedy School, 45–46, 60, 65, 82, 172, 174
Kennedy, Edward, 71
Kennedy, Robert, 42, 87
Kennebunkport, Maine, 5–6, 14, 44–46, 51, 88, 174
Kenny, Meghan and Jerry, 125, 137–40
Kerr, Deborah, 36–37, 38t, 56, 122
Kerrey, Robert, 70
King Foundation, 41
Kirkpatrick, Sam A., 75–76, 88, 90, 94, 183–84
Kissinger, Henry, 143
Kluge, Alexandra, 31
Kollaer, Jim, 12
Korea, 79, 125, 132, 161
Korean Foundation, 41
Kruse, Edward, 41, 181n2, 182n1
Kruse, Evelyn, 41
Kruse, Howard, 41, 181n2, 182n1
Kruse, Verlin, 41
Kuan Yew, Lee, 45
Kuwait, 77, 89
Kvanvig, Johnathan J., 39t

Lahey, Joanna, 82, 104
Larson, Esther, 125, 140–42
law enforcement, 116, 129, 146
Lawrence Livermore National Laboratory, 88, 100
Lay, Kenneth, 5–6, 9, 13, 179n12

Layne, Christopher, 78, 104
Leadership Program, 21, 28, 57, 64, 66, 84–85, 101, 184
leadership skills, 28, 34–35, 65, 132, 137
Leggett, John, 42
Leighley, Jan E., 39t
Liang, Lisa, 71, 130, 143–45
Liberal Arts, College of, 3, 16–17, 21, 26, 37, 39, 40, 46, 48, 54–55, 57, 59, 66, 171, 173, 175, 181
Library Steering Committee, 2–3, 6–7, 9–11, 180–81
Lindsey, John, 2, 30, 40–42, 81, 94, 181n3
Lindsey, Sara, 30, 41–42, 81, 181n3
Linquist, Eric, 108
Liu, Xinsheng, 104, 108
logo, Bush School, 19
Lovett, Lyle, 31
Lu, Xiaobo, 99
Lyndon B. Johnson School of Public Affairs, 36, 62, 72, 109, 168, 186
LBJ Presidential Library, 172
Lynn, Lawrence, Jr., 66–67, 87

MacArthur, Douglas, 164
MacNamee, Richard, 104, 184
MacNeil, Robert, 45
Madrid, Antonio, 80
Maffei, Tony, 146–147
Management, Department of, 26, 38–39
Manhattan Construction Company, 15
Margraves, Ross D., 13, 20, 180n36
Master of Public Service and Administration (MPSA), 8, 26, 48, 56, 60, 62, 67, 69, 80–82, 84, 87, 93–94, 98–99, 101–102, 122, 125, 148, 160, 182
Master's Program in International Affairs (MPIA), 55, 59–60, 68–70, 75, 79–81, 85, 88, 93, 99–100, 102, 109, 116, 120, 125, 183
Mays School of Business, 7, 21, 24, 26, 34, 48, 89
McClure, Fred, 32–33
McCullough, David, 70
McIntyre, David, 79, 104, 117, 120, 183
McKenzie, William, 2, 9, 180n24, 181n1, 181n8
McLane, Drayton, 91, 111, 184n10

Medhurst, Martin, 9, 36, 47, 59
Medicaid, 103, 146
Medicare, 48, 146–47
Meier, Ken, 48
Mellon, Marc, 30
Menchaca, Adriana, 7
Merget, Astrid, 8
Mexico, 45, 48, 68, 101, 106, 167
Meyer, Kathryn, 97
mission statement, Bush School, 23, 25
Mjelde, James W., 39t
Mobley, William, 2–3, 6, 9, 14–15, 182
Moon, M. Jae, 67
Morales, Daniel, 148
Mosbacher Institute for Trade, Economics, and Public Policy, 107, 110–11, 177
Mosbacher, Robert, 48, 107, 110–11
Moynihan, Donald, 67
Mu, Ren, 80, 138
Muller, Catherine, 125, 150–53
Muller, Frank, 91
Muller, Lonny, 151
Mulroney, Brian, 16, 45
Mumpower, Jeryl, 87, 101, 105

Napoli, Roman, 125, 153
Napper, Larry C., 77–78, 92, 94, 109, 129, 184n13
National Association of Schools of Public Affairs and Administration (NASPAA), 8, 80, 96, 101, 183n5 (chap. 5), 185n11
National Defense University, 63, 120
National Science Foundation, 47, 101, 195
National Security Council, 53, 113
Natsios, Andrew, 94–95, 99, 105, 110, 154
Neilson, William, 23, 39t
New York, 64, 140–42, 159, 179, 181, 183
Newman, Louis, 2, 10
nongovernmental organizations, 97, 99, 122
nonprofit management, 82–84, 99, 101, 118, 122, 124–25, 141
nonprofit organizations, 25, 27, 37, 66, 83, 85, 123–24, 142
Norman Borlaug Institute for International Agriculture, 137–38
Norris, William, 99, 105

North American Free Trade Agreement (NAFTA), 48, 60, 68, 110
Nuclear Engineering, Department of, 48, 88
Nye, Earl, 165
Nye, Joseph, 65

Obama, Barack, 91–92, 154
Olson, James, 36, 39t, 48, 56, 68–69, 72, 80, 105, 116–17, 119, 129, 153, 168, 170
Olson, Meredith, 36
O'Quinn, Michael, 2, 186n2
Osmania University, 129

Paarlberg, Laurie, 99
Pakistan, 89, 129, 157
Palestinian, 154
Pan American Health Organization, 160
Pavelka, Lindsey, 65, 85
Peace Corps, 137
Pennsylvania State University, 65
People's Republic of China, 69, 71, 77, 79–80, 99, 104–105, 111, 119, 130, 143–45, 183n2
Persian Gulf War, 15, 69
Peters, Bookman, 2, 10, 179n10
Petraeus, David, 89, 92
Philosophy, Department of, 26, 39
Pichanick, Brandon, 155
Pillsbury, Edmond, 2
Points of Light Foundation, 113
Poland, 70, 156–57
Political Science, Department of: faculty appointments, 7, 16, 23–25, 38–39t, 51, 55–56, 76; link to Bush School, 3, 20, 22, 25–26, 29, 34–35, 48, 54, 57, 59, 66; public administration degree, 23–24, 34, 60–61, 173
Poole, Scott, 23, 39t, 55–56
Popadiuk, Roman, 51, 77
Porter, Roger, 45
Portney, Kent, 104, 108
postdoctoral fellows, 110
Powell, Donald, 40, 45, 49, 52, 181n6
practitioners as faculty, 37, 57, 80, 148, 183
Prechel, Harland, 23, 39t
president, Texas A&M University, 2, 40, 42, 44, 73–74, 174

presidential libraries, 7, 15
Presidential Studies Quarterly, 47, 58–59
Princeton University, 54–55, 100, 173, 183n2
prospective employers, conference with, 27
Psychology, Department of, 28, 35
public administration, 8, 23–25, 35–37, 49, 56, 61, 66, 84, 129
Public Health, School of, 24, 34
Public Service Leadership Program (PSLP). *See* Leadership Program
Public Service Organization, 28, 47, 72, 136, 141
public service, 1, 3, 4, 5, 7, 9, 11, 12, 14, 15, 16, 17, 18, 20, 22, 47, 53, 59, 77, 99, 106, 110, 131, 168, 172, 173, 180n20, 181n1 (chap. 3), 182n11, 182n8 (chap. 4), 182n1(chap. 5), 183n3, 183n5
Public Service and Administration, Department of, 94–95, 98, 101

Reagan Presidential Library, 11, 172
recruiting students, 19, 22, 28, 33, 68, 95, 97, 116, 118
Reeves, Kimberly, 97
Reimer, Dennis, 42
Reinhardt, Gina, 82
Rektorik, Jerome, 91
Rholes, Steve, 12
Rice University, 5–7, 9–11, 13, 56, 165
Rice, Condoleezza, 45, 50, 70, 184n10
Rice, Mitchell, 35, 39t
Robert H. and Judy Ley Allen Building, 43, 73–74
Robert M. Gates Chair, 76, 78
Robertson Foundation for Government, 97
Robertson, Raymond, 100, 105, 111
Robertson, Susan, 184n3
Robinson, Scott, 108
Rodiek, John, 6
Roper, William, 45
Ross, Andrew, 100, 105
Roussel, Peter, 7
Rozell, Griffin, 125, 155–57

Sabino, Michele, 37, 39t
Sandia National Laboratories, 100

Saudi Arabia, 159, 186n6 (chap. 9)
Savings, Thomas, 48
Schlemeyer, Lynn, 46
scholarships, 91, 22–23, 97, 176. *See also* Bush Congressional Scholarships; scholarship fund
scholarship fund, 22, 41, 113
Schuessler, John, 101, 105
Schultz, Charles, 7
Scowcroft Chair in International Policy Studies, 56, 181n3 (chap. 3)
Scowcroft Group, 158
Scowcroft Institute of International Affairs, 77–78, 94–95, 99, 107–11, 177, 185
Scowcroft, Brent, 41, 45, 56, 69, 77, 89, 158, 179n9, 181n18–19
Sellars, Emily, 101, 106
Shi, Lu, 108
Shifrinson, Joshua, 100, 105–106
Sievert, Ronald, 79–80, 106, 119
Silva, Carol, 57
Simon, Paul, 30
Simpson, Alan, 46
Small, Nancy, 68, 116–17
Smith, Brian, 121–22
Smith, Robert, 7, 181n9
Snider, Erin, 100, 106
Sociology, Department of, 17, 23, 50, 66
Southern Political Science Association, 88
Soviet Union, 77
Stallings, Gene, 164
Stanford University, 11, 45, 50, 70, 99–100, 103, 172
State, Department of, 125, 150, 153, 155
state legislature, Texas, 49–50
Stearns, Richard, 138
Stenholm, Charlie, 131
Stewart, Bill, 6
Stewart, Mary, 179n2
Stockinger, Murray, 157–160
Streibich, Ron, 40, 42
student enrollment, 28, 30, 46, 55, 60–61, 66, 74, 81–83, 88, 96–98, 101, 103, 113, 116–18, 122, 125, 174, 176, 185n9
student government, Texas A&M, 11, 47, 72
study abroad, 79, 155, 158
Stuckey, River Burton, 125, 160–62
Sununu, John, 4, 9

Tabaar, Mohammad, 99, 106
Tarrance, Lance, 22
Taylor, Lori L., 67, 106, 111–12, 122, 185n21
Tebeaux, Elizabeth, 116
terrorism, 71, 79, 157, 159, 169. *See also* counterterrorism
Texas A&M AgriLife Extension Service, 108
Texas A&M Engineering Extension Service, 47, 108
Texas A&M Foundation, 40, 43, 91, 162, 165, 175, 185n23
Texas A&M Health Science Center, 108
Texas Agricultural Experiment Station, 47
Texas Higher Education Coordinating Board, 25, 36, 52, 64
Texas Natural Resources Conservation Commission, 57
Texas Sea Grant Program, 108
Texas Southern University, 10
Texas Tech University, 5, 6
Texas Transportation Institute, 47, 108
Thatcher, Margaret, 168
Thompson, Senfronia, 150
Thornton, Gabriela Marin, 80, 106, 138
transfer pricing, 103, 133–34, 165–66
Tucker, Harvey, 7, 9

US Agency for International Development (USAID), 94, 153–55
US Army, 42, 45, 63, 65, 79, 82, 163–64
US Army War College, 63, 65, 109, 119
US Congress, 15, 22–23, 27, 41, 113, 149, 155, 169
US Environmental Protection Agency, 57, 108
US Foreign Service, 77, 89
US House of Representatives, 22, 31
US Navy, 119, 125, 130–32
United Nations, 138–39, 144
United Way of Houston, 135–37
University of Houston, 5–7, 9–11, 13, 130
University of Texas Health Science Center, 10
Upton, Matt, 84, 95, 97, 184n8, 185n10
Uzbekistan, 86, 157

Van Riper, Paul, 23–24, 39t
Vandiver, Frank, 42
Varghese, Adel, 80
Vedlitz, Arnold (Arnie), 9, 16, 20–21, 39t, 42–43, 47, 55–58, 94–95, 100, 106–108, 141, 181n2, 182n8
Verlin and Howard Kruse Founders Associate Professorship, 111
Voelkel, Christi, 164
Voelkel, Eliana, 164
Voelkel, Lily, 164–65
Voelkel, Tyson, 162–65

Wade, Sally Dee, 183, 186
Walesa, Lech, 70
Walker, Robert L., 179n1
Walle, Armando, 150
Watson, Karan, 93
Wegler, Harley, 155
Wehring, Stephanie, 123
Weigand, Courtney, 125, 165–67
Weir, Theresa, 18
Welch, Finis, 48
Welsh, Mark A., III, 112, 174
West, William F., 39t, 56, 61, 66–67, 72, 75, 81, 87, 101, 106, 183n6, 185n11
Wheeler, Joanne, 117
Wilson, Don, 5–7, 9–13, 15, 19–21, 26–27, 29, 41, 51, 54–55, 77, 173, 180n16–17, 180n26–27, 181n1, 181n6–7, 182n11
Wood, Dan B., 39
Wood, Janeen, 97
Woodrow Wilson School of Public and International Affairs, 54–55, 173
World Vision, 137–39, 186
writing program, 28, 54, 73, 86, 122, 183
writing skills, 54, 73, 86, 183

Yale University, 5–6
Younger-Carter Distinguished Policy Maker in Residence, 82

Zardkoohi, Asghar, 39
Zemin, Jiang, 71, 144